Franz Xaver Kroetz

Franz Xaver Kroetz

The Construction of a Political Aesthetic

Michelle Mattson

BERG
Oxford • Washington, D.C.

First published in 1996 by
Berg
Editorial offices:
150 Cowley Road, Oxford, OX4 1JJ, UK
13950 Park Center Road, Herndon, VA 22071, USA

© Michelle Mattson 1996

Berg is the imprint of Oxford International Publishers Ltd.

Library of Congress Cataloging-in-Publication Data

A catalogue record for this book is available from the Library of Congress

British Library Cataloguing-in-Publication Data

A catalogue record for this book is available from the British Library

Cover photograph reproduced by kind permission of Oda Sternberg.
© Oda Sternberg

ISBN 1 85973 079 5

Typeset by JS Typestting, Wellingborough, Northants
Printed in the United Kingdom by WBC Book Manufacturers, Bridgend,
Mid Glamorgan

For Matthias, Rachel, and Samuel

For Matthias, Rachel, and Samuel

Contents

Acknowledgments

As with any extended project, one can never take all of the credit for one's own. I am very indebted to Russell Berman, Andreas Huyssen, Sabine Wilke, and Sabine von Dirke for their help over the last few years. I am especially grateful to Katie Trumpener, without whose diligent and thoughtful readings of the book's various incarnations I would never have been able to complete it. I would also like to acknowledge all of my colleagues in the Department of Germanic Languages at Columbia University. They have offered unfailing support and have my deepest gratitude.

Introduction

Franz Xaver Kroetz: The Playwright and his Paths

Banana-cutter, hospital orderly, warehouse supervisor, fledgling actor, delivery truck driver, tour group leader, gardener, and (West) Germany's most popular contemporary dramatist of the seventies and early eighties. At first glance, it seems hard to believe that the above *curriculum vitae* could belong to one and the same person, let alone to one of the most prominent figures in the German theater world, and yet the various published fragments of Franz Xaver Kroetz's biography would have it be so.[1] Born on 25 February 1946 in Munich, Kroetz attended, but did not finish, a specialized school for aspiring businessmen. After the death of his father, an accountant for the federal government, he chose instead to pursue training as an actor. Without any notable successes, Kroetz found minor roles in various smaller theaters, for instance the Ludwig Thoma Theater in Rottach-Egern, but was forced to support himself with the many and varied odd-jobs listed above. Meanwhile, during the sixties he snatched late night hours and free moments to write a whole string of highly diverse literary texts. Despite his diligence, his efforts to find a publisher for his work were in vain until 1971.

However, in 1970 early versions of two one-act plays, *Heimarbeit* and *Hartnäckig*, so impressed Martin Walser, then a reader for Suhrkamp's theater section, that he passed them on to his friend and colleague Heiner Kipphardt, the chief dramaturg of the Munich *Kammerspiele*, who proceeded to put them on the theater's program and scheduled the premiers for April 3, 1971. Both the stark and dismal content of the plays themselves,[2] as well as the public scandal that accompanied their stagings, had a tremendous impact on the West German theater: its producers, critics and audiences alike. With the receipt of the Suhrkamp stipend for young dramatists and the premier of these two short pieces, Kroetz could finally cast aside his role as a part-time and/or temporary laborer and step into his role as the hot new dramatic talent of the theater season.

Harnessing the enthusiasm that the recent rediscovery of the critical *Volksstück* ("folkplay") from the twenties and thirties had generated,[3] Kroetz then produced a whole string of short, largely one-act theater works that followed closely on the model *Heimarbeit* and *Hartnäckig* had already established. The year 1971 witnessed the further premiers of *Wildwechsel*, *Michis Blut*, and *Männersache*, while the following year solidified his reputation as a dramatist with the premiers of *Stallerhof*, *Dolomitenstadt Lienz*, and, most prominently, *Oberösterreich*. This last piece, centered on a young, working couple whose lives are thrown into confusion by an unexpected pregnancy, was one of, if not *the* most successful of Kroetz's plays. In the next three years alone the play was staged fifty times. It secured for the author the West Berlin Art Prize, and was subsequently filmed and shown on German television.

When in 1972 Kroetz decided to join the German Communist Party (*Deutsche Kommunistische Partei* – DKP), theater critics loosened somewhat their exuberant embrace of the young author, but both he and his work had by then already staked out considerable ground in the theater. At an astounding rate Kroetz continued to churn out play after play, almost all of which were eagerly performed. Nonetheless, his alliance with the DKP instigated what at least seemed[4] to be a new phase of radical experimentation in the playwright's creative endeavours, leading him away from what he felt was the claustrophobic, extreme character of the family-centered, realist one-act play. He wrote two agit-prop works at the behest of the party, *Globales Interesse* (commissioned at the time of the Munich Olympics in 1972) and *Münchner Kindl* (1973), written in ballad form for a DKP tribunal on rental fraud and real-estate speculation.[5] Kroetz also attempted two Hebbel-adaptations, which met with extremely mixed reviews: *Maria Magdalena* (1972) in which he modernizes, but maintains large portions of the original; and *Agnes Bernauer* (1976), which essentially drops all pretence of adapting Hebbel's own text in favour of exploring through the title character the burgeoning of one individual's political consciousness. Even *Dolomitenstadt Lienz* broke with the realist aesthetic confines of such plays as *Heimarbeit* and *Wildwechsel* by introducing the use of songs. Kroetz pursued this early homage to Brechtian dramatic methods in only one other piece, *Sterntaler* (written 1974, premiered 1977).

Amid the formal experiments, all of which met with little if any critical favour, Kroetz also began to expand on the early realist pieces. Beginning with *Oberösterreich* he sought a way out of his so-called early extremism to a more representative dramaturgy. *Das Nest* (1974) explores the same moment central to the later and less successful play

Agnes Bernauer, namely an individual's first step to political awareness and engagement. Kroetz felt that *Oberösterreich*, itself a move away from the abortion, murder, and explosive violence of his first works, failed to push its characters to the point of recognizing the socio-economic and political determinants of their situation. *Das Nest* represents a moment of self-reflection, an attempt to correct the perceived flaws of its predecessors by endowing its cast with the linguistic and intellectual tools necessary to effect an actual change in consciousness. At this juncture Kroetz establishes an experimental pattern that will shape the way he develops as a dramatist throughout his career. Dissatisfied with a successful, but in some way limited, aesthetic model, Kroetz turns back to address his own model, refashioning it as he does so in order to create an effective and successful political aesthetic. Each phase of overt and extensive experimentation leads to a new and relatively stable aesthetic strategy (although the periods of stability become increasingly shorter as he moves into the eighties). The works following *Oberösterreich* and *Das Nest* are good examples of a fairly stable dramatic structure: *Weitere Aussichten* (1974), *Reise ins Glück* (1975), *Heimat* (1975), *Mensch Meier* (1977), *Der stramme Max* (1978).

Disillusioned both with his own position within the DKP and with some fundamental tenets of the DKP's form of Marxism, Kroetz withdrew from the party in 1980. And although this was clearly a decisive step in the playwright's political and artistic career, it was actually only one symptom of a much larger personal and professional crisis. His search for a viable political aesthetic in the years following his entry into the DKP ran afoul of public apathy and the relatively obscure position of literary figures in the German public sphere. Additionally, it became apparent that Marxism's structural analysis of social reality could not address a whole plethora of socio-political and personal (that is to say individual psychological) developments that arose in West German society throughout the seventies and early eighties. Kroetz's attempt to address these factors occasioned another period of extreme experimentation in his work for the theater. His first efforts to reconstruct his own aesthetic history are evident, albeit in only modest alterations of formal strategies, already in *Nicht Fisch nicht Fleisch* (1980) and *Furcht und Hoffnung der BRD* (1983), but the author essentially obliterates the traces of his previous realist aesthetic in both *Bauern sterben* (1985) and *Der Nusser* (1985 – an adaptation of Ernst Toller's *Hinkemann*).

After *Der Nusser*, both Kroetz and his critics seemed to feel that he had written himself out.[6] Kroetz, the actor, took on new roles. He starred in a mini-series about a reporter for a boulevard press. He wrote articles on the Seoul Olympics for the *Bild-Zeitung, the* German yellow rag.[7] The one-time radical communist even offered interviews to *Die Welt,* one of the country's leading conservative newspapers, in which he praised the patriarch of the Federal Republic, Konrad Adenauer, as a positive political and historical figure. In these interviews, the author also pointed in the direction that his artistic interests were then drifting. He states:

> Ich habe Angebote erhalten, Stücke von Thomas Brasch und Peter Turini zu inszenieren. Aber wenn man Brasch persönlich erlebt, ist er viel, viel interessanter als das, was er schreibt. Und Turini ist doch mit seinem Privatleben auch unendlich weit entfernt vom Thema seiner Stücke, etwa von der Vernichtung der eisenverarbeitenden Industrie.[8]

The communication or mediation of socio-economic issues has taken a back seat to the author's interest in individual biography. An even earlier text indicates how this interest will translate into Kroetz's work for the theater. A character from *Furcht und Hoffnung der BRD,* whom Kroetz called "der arme Poet," holds a long and tortured telephone conversation with a friend, in which he tries to explain his current state of mind:

> Ich will nicht ausweichen, überhaupt nicht, ich bin viel radikaler, als ihr euch das träumen könnt *laut:* Ich hab keine Illusionen - ich stelle mein "ich" radikal in den Mittelpunkt und wende mich angeekelt davon ab . . . – MEINE Revolution ist, daß ich zu mir steh, bis es mich zerreißt, das ist die Grundbedingung für Radikalität in unserer Zeit: Zerreißprobe jawohl, im Selbstversuch.[9]

Exposing the self to both public and private scrutiny, seeking the *radical* in the authorial self is in fact that aesthetic project to which Kroetz turned after *Der Nusser.* It has been an experiment that has found little support in Germany's theaters. The first attempt, *Zeitweh* (1986), was performed only in a very small theater near Lake Constance. The second, *Der Dichter als Schwein* (1986/88) has never been staged, and the third, *Bauerntheater* (1991), premiered to decidedly mixed reviews in Cologne.[10] Concurring with "the poor poet" of *Furcht und Hoffnung,* Gerhard Preußen writes of *Bauerntheater*: "Kroetz glaubt sich seiner Unsterblichkeit so sicher, daß er will, was nur die Götter können: Selbstbestätigung durch öffentliche Selbstvernichtung, Beifall noch für den eigenen Bankrott. Ecce homo Kroetz."[11] The sarcastic tone, with which Preußen approaches Kroetz's staging of the personal, provides a glimpse at the playwright's current status among theater critics. What they perceive as excessive and tasteless self-absorption is also something the younger Kroetz rejected out of hand as irresponsible and unethical,[12] and perhaps this phase too is coming to an end.

One of Kroetz's most recent works for the stage is a re-working of one of the very early pieces, *Lieber Fritz* (1971). The first version of the play centers on a character who has been castrated by the state for irremediable exhibitionism. He is released from prison and finds temporary refuge in the home of his sister and brother-in-law. While this version concentrated on how Fritz's attempts to start a new life, an independent life, are thwarted by his family's economically driven concerns, the new play, entitled *Der Drang* (1994), centers on the sexual and personal frustrations of Fritz's sister and brother-in-law. Fritz becomes merely the de-sexed other (here by virtue of drugs, rather than overt castration) in a sexual triangle. Writing for *Theater heute*, Franz Wille describes *Der Drang* as "die grellste Sexualkomödie."[13] Wille also refers to this piece as Kroetz's "comeback," and there is a sense in which this is obviously doubly true: the play may mark the author's return to the German theater, and the theater's renewed acceptance of a playwright who had apparently fallen from grace, but it is also a return to his earliest work for the theater, to the works that made him Germany's most popular contemporary dramatist.

This last comment draws out the dilemma Kroetz has always faced in his artistic production: the seemingly unbridgeable chasm between his desire to create a radical political aesthetic and his equally strong desire to achieve and then cement his popularity with theater audiences. His entrance to the German stage was accompanied by scandal and outrage, but as he worked to develop and elaborate his leftist political aesthetic, he wrote two of his most widely staged and well-received plays: *Oberösterreich* and *Das Nest*. Annoyed and pleased with his success, he found himself at odds with his own project. In an interview with the *Süddeutscher Rundfunk* from 1982 Kroetz talks about his various attempts to break apart what he calls a "spät-hauptmannschen Wohnküchenmilieu-Fantasie" and to move away from the realism of the seventies.[14] He says his attempts were legitimate, but that he essentially chose to respond to those works and the aesthetic strategy to which his public found the greatest access: "Das Publikum hat mehr reagiert auf eine Schreibweise wie 'Oberösterreich', der extreme politische Anspruch wurde nicht angenommen. Es wurde immer mehr der moderate, menschliche Anspruch angenommen. Und ich habe dem einfach auch nachgegeben."[15] Although there is no reason to suggest, as Susan Cocalis does,[16] that Kroetz let himself become a virtual slave to public opinion, the nature of his political aesthetic project forced him to court a wider audience, while at the same time resisting his cooptation as a palatable playwright.

Already in something of an aesthetic pickle, Kroetz was also increasingly writing on the margins of the then aesthetically acceptable. By the end of the sixties, a decade that witnessed the production of large scale, overtly political documentary works for the theater (such as Rolf Hochhuth's *Der Stellvertreter* and Peter Weiss's *Die Ermittlung*), a period of seeming disenchantment with such grandiose political spectacles set in. There ceased to be a dominant aesthetic fashion, but increasingly authors turned away from larger historical questions to ones of a more personal, introspective nature. The search for an overtly political aesthetic drifted off into relative isolation, and it is in this sense that Rolf-Peter Carl says of Kroetz's work already in the mid-seventies, "Mit dem 'Nest' setzt er seine Linie fort, und diese Linie verläuft schon seit 'Münchner Kindl' deutlich quer zur vorherrschenden Tendenz."[17] To say that Kroetz found himself writing against the so-called *Tendenzwende* of German literature tells us very little about his own position in the literary landscape of the time and even less about those authors credited with ushering in the much-touted shift in aesthetic direction. A brief outline of the principal patterns in post-war West German theater will help to contextualize the beginnings of Kroetz's own production history.

West German Theater in the Sixties and Seventies

Certainly one cannot legitimately claim that West German drama of the late forties and fifties was apolitical or that it side-stepped Germany's recent Nazi past, but the most influential plays of the time concentrated on personal experiences of the war, the conflicts of individuals, and the difficulties they had in maintaining an integral sense of self when confronting the future. Two prominent, albeit aesthetically very different, examples of such personalized accounts are Wolfgang Borchert's *Draußen vor der Tür* (1947) and Carl Zuckmayer's *Des Teufels General* (1946). Extensive commentaries and analyses of these plays make a detailed analysis here superfluous. For the present purposes, they are of interest because of the way in which both the despair of Borchert's returning soldier and the personal honour of Zuckmayer's General Harras ultimately serve in a sense to exculpate these individuals and to draw attention away from the social and structural causes of fascism's rise in Germany.[18]

Another important trend in German drama of the fifties was the German version of a theater of the absurd, represented in the main by the dramatist Wolfgang Hildesheimer. Faced with the overwhelming horror of historical developments, absurdist drama refuses the attempt to *make sense* of human existence. Nonetheless, German playwrights of the absurd differed somewhat from the dominant French absurdist paradigms. C.D. Innes describes the German absurdists as follows:

> German absurdists never had the philosophical consistency of the French school. Man remained for them the Aristotelian "political animal" rather than the existential mortal and, as Walser noted, their adoption of absurd principles was really a reaction to the apparently insoluble problem of finding literary perspectives to express contemporary conditions.[19]

Whatever residual political commitment or interests German absurdists may have had, two events from the early sixties drew attention to the social and structural causes of the Third Reich that drama had heretofore been unwilling or, as Innes suggests, unable to address: the Frankfurt Auschwitz trials, along with the Eichmann trial in Jerusalem, and the building of the Berlin Wall. Peter Weiss, who had attended the Auschwitz trials as a reporter, took away from the trials the conviction that there was enormous continuity in German society from the Nazi era, that the Germans had done little to confront their social responsibility, and, aesthetically, that the trial documents could essentially speak for themselves. He claims in *Die Ermittlung* that the piece is nothing but the *concentrated* form of the trials themselves.[20]

With individual authors like Rolf Hochhuth and Weiss leading the way, German drama moved from an interrogation of isolated individuals and their personal responsibility to a broad-scale investigation of German society as a whole. While allowing the defendants in *Die Ermittlung* to maintain their actual names when addressed by other characters, Weiss basically reduces them otherwise to numbers, indicating the move to a collective dramatic character. The dramatist literally puts German society on trial. Indeed, drama as tribunal becomes a prominent aesthetic model in the sixties and seventies.

Whereas the return of documentary theater to the German stage occasioned a politicization of the theater already at the beginning of the sixties, the mid-sixties witnessed an era of extensive politicization and aesthetic experimentation, propelled in particular by the rapidly expanding student movement. Although inspired by the works of the documentarists, authors and artists began to seek new means of aesthetic expression. W.G. Sebald, referring in particular to the initial dominance of documentary theater, writes of the time:

> From the mid-sixties onwards the context changed rapidly. The atrophied body of the *Stadt-* and *Staatstheaterkultur* was rocked by the shock waves of the events of 1968, and it was out of these events and out of the changing consciousness of which they were manifestations that the most important new school of post-war German theatre was born.[21]

Documentary theater may have generated the aesthetic energy that grew at the end of the sixties; nonetheless, it had to make room for other aesthetic innovations. Four dramatists who came essentially to command the German stage of the seventies were Peter Handke, Thomas Bernhard, Botho Strauß, and Franz Xaver Kroetz.[22] While one should not over-emphasize their similarities, particularly given their very real formal and thematic differences, they are worthy of note.

Peter Handke's early works for the theater, such as *Publik-umsbeschimpfung* (1966) and *Kaspar* (1968), initiated a period of intense concern about the character of language, its relationship to individual identity, i.e. how language comes to discipline and constrain the individual, and ultimately about the nature of the individual subject in general. Handke borrows for his piece *Kaspar* the legendary figure of Kaspar Hauser, a young man who appeared as a sixteen-year-old in Nuremberg. Apparently he had been kept until then in total isolation and was essentially unable to communicate with the world around him. Handke takes the historical figure and makes of it an abstract one, using it to demonstrate how language generates the individual.

Additionally, *Publikumsbeschimpfung*, the first of a series of *Sprechstücke* to be staged, pushed the erosion of traditional theatrical conventions even further than had Weiss's grand documentary pieces. Instead of actors donning a role to present before the audience, *Publikumsbeschimpfung* has four speakers hurl increasingly vehement insults at the audience, in essence underscoring the *role* the audience itself had come to play. We can, along with Günther Rühle, paraphrase Handke's central question as follows, "Sind wir nicht alle Schauspieler unserer selbst, Individualität vorgebend, obwohl wir an Rollen fixiert sind, die doch nur Hühlsen und Mechanismen sind?"[23] Actors playing individuals, individuals playing a multitude of roles: Handke's work represents a focus on the individual at the moment when that focus begins to blur. The era of the integral individual or at least the belief in such an individual, so nostalgically evoked in a play like Zuckmayer's *Des Teufels General*, is marked as irretrievably bygone.

Thomas Bernhard's influence on the German stage began in 1970 with the premier of *Ein Fest für Boris* and surely continues today despite his rather early death in 1989. Bernhard pursues relentlessly what one could call a variation of the themes in Handke's work. The subtitle of *Der Berg*, a work that predates *Ein Fest für Boris*, reads: "Ein Spiel für Marionetten als Menschen oder Menschen als Marionetten."[24] Puppets of nothingness, without any possibility of escaping the onrush of nothingness, Bernhard's characters hold tyrannic monologues in the presence of other characters, who seem literally to be co-prisoners on the stage.

Human beings are all crippled by their humanity. Sometimes this is more than apparent, as in *Ein Fest für Boris* in which members of the cast are physical cripples. Sometimes the suffering, devastation, and cruelty that is life is less the physically apparent disfigurement (although that too is a factor in other works) than the web of domination and oppression in which even the powerful figures of human life find themselves, as in *Der Präsident* (1975), *Immanuel Kant* (1978), and *Der Weltverbesserer* (1980). But even these superficially successful characters are ultimately chained to their own destruction. Of Immanuel Kant, the historical herald of reason, tolerance, and man's inherent ability to achieve enlightenment, Bernhard makes a sick, virtually blind, and senile old man on his way across the ocean to an American madhouse. In fact, Dieter Kafitz describes the author's work very aptly as a "Krankheitsbericht des 20. Jahrhunderts."[25] Crippled and sickened by human existence, Bernhard's characters make their way inescapably to death.

Like both Handke and Bernhard, Botho Strauß's early theater works foreground the individual on the stage as alienated, exhausted, and ultimately isolated by and within contemporary society. Although the characters in plays such as *Die Hypochonder* (1972), *Bekannte Gesichter, Gemischte Gefühle* (1975), *Trilogie des Wiedersehens* (1977), and *Groß und Klein* (1978) are caught up in a web of interdependencies, it is not a web that sustains but rather traps the individual in his or her alienated existence. Strauß is often the first example listed for the *Tendenzwende* away from an aesthetic concerned with the political ramifications of certain societal structures to one focused on the condition of the individual in a post-industrial society.[26]

The title of Strauß's first work for the theater indicates both the similarities with the crippled and ailing figures who people Thomas Bernhard's stage as well as the way in which his characters may differ from them. The designation "hypochondria" evokes the question of illness, while at the same time insinuating that said illness is a figment of a neurotic psyche. Buddecke and Fuhrmann describe these neuroses as follows:

Die Hypochondrie der Figuren äußert sich in steigender Angst: Angst sowohl vor einem möglichen Welt- und Wirklichkeitsverlust durch das Schwinden der Sinneswahrnehmungen und anderer Körperfunktionen, als auch und insbesondere vor einem drohenden Entgleiten eigener und fremder Identität, sei es in der Gestalt des Wahnsinns, sei es in der Form des Gefangenseins im Räderwerk einer diabolischen Manipulationsmaschinerie. Als Angst vor dem Verfall des Subjekt-Status oder, anders gewendet, vor der totalen Entfremdung und Selbstentfremdung verweist diese Hypochondrie, absurd verschlüsselt, auf die Situation des Individuums in der abstrakten Undurchschaubarkeit einer verwalteten Welt.[27]

The closed-in spaces of a hotel (*Bekannte Gesichter, Gemischte Gefühle*), various rooms in a huge and anonymous apartment building (*Groß und Klein*), and the display halls of a museum exhibit (*Trilogie des Wiedersehens*) combine with the notion of a perpetual and forced return in the title of the latter to illustrate the sensations of compartmentalization, entrapment and dependency Buddecke and Fuhrmann describe above. Although the world Strauß's figures inhabit is depressingly disjointed, there is, in contrast to Bernhard, a sense in which it is not an entirely hopeless situation (at least not at this point in Strauß's career).

Hypochondria is a relatively mild neurosis compared to the blindness and amputated limbs in Bernhard's work. Furthermore, the pattern of repetition in *Trilogie des Wiedersehens* will not end in total destruction, and, I would argue, there are hints that the pattern can and will ultimately be broken.[28] The disillusionment of West German intellectuals of Botho Strauß's generation after the disintegration of the student movement finds a voice in the introspection of a few alienated individuals, but both the direction Strauß has gone since *Der Park* (at the latest) and the final words of the protagonist in *Groß und Klein* would indicate that this playwright found himself dramatizing a particular historical form of alienation, one that would eventually make way for other conflicts. At the conclusion of *Groß und Klein* Lotte suddenly finds herself alone in a doctor's waiting room. When the doctor asks why she is still there, i.e. if she had not been called for, she replies: "Nein. Ich bin hier nur so. Mir fehlt ja nichts."[29]

Formally, the three playwrights have little in common. Handke's early language plays centered primarily on the language itself, and a play like *Kaspar*, in which the character has become so abstract that one cannot really call him a character, are formally radically different from Bernhard's scenic demonstrations of power relationships in the tyrannic monologues that imprisoned the subject of power and the object of the monologic tirades on the stage with their oppressors.[30] Strauß's first plays were largely realist in form, but often strained the confines of a realism defined too narrowly. Buddecke and Fuhrmann cite the plays' tendency to turn to the absurd, the grotesque or the fantastic. For example, they describe *Groß und Klein* as follows: "*Groß und Klein* verbindet einen konsequent epischen Bau, die lockere, nur durch die Hauptperson verknüpfte Szenenreihe von offener Raum-Zeit-Struktur, mit einem Realismus, der phantastische Grenzüberschreitungen tendenziell einschließt."[31] Not conceived as replicas of empirical reality, Strauß's works confront the perceptions of reality and unreality through which the audience can (re)construct the relationship between their own perceptions and what at least appears to be reality.

Obviously none of the three playwrights, who shared theatrical space with Kroetz, would be adequately described as realists, a label Kroetz and others chose for themselves. Nonetheless, the sixties and seventies were decades of formal experimentation in Germany, and the ultrarealist plays Kroetz wrote, particularly in their extremely limited focus, are part of that period of aesthetic innovation. Thematically, they do share some characteristics: mentioned above were the focus on the power of language to shape the individual, and a challenge to traditional bourgeois notions of an integral and independent individual.[32] The similarities notwithstanding, Kroetz's approach to both of these questions is so different from that of Handke, Bernhard and Strauß as to make comparisons seem overly facile.[33]

Kroetz never really shared his contemporaries' focus on the intellectual. He came to the theater not via the university as they did, but via the theater itself. His conception of the individual and his or her exploitation in late twentieth-century capitalism developed in the context of the relatively orthodox Marxism of the DKP, and not in the anti-authoritarian and neo-marxist groups of the student movement.[34] The debilitation of the individual and the concomitant disfunctionality of language are for Kroetz not (at least not until at the absolute earliest 1980) existential or universal categories, but rather the result of very specific production relations and the logic of capital distribution. The individual *per se* is not damaged, but rather specific individuals within specific social classes. Similarly, language can be manipulative and oppressive, but it is not necessarily the nature of language to be so. Seen in this light, Kroetz's focus on the damaged individual has more in common with Brecht's interest in the divisive effect of capitalism on the individual. However, even this seemingly common ground offers less than sure footing, but in an effort to set some footholds, both language and the individual will form central foci of the discussions about Kroetz's work that follow.

The New Critical *Volksstück*

If he does not fit smoothly into the picture of West German drama in the seventies as sketched above, this is partially owing to the fact that the positioning of Kroetz as one of the four major dramatists of the decade has to do with his status as the most successful representative of a particular kind of drama, namely the so-called new critical *Volksstück* (folkplay).[35] Just as the resurgence of documentary theater in the sixties marked a rejuvenated interest in the theatrical methods developed primarily by Erwin Piscator in the twenties and thirties, so too is the emergence of a new critical *Volksstück* in the mid-sixties to early seventies a result of a new look at the critical realist plays of Ödön von Horváth and Marieluise Fleißer, both of whom wrote their most influential works during the inter-war period.[36]

In fact, the cultural and scientific productivity in the Weimar Republic became the focus of attention for more than Germany's playwrights. Günther Rühle notes that the fascination with Weimar culture ran parallel to a revisiting of sociological theories from and about the twenties and thirties.[37] Of particular interest to the highly politicized student movement were studies done by Frankfurt School theorists on the nature and origins of fascist mentality.[38] Critics felt that Horváth in particular had captured in his work precisely the character of the proto-fascist individual. Helmut Karasek, for example, writes:

> Das, was linke Theorie (Adorno, Marcuse, Reich) in ihrer Analyse von der verinnerlichten Herrschaft, die der äußeren Gewalt nicht mehr bedarf, ermittelt haben, die Versklavung durch die Bewußtseins-Industrie, das ständige Verstoßen der Ausgebeuteten gegen ihre eigenen Interessen, das sie unter anderem für so viele Spielarten des Faschismus präformiert, das alles ist in Horváths Volksstücken dramatische und szenische Wirklichkeit.[39]

The writers of the new critical *Volksstück* turned their focus from the broad-scale documentary productions, that, like *Die Ermittlung*, created images of horrendous and catastrophic events, to the individual and/or localized social groupings and the generation or preservation of a social mentality that made the Third Reich possible.

This refocusing, a zooming in, if you will, was not unique to the *Volksstück* authors: it was definitely part of the larger rejection of the documentary spectacle mentioned above. Martin Sperr, one of the first to rediscover both Horváth and Fleißer and to offer the theater a contemporary version of the critical *Volksstück*, argued that the theater and its grand historical recreations had become just another way of avoiding the problems of post-war German society: "Das Theater wird immer mehr zur sterilen Ablage unserer unbewältigten Vergangenheit. Und diese wird so zu einem angenehmen Mittel, die Gegenwart umgehen zu können."[40] Sperr and others believed that the *Volksstück* offered the theater the opportunity to explore the deformations and extremities of contemporary society in a way that other dramatic forms did not.

For those who are familiar with the history of the term *Volksstück*, such a description may seem questionable. Helmut Motekat offers a concise definition of the *Volksstück* that will create a backdrop for the references to follow:[41]

Introduction

Von spezifischen Ausprägungen abgesehen verband sich im Lauf der Zeit mit dem Untertitel "Volksstück" mehr und mehr die Vorstellung von kaum tragischen, sondern unterhaltenden bis belustigenden Theaterstücken, in denen vor allem landschaftliche oder ständische Eigenarten (z.B. der bäuerlichen Volksschicht) oder bestimmte Typengegensätze (Großstädter under ländlichen Menschen oder umgekehrt) Anlaß zu dramatischen Konflikten, Irrtümern, Verwirrungen und deren Lösung bilden. Häufig dienen Dialekt oder Dialektanklänge dem "Volksstück" als wirkungsverstärkende Elemente.[42]

When one thinks of such works as Kroetz's *Heimarbeit*, Fassbinder's *Katzelmacher*[43] or Sperr's *Jagdszenen aus Niederbayern*, "amusing" (*belustigend*) is not one of the adjectives that come immediately to mind. However, there are elements in Motekat's description that indicate what the writers of the new critical *Volksstück* sought to borrow from their eighteenth- and nineteenth-century predecessors: the focus on rural characters and/or characters from lower socio-economic classes, and the frequent use of dialect for characterization. The traditional *Volksstück* (not to mention its modern-day instantiation in such commercial theaters as the Millowitsch-Bühne and the Hamburg Ohnsorg-Theater) is a necessary foil for both the critical *Volksstück* of Ödön von Horváth as well as the new critical *Volksstück*. Buddecke and Fuhrmann offer a very precise definition of the latter, which includes both its evocation and rejection of more popular forms of the *Volksstück*:

Charakteristisch für das Genre des "realistischen" Volksstückes ist: 1. daß es "Volk" als Gegenstand . . . impliziert; 2. daß es Menschen aus der Unter- und/oder Mittelschicht nicht illusionistisch-unterhaltend wie das Millowitsch- oder Ohnsorg-Theater, sondern – als "Volkstheater gegen den Strich" – kritisch-realistisch darstellt; 3. daß es im Gegensatz zur gehobenen Standardsprache die Umgangssprache aller Schattierungen vom Jargon bis hin zum Dialekt verwendet; 4. daß es sich – anders als das hermetische Theater der Avantgarde – um Gemeinverständlichkeit bemüht und 5. daß es in der Regel als Gegenwartsstück im Unterschied zu den diversen Formen des historischen Dramas auftritt.[44]

Despite these very helpful definitional categories, the differences between the traditional *Volksstück*, the critical *Volksstück* of the twenties and thirties, and the new critical *Volksstück* of the sixties and seventies, and even amongst its most representative playwrights themselves, make a precise generic definition impossible.[45]

A brief description of the differences between Martin Sperr's and Kroetz's approach to the *Volksstück* illustrates this point quite aptly. Critics viewed Sperr's ground-breaking work, *Jagdszenen aus*

Niederbayern (1966) which became part of a three-part study entitled *Bayrische Trilogie*, as the beginning of the critical *Volksstück*'s rebirth.[46] The first play, *Jagdszenen*, features the residents of a small, rural community called Reinöd shortly after the currency reform in 1948. At the center of the conflict is Abram, a homosexual who returns to the community after earlier brushes with the law. Abram's homosexuality puts him outside of the village's shared sense of normalcy, which in turn leads them to view him as a threat to the community. Abram tries very hard to fit in, but manages only to impregnate the girl with whom he hopes to establish a socially acceptable relationship. When she confronts him with the pregnancy, the anger and frustration that has built up in him explodes, and he murders her. The hunt referred to in the play's title is the village's collective effort to track Abram down, turn him over to the authorities and thus rid themselves of the disturbance they believe him to be.

In contrast to Kroetz's plays, which would have focused primarily on the character of Abram, and how the stresses society put on his life led to the eruption of physical violence, Sperr details through language and communal interaction the residual fascist tendencies of the village population and their inability to cope with anything that stands outside the prescribed boundaries of the acceptable. Motekat says of this piece:

> Es geht . . . nicht so sehr um die Schwierigkeiten und das Geschick Abrams, sondern vielmehr um die durch sein Anderssein veranlaßte Demaskierung der sich so ehrenwert und moralisch gebenden Dorfbewohner vom Bürgermeister und Pfarrer über die Metzgerin, die Bauern, die Flüchtlingsfamilie aus Schlesien bis zum Totengräber Knocherl.[47]

Instead of the two-to-three person micro-cast of Kroetz's plays, Sperr's *Volksstück* covers the entire social spectrum. In fact, the scope of the trilogy goes from the above-mentioned grave-digger to student activists to the very affluent and influential owners of a Munich brewery. The second work, *Landshuter Erzählungen* (1967), centers on the conflict between two construction companies in the city of Landshut during the development boom of the late fifties, and the final piece, *Münchner Freiheit* (1970/71), describes both real-estate fraud in Munich and the disintegration of student-movement activism, along with the beginnings of violent forms of protest in the late sixties. Although few critics considered either of the two final plays to be aesthetically or politically as convincing as the first, it is clear that Sperr attempted here to create an inclusive and extensive portrayal of the structures of oppression and exploitation in post-war German society, one that would go beyond the exclusive depiction of fascist tendencies in the petit-bourgeoisie to an exploration of the function of finance capital and its relationship to the state.[48]

One could say that Kroetz's early one-acts come at the same problem of power and exploitation, but from the reverse angle. They literally zoom in on the marginalized individual, whom society has for a variety of reasons forced to its periphery, and highlight the violent results of such exclusion. Innes says of Kroetz's work from this period that the "concentration on minutiae . . . gives this kind of folk play the quality of an anthropological field-study,"[49] a characterization that would align his work with the heightened interest in sociological case studies at the end of the sixties. Günther Rühle points out, however, that the much-analyzed inarticulateness of Kroetz's early characters is in some sense also a response to the rhetorical overflow that was the student movement:

> Mit großer Genauigkeit sind also gezeigt: Rückstände sozialer und psychologischer Art bis zur begriffslos verkümmerten Sprache. . . . Dies geschah in einem Augenblick, in dem gerade Eloquenz und Beredsamkeit neu hervorbrachen und große Wortfluten aus den Megaphonen der Studentenrebellion über die Gesellschaft hinflossen. Das Drama als anschaulich gemachte Feldstudie stand freilich zu dieser Rebellion nicht im Widerspruch; es konnte sie sogar durch seine Verweise auf ungelöste soziale Probleme stützen. Formal aber wandte es sich ganz vom Appellationsstil des revolutionär sich verstehenden Dokumentar- und Appellationstheaters ab. Gegen die zunehmende Utopie bestand es allerdings auf der Besichtigung der Realität, gegen das neue Schwärmertum auf Genauigkeit. Es begleitete also die Revolte und opponierte zugleich.[50]

In other words, the new critical *Volksstück* was both a confirmation and a critique of the student movement's political theories. Rühle's comments hint at the tensions between the group of playwrights classified as neo-realists and certain other tendencies within the student movement: the theoretical complexity eventually led the intellectual leaders of the student movement in a direction the neo-realists did not care to follow. This parting of ways will be the subject for further analysis shortly. One can safely say, however, that the so-called new realism[51] of the critical *Volksstück* assumes a firm position in the German theater at the same time that the prominent figures in documentary theater are beginning to back away from their revolutionary projects. At such a juncture, the new critical *Volksstück* represents not only a new perspective for the German theater, but also in a sense the logical continuation of the project launched by the documentarists.

There should, nonetheless, be little doubt that the renaissance of the critical realist *Volksstück* owed its spread to the political climate out of which both Sperr's early works as well as the renewed interest in Horváth and Fleißer arose. The grand coalition between the Christian Democrats and the Social Democrats (from 1966 to 1969) had created a political climate in which institutional opposition was essentially absent and an extra-parliamentary opposition was forming that would challenge the conceptualization of democracy in West Germany. The year 1968 saw the enactment of the so-called *Notstandsgesetze*, which provided the government with the power to suspend certain democratic rights when it believed the state to be in danger. The extra-parliamentary opposition (APO) saw this as a very real threat to the fabric of democracy and took to the streets in ever-greater numbers. Additionally, Germans were feeling the first effects of an oncoming recession. Even if Kroetz says retrospectively that all of the above played little if any role in the formation of his early works for the theater, their success on the German stage clearly owed much to the highly politicized culture of West Germany in the sixties.

However, by the time his first plays premiered in 1971, there was already a marked decrease in the literary public's interest for overtly political literature. Writing about Kroetz and his relationship to the genre of the new critical *Volksstück*, Moray McGowan notes that by the time Kroetz first actually labelled a work *Volksstück* (*Das Nest*, 1974) "most directors were already bored with what was for them a passing fashion."[52] Wend Kässens and Michael Töteberg also note that the popularity and productivity of the *Volksstück* had begun to stagnate by 1975.[53] I would argue, however, that the waning popularity of the *Volksstück* had to do with more than just the aesthetic *Tendenzwende* mentioned above or the end of the grand coalition.

The playwrights of the new critical *Volksstück* were part of a larger group (although the group as a whole was never that large relative to other aesthetic trends in Germany): the neo-realists. These authors were committed to creating a political aesthetic that would appeal and be accessible to a large number of readers. Their efforts faced considerable resistance among literary circles and heated discussions about the adequacy of a realist aesthetic accompanied their work from the early sixties through the mid-seventies.

Excursus on Realism and the Realism Debate of the Seventies

Obviously, both the character and the success of Kroetz's work during the seventies are rooted in the literary-historical configuration and the literary discourse of the late sixties and early seventies. A brief look at where that discourse originated and how it developed in the Federal Republic provides a context for Kroetz's work that further helps to explain why he became the most successful dramatist of the seventies. However, given Kroetz's personal political affiliation with the DKP, an analysis of his work must also then take into consideration the influence of "official" communist aesthetic theory on Kroetz's production as he moves into the seventies. Kroetz's creative efforts throughout the decade are positioned somewhere between the highly politicized socio-political constellation in West Germany during the late sixties and the early seventies and the theoretical demands placed on him by his chosen party during his development as an author.

The Politicization of Art in the Sixties

A general aversion to a politicization of art in the wake of both the Nazis' and the communists' subjugation of art to the needs of their respective movements dominated the West German literary world in the fifties. Virtually all attempts to work at a viable political aesthetic in Germany came under the rubric "ideologically suspect." Several developments occurring throughout the fifties and into the early sixties did, however, gradually make possible a radical revisioning of art's relationship to the political.

As the physical, economic and emotional re-building of Germany took hold, a new generation of Germans began to come of age. Born toward the end of or shortly after the war, this generation had no immediate or extensive experience as adults of either the devastation the war had wrought on German society or the sacrifices Germans had had to make in order to reconstruct their country. These individuals grew into a society they saw as lacking in democratic structures, as overly determined by economic and material concerns, in short as needing a thoroughgoing reform of most social structures and institutions. As mentioned above, the advent of several high-profile war crimes trials in the early to mid-sixties (the Frankfurt Auschwitz trials and the Eichmann trial in Jerusalem) also served to refocus public attention on Germany's Nazi past in a way that was new to post-war German public discourse. In essence the material success of the *Wirtschaftswunder* made possible the critique of its success: with the daily struggle for physical existence at an end, people finally began to turn back, to reflect on what had happened, both during the war and after.

At the same time, on a more global level, the Cold War had spawned several international conflicts, in which the interests of two competing superpowers took precedence over the concerns and, in fact, the very lives of innocent individuals: Korea, Chile, Vietnam. In such a way, the

Cold War reached into the lives of individuals who were in many ways not party to the conflict. After the chancellorship of Konrad Adenauer, the United States had become the dominant extra-national influence on the government of the Federal Republic and, one could argue, on German society in general. The United States had during the fifties gradually stepped into the role of protector and fosterer of democracy. However, with the outbreak of the Vietnam War and the interference and intervention of the U.S. government in Chilean affairs, the image of America as benevolent was tarnished. Nonetheless, the West German government continued to pursue a strong allegiance with the United States.

Both the international and domestic developments of the early sixties became the subject for increasingly intense criticism. German university students, confronted with rigid hierarchical structures within the German university system and what they perceived to be outdated and irrelevant courses, fostered a rebellion that quickly expanded its attentions to German society and then to the international arena. The rebellion also spread to the world of art.

The most vocal and critical constellation of authors in Germany of the fifties was the so-called *Gruppe 47*. Although the group was politically influential, the generation coming of age in the sixties saw its representatives as too comfortable with the establishment, as thematically too reactionary (and reactive) and formally too dull for the present situation. The discussion of German theater in the sixties noted that with the premiers of Rolf Hochhuth's *Der Stellvertreter* and Peter Weiss's *Die Ermittlung* art became aggressively accusatory, sparing no one its authors saw as implicated in some way in either the atrocities of the Third Reich or the continued disinterestedness of German society in the implementation of effective democratic political structures. Documentary theater was also arguably the first native innovation in the theater world since the very productive period of the Weimar Republic.

The resonance documentary literature found among a younger West German audience certainly caused a general reevaluation of art's social function. Lamenting the distance that separated art from everyday life, the aesthetic innovators of the sixties called for both a reintegration of art into a life-praxis as well as an exploration of new aesthetic strategies. In a now famous *Kursbuch* edition, Karl Markus Michel calls for the pursuit of non-traditional aesthetic experiences that transcend the boundaries of art's institutionalized isolation and attempt to draw in together the aesthetic and the political.[54] Thus, although Kroetz himself was not involved in either the university-centered student movement or the efforts of the West German theater to confront its audiences with its own sullied past, his first dramatic works found much acclaim in this political climate. In fact, as noted above, both Martin Walser, one of the preeminent figures in the theater's politicization, and Heinar Kipphardt, one of the most prominent playwrights of documentary theater, were instrumental in Kroetz's introduction to theater audiences.

The extremely politicized atmosphere of the late sixties began, however, to crumble as soon as the student movement itself fragmented and dispersed, at the latest in 1970 with the official disbanding of the SDS (*Sozialistischer Deutscher Studentenbund*). The relative isolation of the student protesters and organizers within the universities, the formation of various factions within the student movement itself (of primarily anti-authoritarian or Marxist-Leninist orientations), the emergence of violent protest and the end of conservative political hegemony with the rise of the Social Democratic/Liberal Democratic reform-minded coalition in 1969 are just some of the factors that led to the gradual defusing of the explicit and aggressive politicization of art and culture in West Germany. Not that there ceased to be artists and artworks that pursued a political agenda, but there was no longer a general consensus either on whether art should in fact attempt to be political, or on what aesthetic strategies would be appropriate, should art maintain its active participation in the political discourse of the time.

The Split in Germany on the Character of Aesthetic Expression

A certain bipolarity developed at the time around the question of art's political character and the means appropriate to aesthetic expression in the second half of the twentieth century. A substantial number of artists and literary critics expressed the view that whatever political function art might have, it was not an immediate one that could be centered on the actual content of the work of art. Based theoretically primarily on the work of Theodor W. Adorno, these individuals insisted that any attempts to portray contemporary reality through a realist[55] strategy could not do justice to the highly complex and differentiated character of post-monopoly capitalism. They felt instead that art could only explore this complexity and fragmentation through its own particular formal possibilities.

Other artists maintained that such a position was essentially a capitulation to the structures of domination and oppression, and that an (over)emphasis on highly formal art was necessarily elitist in character, and implicitly (if not in fact explicitly) excluded large portions of society from active participation in art's reception. Although certain literary groups, such as the *Gruppe 61* and the *Werkkreis Literatur der Arbeitswelt* used both realist and non-realist aesthetic strategies in the sixties, the discussion of realism as an adequate aesthetic tool intensified in the late sixties and early seventies. The debate about realism and reality in art reached a high point in 1974 around the formation of the *AutorenEdition* (founded by Uwe Timm, Richard Hey, Uwe Friesel, Hannelies Taschau and others). Given Kroetz's own expressed allegiance throughout the seventies to a realist aesthetic paradigm, a rough sketch of the literary-theoretical terrain will help to explain the fertile ground on which his work initially fell, and to outline the issues that would ultimately lead to the gradual waning of his popularity in the eighties. However, in order to set the parameters of the realism debate of the seventies, I would like first to go back to positions articulated by two of the dominant influences on aesthetic theory in Germany of the sixties and seventies: Theodor W. Adorno and Bertolt Brecht. They were arguably the most important literary theoretical ancestors of the realism debate in Germany of the sixties and seventies. Outlining their basic aesthetic suppositions will help to clarify the positions assumed in the later debate, and will, in turn, account in a large part for Kroetz's position within the literary terrain of the seventies and eighties.

The Literary-theoretical Ancestors of the Realism Debate in the Sixties and Seventies – Adorno and Brecht

I have chosen to include and to begin with Adorno because he is the most challenged and the most championed voice in the ongoing struggle to determine art's political character. His adamant insistence on aesthetic autonomy (albeit as only part of art's double nature) engendered countless counter-arguments and a ceaseless intellectual battle to define the boundaries and characteristics of the aesthetic. The discussion of Adornian aesthetic theory in this chapter will highlight moments in a very complex and involved theoretical argument in order to clarify the implications of an aesthetic theory based on the absolute autonomy of the work of art. Although not focusing exclusively on the question of realist versus non-realist aesthetic strategies, Adorno's views on aesthetic autonomy and/or the political function of art in society bear directly on whether realist representational paradigms can do justice either to a particular political program or to social reality more generally.

The word "autonomous" in its original Greek sense means having the characteristics of self-legislation – or self-determination, as it were. For Adorno, on the other hand, aesthetic autonomy in the modern world is art's freedom *from* the dictates of the capitalist market, its freedom *from* the regulatory instances to which all other commodities are subjected.[56] A simple reversal of this description obviously yields a definition similar to the one above. However, the emphasis here is on the negative nature of aesthetic autonomy. As a distantiation from the prescriptions of commodity exchange it tells us nothing of itself: it is a definition in purely negative terms. Why is this distinction crucial?

It is important because of the loss (even if not the complete loss) of the self-regulatory or self-determinative aspect of autonomy. Autonomy relates, of course, not only to art, but also to its producers, human beings. Although Adorno insists on aesthetic autonomy, he sees individual autonomy as completely restricted, subject to a process of erosion commensurate to the gains won by the ever-multiplying and regenerating powers of the culture industry. To facilitate the smooth functioning of the market, to ensure the fluid exchange of commodities, the individual too has been standardized, ready-made so to speak, to fill the needs generated by the machinery of the culture industry: "In der Kulturindustrie ist das Individuum illusionär nicht bloß wegen der Standardisierung ihrer Produktionsweise. Es wird nur so weit geduldet, wie seine rückhaltlose Identität mit dem Allgemeinen außer Frage steht."[57] The autonomy of the individual is an illusion because it only obtains when the individual has given it up. What any given individual thinks, feels and needs is created by the culture industry, and the products to fulfill those needs appear on the shelves of the customers' freely selected department store.[58]

Although the term "culture industry" would seem to limit its own descriptive powers in terms of human society as a whole, it is difficult if not impossible to discern those bastions of non-industrialized culture left. In fact, the process of bureaucratization largely to be credited with the management of today's society in global dimensions has left little room for non-regulated social behaviour, thus providing the societal structures necessary for broad-scale marketing of any sort. The negative consequence of this management, as seen above, is the destruction of the individual as it had previously been known:[59] "Die Kulturindustrie hat den Menschen als Gattungswesen hämisch verwirklicht. Jeder ist nur noch, wordurch er jeden anderen ersetzen kann."[60]

What possible purpose could political art have in a society peopled by interchangeable parts? Although a question of paramount importance for this particular study, for Adorno, it is, if not totally irrelevant, at least a completely misformulated question. To insist that art have a purpose or, if you will, a function within society, is to subject it to the same principles of exchange that have reduced everything else to mere commodities. Adorno writes, "So weit von Kunstwerken eine gesellschaftliche Funktion sich prädizieren läßt, ist es ihre Funktionslosigkeit."[61] This further underscores the idea that one cannot view art as either completely autonomous or as unmitigated social fact; to do so would mean to employ a completely false dichotomy. Art rejects the instrumental rationality (*Zweckrationalität*) that governs the workings of the market and all reified societal relationships: it maintains its autonomy by its refusal to serve a purpose. The autonomy of art itself is thus a critique of existent societal structures, "Die rücksichtslose Autonomie der Werke, die der Anpassung an den Markt und dem Verschleiß sich entzieht, wird unwillkürlich zum Angriff."[62] Aesthetic autonomy, in a sense, becomes the place-holder for the autonomy of the individual, for the individual's freedom to be identical within itself and not with something else for which it could then be exchanged:[63] "Kunstwerke sind die Statthalter der nicht länger vom Tausch verunstalteten Dinge, des nicht durch den Profit und das falsche Bedürfnis der entwürdigten Menschheit Zugerichteten."[64] Artworks, although social products themselves, must shut themselves off from empirical world.[65] They deny the supremacy of that which is external to them, but, at the same time, the negation implicitly reaffirms the prevalence of that external reality.[66]

Perhaps it would help to step aside for a moment and examine the way in which works of art both reject and incorporate existing reality. In Adorno's view, as the universe of bourgeois enlightenment began to crumble, after rationality, unreflected in itself, stagnated into the dominance of instrumental rationality, it became increasingly difficult for art as mimetic to consolidate into conceptually meaningful constructs: "Aber den Kunstwerken wird es immer schwerer, sich als Sinnzusammenhang zusammenzufügen. Darauf antworten sie schließlich mit der Absage an dessen Idee."[67] Gradually art came to refuse to synthesize the elements of the reified world. It refused to present an immediacy of meaning. Instead artworks, according to Adorno, exhibit meaning by excluding it.

A frequent example for Adorno is the work of the playwright Samuel Beckett. In both *Endgame* and *Waiting for Godot* there are characters, but they do not constitute individuals, they act by not acting, they speak, but they do not communicate. In essence meaning can be extracted from these "dramas" solely *ex negativo*. Not only is the internal mediation of the parts to the whole made oblique, external discourse of the work of art with the world beyond it is also abandoned, replaced by a steadfast refusal to participate in the thoroughly rationalized sphere of communication.[68] In other words, art cannot fulfill its function as place-holder if it attempts to recreate reality, even as an obvious illusion. Instead it must sever all apparent ties to empirical reality. Once again, Adorno argues that this act of distantiation represents a more powerful critique of society than blatant social criticism, "Die hermetischen

Gebilde üben mehr Kritik am Bestehenden als die, welche faßlicher Sozialkritik zuliebe formaler Konzilianz sich befleißigen und stillschweigend den allerorten blühenden Betrieb der Kommunikation anerkennen."[69]

The paradox in this is precisely the duplicitous character of art's renunciation of manifestly intelligible discourse. For in its rejection lies recognition and acknowledgment, though not approval of the other. This is the key that distinguishes most clearly between (for lack of more subtle terminology) autonomous and engaged art. Engaged works of art, in order to avoid the trap of amorphousness, are forced to participate actively in the "allerorten blühenden Betrieb der Kommunikation."[70] For Adorno participation necessarily entails sanction, and this implicates such works in the violence of society as dominated by instrumental rationality. Thus any work of art that even attempts to initiate communication with the external world is doomed from the outset to function as an accomplice in the all-pervasive oppression within contemporary society.

Adorno's rebuttals to Bertolt Brecht's work illustrate these points. Adorno concedes, as it were, the "good intentions" of the author and directs his critique towards the products themselves. As he works through them he illustrates their inner contradictions, which both exemplify the impossibility of their premise as well as make a case for non-referential art. In his brief essay "Zur Kritik des Engagements" Adorno dedicates over eight pages to a commentary on and critique of Brechtian literary theory and practice. He maintains that Brecht had grasped the truth of capitalist society, had recognized the demise of the bourgeois subject and had made efforts to reveal the reality beneath the surface. Adorno's essential criticism is that Brecht was forced to reduce this political reality in order to fit it on to the stage. This reductionism, in turn, renders his material infantile:

> Aber der ästhetische Reduktionsprozeß, den er der politischen Wahrheit zuliebe anstellt, fährt dieser in die Parade. Sie bedarf ungezählter Vermittlungen, die er verschmäht. Was artistisch als verfremdender Infantilismus sich legitimitert . . . wird zur Infantilität, sobald es theoretisch-gesellschaftliche Gültigkeit beansprucht.[71]

In Adorno's eyes Brecht's own method of reduction and abstraction turns against his intentions, serving only to trivialize political reality. However, Adorno contends that Brecht's dramatic work goes beyond a trivialization. Brecht did not find a way to depict the actual machinations of capitalism (eg. the "Appropriation des Mehrwerts in der Produktionssphäre," p. 417); instead his subjects were

"Epiphänomene", mere by-products, miserable little parasites on the social body.

Referring here specifically to Brecht's farce *Der aufhaltsame Aufstieg des Arturo Ui*, Adorno writes, "Anstelle der Konspiration hochmögender Verfügender tritt eine läppische Gangsterorganisation."[72] In the minimalization of the opponent, so Adorno argues, Brecht has actually portrayed a political untruth. He further contends that the few moments of truth Brecht manages to bring to the stage are self-evident and that there is essentially no one who would be unfamiliar with them.[73] Although it would be a problematic (mis)representation of Brecht's work to label it realist, Adorno's critique of realist techniques would underscore that a realist pretension to represent reality would also only result in a misrepresentation of reality, a reduction of the empirical possible and real within the aesthetic. Instead the effort would merely sully the work of art.

Beyond that, as Adorno's biting critique of Georg Lukács demonstrates, realism as an aesthetic strategy promises or pretends to an adequate portrait of reality, generating the image of a comprehensible totality, when in fact twentieth-century reality is far from constituting an intelligible whole and art is therefore itself incapable of rendering a whole within a single work. What the realist work of art then does is offer an "extorted reconciliation." Realism in the artwork shows itself conciliatory to the oppression and virtual destruction of the individual in this century. In his essay on Paul Valéry, Adorno implicitly contrasts the aesthetic vision of the poet with more representational aesthetic forms such as realism:

> Die dicht organisierte, lückenlos gefügte und gerade durch ihre bewußte Kraft ganz versinnlichte Kunst, der er nachhängt, läßt sich kaum realisieren. Aber sie verkörpert die Resistenz gegen den unsäglichen Druck, den das bloß Seiende übers Menschliche ausübt. Sie steht ein für das, was wir einmal sein könnten. Sich nicht verdummen, sich nicht einlullen lassen, nicht mitlaufen: das sind die sozialen Verhaltensweisen, die im Werk Valérys sich niedergeschlagen haben, das sich weigert, das Spiel der falschen Humanität, des sozialen Einverständnisses mit der Entwürdigung des Menschen, mitzuspielen.[74]

This passage goes to the heart of art's only social function in Adorno's view: it creates a preserve for the human, and it does so by refusing to pretend to be human or real. Art refuses to participate in the destruction of humanity by recreating it. Instead art must focus in on its own inherent logic, irrespective of how it is received or understood *vis-à-vis* social reality. In the essay on Lukács Adorno contends:

Kunst selber hat gegenüber dem bloß Seienden, wofern sie es nicht, kunstfremd, bloß verdoppelt, zum Wesen, Wesen und Bild zu sein. Dadurch erst konstituiert sich das Ästhetische; dadurch, nicht im Blick auf die bloße Unmittelbarkeit, wird Kunst zu Erkenntnis, nämlich einer Realität gerecht, die ihr eigenes Wesen verhängt und was es ausspricht zugunsten einer bloß klassifikatorischen Ordnung unterdrückt. Nur in der Kristallisation des eigenen Formgesetzes, nicht in der passiven Hinnahme der Objekte konvergiert Kunst mit dem Wirklichen. Erkenntnis ist in ihr durch und durch ästhetisch vermittelt.[75]

Although one could certainly take exception to many of the points Adorno makes here (e.g. that realist art would be in any way capable of simply "passively" reflecting an object-reality), what is of interest in this context is the claim that only the logic of aesthetic form mediates knowledge.

An essay on the position of the narrator in the contemporary novel reinforces both the moral component of the Valéry quote above and the concomitant formal argument. One passage from it is even italicized in the original, drawing physical attention to the point Adorno is trying to thrust home: "Will der Roman seinem realistischen Erbe treu bleiben und sagen, wie es wirklich ist, so muß er auf einen Realismus verzichten, der, indem er die Fassade reproduziert, nur dieser bei ihrem Täuschungsgeschäfte hilft."[76] On just about every conceivable point, Adorno finds realism lacking. As a representational strategy, it is inadequate to the complexity of contemporary social reality, producing only a superficially comfortable rendering of conventional reality. Further, its claim to mediate the truth about reality reveals itself to be implicated in the business of deception.

There are many ways in which Adorno is right: art can never be a complete introduction to the inner structure of any political/economic system. It would be virtually impossible, for example, to dramatize adequately the appropriation of surplus value in the realm of production. This does not mean that attempts to do so should be abandoned. It does necessitate, in my view, the recognition that all art reduces and to a certain extent trivializes reality by transfiguring the real into that which it is not, namely the aesthetic. Adorno himself saw this as a problem, albeit from a different perspective. His repeated critique that the aestheticization of suffering, for instance in Arnold Schönberg's composition *Überlebende von Warschau*, transformed it into the sublime, thereby detracting from the intensity and truth of that suffering, is simply another side to the same phenomenon.

This review of Adorno's basic stance *vis-à-vis* manifestly committed and realist literature calls attention to three major issues. First, for Adorno the once-autonomous subject has been rationalized into virtual non-existence. This means that there is essentially no longer a potential instigator or bearer of political change. Second, this rationalization also logically dominates the structure of human communication and interaction. Thus, the transference or practice of intentionally political discourse serves only to reinforce the process of oppression in society. This means, finally, that art can no longer function as a traditional mode of communication, effectively shutting out reception as a constitutive element of the aesthetic object. Indeed, art's function, as it were, is to safeguard a sphere for non-instrumentalized rationality. Its function/lessness protects a preserve, in a sense, for the lost autonomy of man. The participants in the so-called realism debate of the sixties and early seventies who took positions against realism as a viable contemporary aesthetic strategy relied heavily on Adorno to stake their territory.

Ironically, they also used Brecht to make their arguments, even though Brecht was the target of an impressive and extensive Adornian critique. That the proponents of a contemporary realism drew substantially from Brecht to shore up their own case only adds to the confusion. It is a testimony to the fact that there was no longer any way around Brecht, so to speak, in a discussion of political aesthetics. Whether one chose to reject Brechtian aesthetics, as did in fact Handke, Kroetz and Fassbinder in the early seventies, or whether one embraced Brecht's theoretical work, there had to be at some point a critical evaluation of his ideas. Just ignoring him was not an option – for them or for this study.

The apparently multi-purpose or multi-valent character of Brechtian aesthetic theory is inherent to the double-fronted strategy Brecht was pursuing in his pronouncements on realism. Clearly, Adorno and Brecht would seem to view the subject of aesthetics and political commitment in the work of art in radically opposing ways. On closer inspection, however, it becomes less and less a question of polar opposites and more and more a problem of degree, of mediation, and, ultimately, of perspective and persistence. To create a symmetry in presentation it will prove helpful to delineate first Brecht's perspective on the political subject as the addressee of any political aesthetic before moving on to a portrayal of his aesthetic theory.

Despite Brecht's insistence on the political mission of the proletariat, he does not harbor any naive notions that the development of capitalism has left the individual unscathed. He sees, rather, a political subject greatly compromised by the manipulative and suppressive powers of a society, intent solely on the maximization of profit and the eventual perfection of efficiency, with all of the related implications for human beings. He is, on the other hand, unwilling to abandon the individual in this process, maintaining that capitalism entails both the destruction as well as the creation of humanity:

> Der Kapitalismus entmenscht nicht nur, er schafft auch Menschlichkeit, nämlich im aktiven Kampf gegen die Entmenschung. Der Mensch ist auch heute keine Maschine, er funktioniert nicht nur als Teil einer Maschinerie. Er ist auch vom sozialen Standpunkt aus nicht zureichend beschrieben, wenn er nur als politischer Faktor beschrieben ist.[77]

The struggle against oppression and alienation generates a new form of individuality and political subjectivity. Indeed, if the progression of history is dialectical, and that was Brecht's working assumption, then no destruction can be complete. The ramification this had for his own aesthetic theory and production was that knowledge could be attained in a process of mutual education. A description of Brecht's pedagogical intentions follows later.

Of paramount importance here is the fundamental tenet of education that communication between individuals is possible. In stark contrast to Adorno, Brecht believed in the powers of language as a communicative tool. Indeed, it is a necessary tool in any attempt to reveal oppression, which, as we shall see, is the first step in Brechtian pedagogy. The assertion that language might somehow be irreparably damaged was not only improbable, but also counter-productive.[78]

Language serves not only the purpose of uncovering the character and structures of oppression, but also functions in the actual triumph over oppression.[79] Language, of course, ceases to exist in a vacuum. That is to say, the role of language on the stage is an integral part of the production itself, but also of its reception in the audience. This is the point at which language becomes the tool of the spectator in the process of three-way communication, namely between the stage and the viewer and vice versa, and within the spectator as an individual. In abstract, this is the moment of self-production so crucial to Brecht's conceptualization of the theater's socio-political role.

The issue of reception constitutes one major difference between Brechtian and Adornian aesthetic theory. For the former, reception is not simply one element of the aesthetic experience. It would indeed be impossible to separate it from the aesthetic object as a whole. Without the phenomenon of the spectator, viewer or reader, a work of art would have no social significance. In fact, without the element of self-production within the aesthetic experience for the audience of an artwork, art itself becomes, as Brecht so eloquently states, a mere exercise in futility, the painting, as it were, of murals on the inner walls of ships already demolished in battle and sinking.[80] The aspect of self-production will provide the key to an understanding of Brecht's conceptualization of autonomy, both human and aesthetic as this discussion develops.

In order to establish the terrain, it is important first to recognize that Brecht operates on the basis of a greatly extended definition, in a sense redefinition, of art as a whole.[81] The expansion of the category of art to include such activities as dam construction, the development of hybrids and the transformation of a state[82] was a necessary prerequisite to his introduction of the concept of labor and self-production into aesthetics. Brecht writes:

> Es wäre viel nützlicher, den Begriff "Kunst" nicht zu eng zu fassen. Man sollte zu seiner Definierung ruhig solche Künste wie die Kunst des Operierens, des Dozierens, des Maschinenbaus und des Fliegens heranziehen. Auf diese Weise geriete man weniger in Gefahr, von etwas, genannt "Bezirk der Kunst", zu faseln, von etwas sehr eng Umgrenztem, von etwas, was sehr strenge, wenn auch sehr dunkle Doktrinen erlaubt. (GW19,350)

This expansion of the realm of aesthetic production was a way to include art in the processes of political and societal change occurring during Brecht's life. In the twenties there was the growing strength of the labor movement and later the perversion of that movement in fascism.[83] Authors such as Brecht and Benjamin saw in fascism efforts to aestheticize political life and they considered the politicization of aesthetics to be one appropriate response to such attempts.[84] Abandoning the comfort of their previously well-guarded autonomy, works of art were to become additional tools in the service of the working class. Indeed, the exigencies of the historical situation made any other role not only ridiculous, but even unethical. This is the sense behind the famous lines in the poem *An die Nachgeborenen*: "Was sind das für Zeiten, wo/Ein Gespräch über Bäume fast ein Verbrechen ist." (GW 9,723)

The politicization of art did not, however, come about solely from the left. In fact, it is crucial for Brecht that one recognize the perpetual political character of aesthetic objects. The subject of art as "ein Geflecht gesellschaftlicher Beziehungen" (GW15,257) of necessity includes the sphere of activity traditionally labeled as political. It is simply a matter of whether art chooses to ignore, energetically disavow or emphatically affirm its own political character and substance. The first two options implicitly place art in the service of oppression, "So heißt *unparteiisch sein* für die Kunst nur: *zur herrschenden* Partei gehören" (GW16,687, his italics). Brecht's redefinition of art represents an attempt to explode the restrictions placed on aesthetic production by an all too adamant separation of art from the rest of society.[85] Only if art yields its privileged status can it even begin to meet the challenges facing the world of the twentieth century.

In contrast to bourgeois theater, the goal of Brechtian theater is to go beyond the individual appearance or occurrence. The theater piece or any given artwork must reveal the structures underlying any particular phenomenon: "den motiven menschlicher handlungen muß in einem tieferen stratum nachgegraben werden, als dem subjektiven bewußtsein des handelnden, nämlich der sphäre des gesellschaftlichen seins [*sic*]."[86] Whereas in bourgeois theater it is largely the individual and his or her actions that constitute the focus of the play, it is in fact society, made concrete in the exposure of its structures, that forms the actual subject of Brecht's theater. The identification of the audience with the characters on the stage has become not only superfluous, but also counter-productive. Any emphasis on the accidental or individual merely serves to mask the structural problem at hand.[87]

Once the audience, with the help of the play, has peeled off the layer of the abstract or superficial, the aesthetic process becomes an enterprise of reconstruction. This process does not end in the simple portrayal of societal structures. That would, in essence, be fatalistic, in so far as it would tend to produce a picture of society as unalterable. In its efforts to formulate the substance beneath the surface, the audience must come to recognize that such a formulation is already a reformulation or modification of the configuration at hand.[88]

A different approach to the same concept would be to view the work of art as a model. A model is a provisional reconstruction of essential elements in reality on a smaller scale. It is always temporary, because, as reality changes, it also must change. Benjamin offers an insightful description of the functional model in aesthetic production:

> Also ist maßgebend der Modellcharakter der Produktion, der andere Produzenten erstens zur Produktion anzuleiten, zweitens einen verbesserten Apparat ihnen zur Verfügung zu stellen vermag. Und zwar ist dieser Apparat um so besser, je mehr er Konsumenten der Produktion zuführt, kurz aus Lesern oder aus Zuschauern Mitwirkende zu machen imstande ist.[89]

Thus, the work of art as model serves a dual purpose: it offers not only a flexible, creative perspective on certain social structures, it also acts as a process of enablement, guiding the spectator or reader out of a passive, receptive stance into a position from which he or she can actively work on the present situation. It facilitates, in other words, the conversion of the spectator from the recipient of political action into an actual agent for political change. Brecht never assumed that the members of his audience had come into the theater already able to make that step from passivity to active participation, but he did assume that they were capable of such.[90] The aesthetic experience was always to be a mutually educative one, and as such the theater was to become an integral part of a society in permanent revolution.

Do these goals find expression in a well-defined aesthetic program? In incessant efforts to save modern art from what he perceived as the all too possessive and dogmatic claws of the proponents of socialist realism, Brecht establishes a general framework for how he envisions twentieth-century theater and art ought or ought not to be. Although he repeatedly underscores the necessity of realist or realistic art, he nonetheless emphasizes that such terms make sense only within the given historical context. His attempt to salvage the concept of realist writing, in the sense of adequately portraying reality, pitted him against Lukács, whom Brecht (agreeing in this case with Adorno) saw as restricting art within the confines of an aesthetic technique inappropriate for twentieth-century audiences: "Die einzelnen Werke müssen danach beurteilt werden, wieweit sie die Wirklichkeit im konkreten Fall erfassen, nicht danach, wieweit sie einem vorgestellten Muster historischer Art formal entsprechen" (GW19,339). Brecht considers it a positive trade-off to sacrifice the illusion that the reader actually experiences reality in a work of bourgeois realism for aesthetic techniques that render readable more of reality itself. In other words, realism is to lay bare the structures of our reality instead of providing a convincing and deceptive portrayal of an individual section of that reality.[91] In fact he insists that within the traditional realist work those structures, although lurking below the surface, are virtually impossible to uncover.[92]

Brecht is offering a two-fronted argument here. On the one hand, in the interest of a greater freedom of experimentation and expression for leftist artists he wants to overturn the dicta of an aesthetically conservative cultural program represented by most orthodox Marxist functionaries. On the other hand, he wishes to respond to critical dismissals of both his work and that of others as formalist, and oppose an exaggerated concentration on form to the detriment of content. In one of the *Kalendargeschichten* Brecht explains the dangers of a preoccupation with form. In Herr K's attempts to shape a tree into a perfect sphere, he leaves little of the tree itself. The gardener views the work Herr K has done and exclaims: "Gut, das ist die Kugel, aber wo ist der Lorbeer?" (GW12,385). Brecht does not share Adorno's optimism that the careful cultivation and observance of the formal logic in an artwork will in and of itself expose the structures of oppression in contemporary society.

Brecht's critics often accuse him of being dogmatic. There is a sense in which this is true politically, but such a criticism does not hold water in terms of aesthetic techniques – at least not on a theoretical level. Brecht writes, "Wir dürfen nicht bestimmten vorhandenen Werken *den* Realismus abziehen, sondern wir werden alle Mittel verwenden, alte und neue, erprobte und unerprobte, aus der Kunst stammende und anderswoher stammende, um die Realität den Menschen meisterbar in die Hand zu geben." (GW19,325, his italics)

In fact, Brecht's apparently undogmatic stance in the previous citation does translate into a relatively rigid view of acceptable and unacceptable aesthetic practices. As we have seen, Brecht rejects traditional realist techniques as inadequate for a representation that would enable the audience to master the political reality of this century. Brecht writes of aesthetic production in the early twentieth century:

> Die Lage wird dadurch so kompliziert, daß weniger denn je eine einfache "Wiedergbe der Realität" etwas über die Realität aussagt. Eine Photographie der Kruppwerke oder AEG ergibt beinahe nichts über diese Institute. Die eigentliche Realität ist in die Funktionale gerutscht. Die Verdinglichung der menschlichen Beziehungen, also etwa die Fabrik, gibt die letzteren nicht mehr heraus. (GW18,161f)

Any artwork, not just photographs, that creates the impression of empirical reality runs the risk of deception and over-simplification. Brecht has, further, disallowed any devices that might unnecessarily distract, so to speak, from very serious problems and topics.[93] What, in effect, he does condone is his own epic techniques, eclectically, but carefully collected to comply with his highly specific understanding of the demands modernity places on the work of art. It is possible, however, that Brecht's refusal to be truly eclectic effectively hampered his attempts to reach his targeted audience.

On the one hand, Brecht's goal in the expressionism debates with Lukács was to secure for artists the full realm of techniques they might need to offer what they considered to be an adequate and true representation of the reality at hand. On the other hand, Brecht objected to realist techniques because they served only to obscure the structures underlying the surface. Along with Adorno, Brecht maintained that the artist had to avoid conveying the image of wholeness, of a society completely integrated and intact. (GW12,414) An artist cannot present social reality as malleable if the seams at which it is stitched together are not visible.

In this context Brecht was insistent that any given aesthetic project create the possibility of abstraction and generalization. (GW10,

348,359) His critique of naturalism outlines the differences between naturalism and what he considered to be a fruitful and true realism. The naturalist authors, he contends, offered only one small piece of reality, whereas realism, as he saw it, illustrated the entire social system through a variety of aesthetic tools. Naturalism proffered only milieu, while realism laid bare the system.[94] Anyone, therefore, who purports to have escaped the naturalist trap is thus at least theoretically justified, as are those who wish to underscore methodological tolerance and propose on this basis to experiment within a loosely defined realist aesthetic. Those late twentieth-century realists, who struggled to formulate their own political aesthetic, seized on this moment in Brechtian theory in order to recuperate for themselves the most influential dramatic force in post-war Germany, while retaining an aesthetic paradigm he would probably have rejected. The tug-of-war over the intellectual rights to Brecht is an explicit component of the realism debate.

Up to this point the discussion has revolved around the question of art's involvement in the political and the appropriate expression of this involvement. The split in the sixties between those who wanted to strengthen and deepen the socio-political function of art and those who insisted that art could only function socially outside of society developed over time into the above-cited "realism debate." Although there were obviously other literary predecessors than Brecht and Adorno (Lukács, Marcuse, Freud, Piscator – to name just a few), without them one does not have a full literary-historical picture of the arguments from the debates in the sixties and seventies.

The "Realism Debate" of the Early Seventies

In *Realism Today* Keith Bullivant writes that the German novel of the sixties employed predominately abstract aesthetic methods, further breaking it down into the "literary exploration of the theme of identity," and a number of neo-picaresque works that sought to exploit the success of Günter Grass's *Die Blechtrommel*.[95] With the advent of documentary theater, the growth of the student movement and the concomitant politicization of the cultural sphere, a number of young authors began to seek literary forms they felt related more directly to their political aspirations. In Austria, as a counter-reaction to the literary avantgarde of the "Wiener Gruppe," politicized authors coming from the student movement propagated and created a type of proletarian realism.[96] In West Germany Dieter Wellershoff, an editor for the publishing company Kiepenheuer & Witsch, launched an attack on Günter Grass's supposedly grotesque style, proposing instead a new realist literature.

Bullivant refers to this confrontation as the opening "salvo of a conscious campaign by Wellershoff for recognition of the merits of realist writing."[97] Reflecting back on his own words from 1965, Wellershoff writes of the reaction to his statements:

> Überall stieß ich auf Vorurteile. Sie lagen wie Krokodile auf ihren Sandbänken und schnappten, wenn ich das Wort "Realismus" gebrauchte. Ich war etwas überrascht von dieser Reaktion, bis mir allmählich deutlich wurde, daß man unter Realismus nicht eine unabschließbare Tendenz verstand, die fortschreitende, und sich dauernd verändernde Artikulation der grundsätzlich unausschöpfbaren Wirklichkeit, sondern dabei an erstarrte Konzepte dachte, etwa an die oberflächliche Milieutreue und die schablonenhafte Psychologie, wie sie zum Beispiel heute im Kriminalroman üblich ist. Sicher war der Begriff in Deutschland auch durch die Nachbarschaft des sozialistischen Realismus tabuisiert. Und schließlich fand ich heraus, daß sich damit die Vermutung einer erkenntnistheoretischen Naivität verband: man unterstellte, ausgehend von der statischen Vorstellung, die man sich vom Realismus machte, daß hier eine Sichtweise verabsolutiert werden sollte, die sich ihres perspektivischen Charakters nicht bewußt sei.[98]

This passage contains a number of issues that are key to understanding the various positions within the realism debate of the seventies. Above all Wellershoff indicates how intense and entrenched anti-realist sentiments were. The rejection of realism rested on the conviction that the term specified a particular stylistic canon, whereas Wellershoff, and indeed many of the pro-realist writers of the early seventies, believed that the term implied a particular epistemological and moral stance. Many opponents of a new realism read this moral stance as a political statement of alliance with and support for East European communism.[99] They found not only political sympathies with communist countries suspect, but also, given the highly rigidified character of official socialist realist aesthetic theories, considered the literary manifestations of this aesthetic paradigm to be of negligible aesthetic quality.[100] The authors, who were actively seeking a realist aesthetic appropriate to the demands of the day, reacted to such criticisms angrily and vociferously.

Despite Stephan Kohl's assertion in *Realismus: Theorie und Geschichte*[101] that the debates of the sixties and seventies in no way approached the sophistication of the arguments proffered in the debates about realism from the twenties and thirties, they are nonetheless helpful in contextualizing Kroetz's development as a dramatist. This is particularly true given that the work he did before his ultrarealist plays met with such success was, as Otto Riewoldt documents, highly eclectic, ranging from pieces similar to dadaist works (*Tiroler Elegien*) to experimental adaptations of Shakespearian texts (*Julius-Cäsar-*

Collage), to a relatively simplistic *Bauernschwank* (*Hilfe, ich werde geheiratet*).[102] Kroetz himself admits that the popularity of the realist pieces essentially convinced him to move in that direction instead of continuing to experiment with such highly divergent forms. His own theoretical musings about aesthetics in general and his own aesthetic project also developed around these pieces. And although the so-called realism debate did not dominate literary discourse at the time, the support his work received from pro-realist quarters cannot have gone without influence.

Such influence justifies a brief explication of what was at stake in the debate. However, in order to avoid redundancy and limit its own expanse, this examination focuses in on only the confrontation between Uwe Timm, one of the founders of the *AutorenEdition*, and Jörg Drews, a literary critic, as it appeared in a volume edited by Peter Laemmle entitled *Realismus – welcher?*[103] In conclusion, I will draw out how Kroetz's own thinking about realism developed and where it went from the early seventies to the mid-seventies.

In the writings of both Adorno and Brecht, literature and art in general clearly have a quasi-moral function. For Adorno it is to safeguard an area free from the oppressive and destructive character of modern society. For Brecht it is to participate consciously and intentionally in the political struggles of the day and in the development of a viable and active political subject. Their respective aesthetic theories are replete with references to art's higher calling. The proponents of realism at the time Kroetz launched his literary career also maintain a sense of moral righteousness, which they see bound up with the practice of writing.[104] It is, however, largely absent in the attacks on realism (other than the aforementioned distrust of communist ideology). Kohl even cites the conscious mediation of a moralist idea as one standard element of realist works.[105] Laemmle, the editor of *Realismus – welcher?* also claims that realism is always an ethical moral category, marking the relationship of the author to empirical reality.[106]

Jörg Drews's assertion that literature, in a fashion similar to the development of technology, has gotten technically so sophisticated as to be accessible only to a small, well-educated public, elicited a response from Uwe Timm that clearly reveals a moralist stance. Timm writes:

> Diese Einteilung in zwei Literaturen wird von der vorherrschenden bürgerlichen Kritik täglich durch neue Verdikte verfestigt und verschärft: auf der einen Seite die gehobene, feine Literatur, die sich mehr und mehr von der Wirklichkeit zurückzieht – weil diese angeblich nicht mehr anschaulich dargestellt werden kann, auf der anderen Seite die zynische

massenhafte Vermarktung jener Literatur, die ihren Lesern eine heile Welt vorgaukelt, um sie dadurch von der kaputten Welt abzulenken.[107]

The *de facto* abandonment of the general public by so-called high culture (i.e. non-realist art) amounts to the betrayal of that public to the sinister intentions of the culture industry, which would have the average reader believe that there is in fact nothing at all wrong with "the way things are." Timm argues further that the way for an author to participate actively in the political struggles of his/her time, to take a position in the class conflicts of the late twentieth century, is to pursue an aesthetic strategy that renders individual reality intelligible.[108]

At the risk of reductively exaggerating their positions, one could say that the *realists* of the realism debate argued from an ethical social position, the opponents of realism argued from an *ethical* (the italics are to denote caution) aesthetic position, i.e. the explicit inclusion of contemporary political realities would, because of its aesthetic and epistemological naiveté, sully the work of art. Jörg Drews argues:

> Der Wunsch nach einer neuen *realistischen* Literatur läuft weitgehend auf den Wunsch nach einer Entlastung von der ganzen Bürde der Erkenntnisse hinaus, die das naive Erzählen immer schwieriger machen. Er ist fast gleichzusetzen mit dem Wunsch nach Entlastung von intellektueller Anstrengung, mit der Sehnsucht nach einer Welt, die endlich weniger kopflastig wäre. Was dabei nicht gesehen wird, ist am Ende wohl einfach die Tatsache der Arbeitsteilung. Literatur soll ein Bereich des Unmittelbaren bleiben, der komplikationslosen Kommunikation, des common sense, ein Bereich, in den die Spezialisierung nicht eindringen soll. . . .Es ist, als wollte man die Philosophie wieder aus ihren Abstraktionshöhen herabholen und sie auf den gesunden Menschenverstand einschwören als der Basis, da sie doch gefälligst für alle verständlich sein müsse. Aber wie etwa die sprachanalytische Philosophie nicht mehr umgangssprachlich, wie Atomphysik, Gesellschaftslehre und Kybernetik nicht mehr allgemeinverständlich formulierbar, sondern höchstens – um den Preis der Simplifikation – popularisierbar sind, so führt auch bei der Literatur kein Weg mehr zurück in eine neue Einfachheit, die man nur wollen müßte, damit sie sich alsbald und ohne gravierende Qualitätsverluste einstellt.[109]

In this passage alone, Drews launches a multi-fronted polemic against the proponents of a late twentieth-century realism. He calls into question not only the intellectual capabilities of such individuals, citing conceptual laziness and incompetence on their part, he also accuses them of being unwilling to recognize that the division of labor in industrial societies has led to the increasing specialization of all areas of human production. Trying to reverse the process in art can only result in simplification and/or a loss of aesthetic quality. Thus he ends here with an indirect critique of contemporary realist literature as bad literature. Obviously one can hear several echoes of both Adorno and Brecht in Drews's words, and Adorno did make the argument about increasing specialization. Brecht, however, would never have concluded that the consequence of specialization must be increasingly restricted intelligibility.

Brecht, in fact, insisted on art as a form of political praxis for all of those involved: readers, writers, dramatists, theater public, sculptors, painters and spectators. As Benjamin states in the above-cited passage from *Der Autor als Produzent*, the function of art is to be a model, one which would move ever more (not ever fewer) consumers into the position of cultural producers. The notion of art as indissolubly linked to praxis is definitely one Timm and his fellow realists share. Timm stakes literature's claim to be a form of praxis in the following excerpt: "Der politische Realismus unterscheidet sich vom bürgerlichen gerade dadurch, daß seine Figuren nicht nur eine kritische Haltung gegenüber der gesellschaftlichen Realität einnehmen, sondern daß sie eine bewußte Veränderung dieser Gesellschaft versuchen."[110] Not only the fictional characters, but the authors too participate in the effort to change society for the better. In an interview from 1973 Kroetz himself stated: "Ich glaube an die Möglichkeit, daß sich durch das Ansehen eines realistisch gestalteten Geschehens im Zuschauenden etwas verändert" (WA, 601). The proposition that reality is changeable and that literature participates in this process is one to which most of realism's proponents would agree. Timm, for example, writes:

> Ich möchte hier zunächst davon ausgehen, daß Wirklichkeit sich bewußt verändern läßt. Das ist kein politischer Glaubensakt, sondern läßt sich in der Realität belegen. Deutlich wird das beispielsweise im Überbau, seit der Studentenrevolte 1967, an der Basis verstärkt seit den spontanen Streiks von 1969.
>
> Wie veränderbar unsere gesellschaftliche Wirklichkeit ist, kann auch an der Reaktion derer abgelesen werden, die sich gegen jede Veränderung stemmen, die das, was da in Bewegung gekommen ist, mit allen Mitteln versuchen abzudämmen, mit Berufsverboten, mit antikommunistischen Slogans, mit Stimmungsmache und mit Diffamierungen.[111]

Whether one chooses to believe that the student movement and the concomitant efforts to democratize society had any lasting impact on West German society, from Timm's perspective there had been concrete achievements and concrete and concerted opposition to the work of social activists in the sixties.

However, it is probably already obvious that Drews, Timm's opponent in the realism debate, does not share the political optimism generated briefly in the wake of the student movement, at least not *vis-à-vis* art's participation in socio-political change. Instead Drews maintains, as does Adorno, that contemporary society is enshrouded in what I would call a "cloud of unknowing." In a move that implies a type of historical condescension, Drews argues that while Balzac's reality was still simple enough to understand, contemporary reality exceeds human comprehension:

> Balzacs Spekulanten und Finanzmakler waren noch plastische Gestalten, aber was geben moderne Industriemanager, die mit Millionen jonglierenden *plastic people* des Big business noch her an sinnlicher Anschaulichkeit, an unverwechselbarer Individualität? Bei Balzac konnten ihre Liebesaffären noch ihre Firmen ruinieren; wenn heute der Manager aber nicht mehr von seiner Person abstrahieren kann, so wird er gefeuert, und die Firma wird höchstens ruiniert durch ökonomische Trends, auf die der einzelne Manager kaum noch Einfluß hat, durch Beschlüsse, bei denen nicht mehr seine Mätresse, sondern der Staatshaushalt, der Weltbankrat oder die OPEC mitbestimmen.[112]

The extended implication of Drews's argument is that in a time when abstract things such as economic trends and state budgets determine both the course of world markets and world politics, the individual can only react. Thus, any aesthetic proposing that art can have an impact on socio-political reality is hopelessly anachronistic. Although Timm rightly points out that Drews's concept of history is virtually fatalistic, there is a sense in which some proponents of a contemporary realism do sound politically outdated.

Relying on in many ways rigid Marxist ideas about the character of society, Timm and others often seem to have missed how the society they wish to change has already changed since early Marxism described it. One passage in Timm's response to Drews captures the apparently anachronistic tendency in his political philosophy. In it Timm argues that an author must learn more about scientific theories of society in order to avoid both an overly subjective as well as an overly fatalistic portrait of contemporary reality: "Eine solche Einsicht wäre, wenn er erkennt, daß er nicht einem alles durchwaltenden abstrakten Sachprozeß nachzuschreiben hat, sondern, daß hinter diesem scheinbar so sachlich abstrakten Prozeß höchst unsachliche konkrete Interessen stehen: Klasseninteressen."[113]

Class struggle as the engine of social change is a notion very much contested today, but it is one to which Kroetz himself also ascribed.[114] His own theoretical pronouncements often revealed an epistemological and representational naiveté that Drews could have called on to support his own ideas. When Kroetz decided that his early plays were too narrowly focused, seldom portraying any part of society that went beyond the nuclear family, he repeatedly stated that he needed to find the craft necessary to put capitalists on the stage. During a 1973 interview with *Theater heute* Kroetz pronounced: "Ich muß die dramatische Kraft mir erwerben, einen Firmenchef, einen Polizeipräsidenten, einen CSU-Bundestagsabgeordneten, einen SPD-Bürgermeister darzustellen. Wenn ich über die Macht Aussagen machen will, muß ich die Mächtigen zum Reden bringen" (WA, 590f).

Nonetheless, although one can point out the apparent anachronism in Kroetz's and Timm's position, there are other responses to the complexity of contemporary social reality than Drews's apparent socio-political fatalism. Wellershoff, a proponent of what he loosely refers to as realist literature and the founder of the so-called *Kölner Realismusschule*, shares Drews's scepticism about art's ability to render social reality *in toto*. In *Literatur und Veränderung* he writes:

Wenn die Wirkungszusammenhänge von Industrie, Verwaltung, Geldwirtschaft und Politik so weitläufig, indirekt und abstrakt geworden sind, daß sie sich der Anschauung, Kompetenz und dem Einfluß jedes einzelnen entziehen, ist nicht mehr der Handelnde exemplarisch für die Gesellschaft, sondern der Betroffene, der nicht einmal weiß, wie, warum und wovon er bestimmt wird, der den gesellschaftlichen Druck als Privatsituation erfährt und mehr oder minder glücklich individuell zu verarbeiten sucht. So kann auch der Schriftsteller kaum noch ein konkretes Gesamtpanorama der Gesellschaft schreiben. Er weiß zu wenig dazu. Auch seine Erfahrungen sind zufällig und privat, und das Allgemeine liefert ihm wie allen anderen die Informationsindustrie. Es ist ein unübersichtlicher, dennoch schon selektierter und durch mitlaufende Meinungen flüchtig und schematisch geordneter Nachrichtenstrom, in dem sich die Gesellschaft alltäglich repräsentiert und immer wieder konkretistisch verflüchtigt. Als strukturelle Entsprechung des zugehörigen Bewußtseins und des Zitatcharakters seiner heterogenen Inhalte ist die Collage aktuell geworden. Sie hat als deren Negation die metaphysische Attitüde einer Deutung des Ganzen abgelöst.[115]

In essence, he suggests that realist literature shift its focus from Balzac's economic giants to those individuals subjected to the day-to-day ramifications of world economic policies.[116] One thinks immediately of the hapless, helpless but violent victim/victimizers of Kroetz's early plays, and the author's consistent focus on the family would be one interpretation of Wellershoff's proposition. And, in fact, when Kroetz abandons his attempts to write the grand social portrait, he comes to formulate a very similar position:

Politik hat immer mit dem einzelnen zu tun und immer wenn ich Schicksal darstelle, stelle ich eine Zeitgeschichte dar, aber eben erfahrbar für den, der der Behandelte in dieser Geschichte ist. Weniger die Händler der Geschichte. Wie in allen meinen Stücken treten ja keine Betriebsleitungen, keine Aktienbesitzer oder keine Bosse auf, es treten da nur die Behandelten auf.[117]

In other words, an artist does not have to fashion a prototypical late capitalist industrialist in order to create representative characters.

Nor does one, as Wellershoff goes on to point out, have to limit the tools available to a contemporary realism to those at the disposal of earlier realist literatures. Although he later comes to lessen the emphasis he puts on collage, it is apparent that he and other proponents of realism in the sixties and seventies were aware that the spectrum of choices open to them *vis-à-vis* aesthetic means had expanded considerably. Uwe Timm also touches on this point: "Daß sich das, was als politischer Realismus zu bezeichnen wäre, in verschiedenen stilistischen Richtungen abschattet, ist für jeden selbstverständlich, der einmal begriffen hat, daß es sich beim Realismus um eine Methode handelt, nicht um die Kanonisierung eines Stils."[118] One could argue that the word "method" was an unfortunate choice here as it does imply a particular way of doing something, but one cannot meaningfully accuse the proponents of a new realism of stylistic rigidity.

However, along with Drews and others, one might question whether the term "realism" is itself a meaningful term.[119] Particularly if the non-stylistic definitions offered seem rather vague. A good example of this is one of the definitions Timm puts forth in his rebuttal to Drews: "Zur realistischen Methode gehört wesentlich das Moment der an Personen gebundenen Entwicklung, die sich in einer historischen Dimension entfaltet."[120] Albeit stylistically inconclusive, Timm's definition could be helpful in returning full circle the discussion of the realism debate, which served as one of the backdrops for the reception of Kroetz's early work.

This description of the literary debate on realism began with the assertion that proponents of a new realism in the late sixties and early seventies underscored the ethical obligation and implication of literature, in fact art in general, to society. It is – however methodologically diverse – not a literature that debates abstract philosophical questions on a level above or outside of the questions concerning contemporary society. Stephan Kohl outlines this emphasis on contemporary reality quite aptly when he writes:

Als realismusspezifisches Merkmal ist damit Aufklärung über die Wirklichkeit der jeweiligen Zeit anzusetzen. Nicht-realistische Literatur vermittelt zwar durchaus auch Einsichten in den Gang der Welt, aber auf einer allgemeinen Ebene durch Bezug auf immer Gültiges. Solche Verallgemeinerungsfähigkeit eignet auch der Mehrzahl der realistischen Werke, die Anwendung auf eine konkrete historische Situation geht aber darüber nicht verloren: Realistische Literatur nimmt die Zustände einer datierbaren und lokalisierbaren Situation in die Kunst auf. Insofern ist freie Schöpfung oder gar Abkehr von der Wirklichkeit realismusfremd.[121]

The ethical or moral position of the author, the emphasis on the individual in contemporary society, and a commitment to and belief in the possibility of societal change directed toward improving the lot of society's members are all constitutive elements of the arguments in favour of a new realism. And, although it is not always clear how the term realism applies to works for the theater, it is clear that Kroetz shared these sentiments and that his work was well-received by most realism proponents. Indeed many critics consider him to be the most consistent and persistent of the new realists.[122]

Nonetheless, the political and aesthetic scepticism that comes out in the arguments of someone like Jörg Drews (or Adorno) accompanied Kroetz's career as well. As the political optimism of the late sixties faded into the political fragmentation and resignation of the seventies and early eighties, Kroetz's realist aesthetic became stale, even in his own eyes. From (at the latest) the mid-seventies onward, the playwright found himself defending an aesthetic that had increasingly fallen into literary disrepute. He acknowledges the critical voices that label realism an "überlebte Mode," but attributes the rejection of realism to a flight from personal responsibility into an historical defeatism. Clearly revealing frustration and anger at literary colleagues like Drews, Kroetz writes in 1980:

> Man flieht aus der Verantwortung in die defätistische Crux, daß Wirklichkeit "sowieso unverantwortbar" sei, man sich also − wieder mal − am besten gar nicht auf sie einlasse, da sie einerseits Moloch sei, der einen auffresse und andererseits Betonwand, an der man sich nur den Schädel einschlagen könne.[123]

Already then Kroetz sensed, consciously or unconsciously, the onset of his own exclusion from the West German stage. The theaters were, he claimed, squeezing out realism to make room for a celebration of the *Neue Innerlichkeit*. What they lost by doing so was the re-awakening of the stage by the Horváth/Fleißer renaissance at the transition point from the sixties to the seventies. It was for Kroetz not only a re-awakening but also a rejuvenation that had regained for the West German stage a position of social importance.[124] Although he is here still bitter and dismissive, the eighties marked a shift in his own work distinctly away from realist aesthetic strategies. But what came between his initial work of ultrarealism and the phantasmic realism of the mid-eighties?

Socialist Realism as a Theoretical Influence

While Kroetz's work debuted in a literary climate that had some room left and a modicum of sympathy for his early ultrarealist one-act plays, as the dramatist moves into the seventies, his aesthetic program seems increasingly to come under the theoretical influence of socialist realism.[125] The realism proponents in the West German debate shared many basic tenets with socialist realism, which was also the official aesthetic of the West German communist party, but it would be unfair to posit a direct link aesthetically or politically between all leftist authors in West Germany and Eastern European institutional communism.

In fact, I believe it would be inaccurate to label all of Kroetz's work as socialist realist, but certain general principles do weigh heavily in his aesthetic project during the early seventies, beginning at the latest with *Oberösterreich*. Rolf-Peter Carl writes of Kroetz's relationship to the aesthetic theory of socialist realism: "Daß sich Kroetz vom Weg des sozialistischen Realismus im Drama zugleich angezogen und abgestoßen fühlen kann, findet seine Erklärung vielleicht darin, daß er seiner Wirkungstheorie zuneigt, seine dramaturgischen Mittel aber als nicht ausreichend erkennt."[126] One should add that Kroetz may not have been as restrictive in his choice of the aesthetic means he saw offered by socialist realism, but he certainly did subscribe to the theoretical assumptions behind those choices.

Furthermore, he also saw his work from 1972 to at least the late seventies as in the service of the DKP's political platform. This is not to imply that Kroetz sold his aesthetic soul to the DKP, but he does acknowledge the influence of the party on his writing after 1972. He writes: "Wenn ich heute ein wenig anders schreibe, als ich früher geschrieben haben, dann ist das nicht zuletzt das Verdienst meiner Partei, die mir auch da vorangeholfen hat" (WA, 608). Again, it is the role of an aesthetic guide that the party filled for Kroetz. Ernst B. Hess-Lüttich comments on the changes in Kroetz's realism paradigm from the early ultrarealism to the realism of *Oberösterreich* or *Das Nest*:

Empirie als Appell, zeit-kritisches Engagement in deskriptiver Präzision verwirklicht, ohne dem Publikum fertige Programme und beispielhafte Modelle politisch vorzugeben. Diesen naturalistisch instrumentierten

Realismus seiner Anfänge wird er wenig später, nach seinem Eintritt in die DKP, als bloß "beschreibenden Realismus" denunzieren und ihm seinen "westlichen sozialistisichen Realismus" gegenüberstellen. . .[127]

His early reliance on the ability of the naturalistic detail to speak volumes on the systemic exploitation of the individual in contemporary society has given way to a more focused realism.

There are, however, only a few aspects of socialist realism that are particularly important for Kroetz's work. They are *Parteilichkeit* (i.e. relying on a firm belief in and adherence to communist party principles to guide one's productive efforts), *das Typische* and an insistence that the work of art portray not only the way society is now, but also reveal trends that indicate in what direction society should and will be moving. Although these are principles that literary theorists of socialist realism date back both to Marx and Engels as well as Lenin, Kroetz struggled to do justice to all of them after his entry into the DKP. Since they are at the very least implicitly always in the background of his theoretical pronouncements from *Oberösterreich* up through *Nicht Fisch nicht Fleisch*, they merit a short definition.

Parteilichkeit

Theoretically, *Parteilichkeit* goes well beyond a simple political or philosophical commitment to the goals and practices of the communist party. It becomes a structuring principle in works of art that determines not only the selection of topics or stylistic means an author chooses, but also the perspective that the work assumes. In a collection of essays about socialist realism, one finds the following definition of *Parteilichkeit*:

> Mit dem Begriff "sozialistische Parteilichkeit" erfaßt die Theorie des sozialistischen Realismus den ästhetischen Ausdruck der offenen und tiefen, zur persönlichen Überzeugung gereiften Übereinstimmung des Künstlers mit den gesellschaftlichen Zielstellungen, den Aufgaben und der revolutionären Praxis der marxistisch-leninistischen Partei der Arbeiterklasse.[128]

Although the authorial collective here emphasizes that it is the aesthetic expression of the author's personal commitment and concurrence with the party's goals, it also entails a socially productive moment, whereby the author's active reflection of society, governed by *Parteilichkeit*, becomes a co-generative power in social development.[129]

Parteilichkeit also goes hand-in-hand with an epistemological surety, one which the majority of West German proponents and opponents of a contemporary realism did not share. Based on the notion that historical materialism not only recognizes, but also acknowledges objective reality, an aesthetic constructed on historical materialist foundations offers a productive recognition of reality's totality. That is to say, socialist realist works produce a slice of reality that allows for a generalization to reality as a whole.[130] The expression "slice of reality" is actually somewhat inadequate here. A better choice would be a *typical* moment. In fact, *Parteilichkeit* and *das Typische* are essentially inseparable principles. Claus Träger writes:

> Der Realismus beweist sich schließlich dort, wo in einer individuellen Geschichte die Triebkräfte und Tendenzen des Zeitalters transparent werden, wo der Held nicht mehr in sein "Milieu" eingesperrt scheint: wo unter der Hülle einer bestimmten Lebenstätigkeit *das wirkliche Subjekt* perspektivischen gesellschaftlichen Handelns sichtbar wird. Darin erweist sich die Parteilichkeit des Autors wie seine Gestalten. Sie ist eine Kategorie von welt-historischer Dimension, in welcher sich die Hauptkraft und-richtung der Epoche ausdrückt; sie kann deshalb nur zum Schaden des Realismus dieser Epoche, in der die Wege zum Sozialismus führen, in ihrer Bedeutung jeweils auf bloß eine durch ihre unmittelbaren Tätig-keitsmerkmale charakterisierte Menschengruppe ästhetisch eingegrenzt werden.[131]

Träger here touches on all of the points discussed so far. He notes that realism reveals the true driving forces of an era, including the real subject of history, and that realist literature points in the direction history is moving. This feat, he claims, is what constitutes an author's *Parteilichkeit*. This passage also introduces the concept of *das Typische*, and begins to distinguish it from such seemingly related concepts such as the average or the normal.

Das Typische

When Kroetz sets out to alter his first aesthetic model (well-repres-ented in such plays as *Heimarbeit* or *Stallerhof*), he seeks a more representative dramatic model, with all of the aforementioned implications. According to socialist realist theory, the typical must fulfill the following criteria:

> Die realistische Typisierung ist wesentlich darauf gerichtet, die Wirklichkeit überschaubar zu machen. In der Verallgemeinerung individueller Verhalt-ensweisen und Eigenschaften stellt sie deren soziale Bedeutung heraus, sie setzt den einzelnen zum gesellschaftlichen Ganzen, die Persönlichkeit zur jeweiligen sozialen Gemeinschaft in Beziehung und erkundet auf diese Weise die mögliche und wirkliche Größe des Menschen, aber auch die

mögliche und wirkliche Größe der Gesellschaft, die eine Lebensgrundlage ist.[132]

This definition stresses the role typification has in allowing the reader to see reality in its entirety. The relationship of such a definition to Kroetz's own is blatant. The author writes:

> Der Realismus muß sich aber nicht nur mit dem Volk, er muß sich mit dem staatlichen Ganzen, der Gesellschaft, so auseinandersetzen, daß, einfach gesprochen, der Seufzer der Frau Meyer nicht der Seufzer *einer* Frau Meyer bleibt, sondern der Seufzer aller in der Situation der Frau Meyer befindlichen Frauen eines Staatsgefüges (also der BRD) ist, und der Realismus muß erklären, wer die Frau Meyer seufzen macht und was.[133]

However, in order for a character or situation to be *typisch* it must also bring out the direction society is going, which, in turn, is determined by *Parteilichkeit*. Stephan Kohl describes *das Typische* as follows: "Methodisch wird die Zukunft in der Gegenwart durch die zentrale Kategorie des Typischen gestaltet. Als 'typisch' werden dabei nicht das Durchschnittliche, am häufigsten Vertretene bewertet, sondern jene Charaktere und Tendenzen, die in der Gegenwart die Zukunft am deutlichsten vorwegnehmen."[134]

The term is, to say the least, overburdened. The theoretical demand, however, that the author find and then aesthetically recreate *das Typische* is essential if socialist realist works hope to be as actively productive socially as party theorists and officials assert they are. Rolf-Peter Carl maintains that it was Kroetz's political schooling in the DKP that led him to expand his aesthetic horizons to include a perspective to the future.[135]

The element of socialist realist theory that ultimately can be either the most powerful or the most frustrating for the artist is this expectation that art will in fact generate further impulses in its readers to participate actively in the generation and realization of socialist goals. These impulses must already be so shaped by the author that they can yield only behaviour conducive to such goals:

> denn der "pädagogische Charakter" der Konfliktgestaltung besteht gerade darin, daß in ihr typische geistige und emotionale Spannungen der Epoche eingefangen sind und damit dem Kunstaufnehmenden eine Darstellung des historischen Prozesses ausgeliefert wird: Sie zeigt ihm den Spielraum eigener Betätigung, Bewährung und Entscheidung. Diese Möglichkeit, Leser, Zuschauer und Hörer in das Konfliktgefüge auf solche Wiese einzubeziehen, erweitert sich in dem Maße, wie sich das gesellschaftliche Bewußtsein entwickelt. Der Künstler macht den Konflikt nicht nur in seiner Gegenständlichkeit nachvollziehbar, sondern auch in seinem

gesellschaftlichen Bezug bewußt und damit den Kunstaufnehmenden zum "Mitverantwortlichen".[136]

Good socialist realist literature therefore not only shows historical processes, it also essentially tells the readers what options are available *vis-à-vis* their own behaviour. It involves the readers to such an extent that it infuses them with more than just a feeling of responsibility for the direction of history, it actually makes them responsible − at least theoretically.

True socialist realism is, so some would argue, only possible within a socialist society. Nonetheless, Kroetz talked expressly about the creation of a *Western* socialist realism. He explicitly directed his aesthetic production for at least eight years according to communist party philosophy; he actively sought out ways aesthetically to pin down the typical dramatic character and the typical dramatic conflict in order, finally, to point out the way to what he believed would be the social equality obtaining in a socialist society.

Again, in outlining these few principles of socialist realism, I do not wish to assert that Kroetz wrote all of his work according to a socialist realist paradigm (although some pieces, like *Das Nest*, resemble the works of Friedrich Wolf, an earlier proponent of socialist realism). Instead I would argue that the production and reception of Kroetz's work throughout the seventies benefits or suffers from its close alliance to either the debate about realism in West Germany of the sixties and seventies or to at least the theoretical demands of socialist realism. His theater works premiered during a time when the political quality of art and literature was the focus of heated debate, and manifold experiments to create a political aesthetic abounded. Although Kroetz's earliest literary attempts did not go in any one direction at all, the success of his realist plays prompted him to pursue that particular aesthetic strategy. Upon joining the DKP, Kroetz's political aesthetic project was subject to refinement according to certain theoretical principles of socialist realism. His work is thus positioned between two different, albeit related, discourses about the relationship between politics and aesthetics.

As other political and aesthetic strategies supplanted the political culture specific to the sixties and then to the era of the student movement, arguments such as those offered by Adorno or Drews gained influence in Kroetz's thoughts about his work. He began to experiment again, moving further and further away from the ultrarealism characteristic of those pieces that earned him his reputation. It has not been an easy move for him to make, and his work has certainly met with considerably less success in the eighties and early nineties.

Structure and Focus of the Following Analyses

Needless to say, many of the issues that surfaced above will come up again in the following chapters. This treatment of Kroetz's work centers on the process of constructing a political aesthetic. Because the playwright repeatedly found himself dissatisfied with certain representational strategies he had pursued (be they characterization, dramatic language, thematic focus, or form), his work is marked by several breaks in established dramatic models. Each major political or aesthetic realization led to a reconceptualization of his dramatic project. The plays chosen for this study all represent such a moment of reevaluation and, very literally, retooling.

Oberösterreich and *Das Nest* were Kroetz's first successful attempts to address issues relevant to his new interest in creating a theater accessible and pertinent to Germany's working class. Although plays like *Heimarbeit* and *Hartnäckig* premiered in a highly politicized atmosphere and were then essentially coopted by the German left as examples of the wretched circumstances two decades of conservative government had bred, it would be a mistake to assume that Kroetz wrote them with this in mind. Kroetz did not really begin to develop a comprehensive political and aesthetic vision until the early seventies, a good five years after he had written many of the earliest works. Nonetheless, his retrospective readings of the early one-acts do provide valuable insights into what occasioned the much-touted move toward what he saw as the demographic center of German society. Although both pieces were huge public and critical successes, the methods of characterization he used in *Oberösterreich* and *Das Nest* made it obvious that the formal restrictions of both plays, particularly language, were inadequate for his envisioned purposes. As Kroetz moves through the seventies, he perfects the model he provisionally adopted with *Das Nest*, but a renewed evaluation of German society and the role of political art therein brings about the next major stylistic break in his primary formal venue.

One could legitimately argue that the formal changes in *Nicht Fisch nicht Fleisch* are minimal, and yet they are significant enough to mark a turn in his aesthetic strategies that only increases in the following plays. The changes in *Oberösterreich* and *Das Nest* did not go much beyond a slight shift in focus *vis-à-vis* the main characters and an even slighter expansion of their linguistic capacities. *Nicht Fisch nicht Fleisch*, on the other hand, introduces a whole array of innovations: an expanded and more differentiated cast, more variety in the loci of the many scenes, and a departure, however brief, from the standard realist paradigm in the almost surreal concluding scenes.

Apparently still dissatisfied with the aesthetic changes introduced in *Nicht Fisch nicht Fleisch*, Kroetz begins his 1985 work, *Bauern sterben*, by citing his erstwhile realism in the opening scene, only to jettison realist representation for the remainder of the play. *Bauern sterben*, borrowing from various aesthetic paradigms, but primarily parabolic in form, creates an horrific vision of contemporary reality. This vision clearly no longer entails any vestiges of Kroetz's revolutionary optimism from the early seventies. Instead it reveals a growing sense of disillusionment with society and a trenchant pessimism about the future of humanity.

In contrast to Ingeborg Walther's recent examination of Kroetz's work that sought to highlight the continuities in the author's work, I am particularly intrigued with the ruptures and the inconsistencies that move his aesthetic project of experimentation forward. What causes Kroetz to modify, even abandon, stable and (relatively) successful representational strategies? This question constitutes the primary interest in each analysis. However, an answer to the question is accessible only through a number of other questions. Although not the exclusive focus of the following readings, both Kroetz's understanding of the political subject and an assessment of how well a realist aesthetic can capture social reality return to the foreground of the discussion repeatedly, and many of the other issues covered ultimately relate back to these two central issues. Given these parameters, the following readings look at each stylistic and thematic modification to see how it does or does not overcome the perceived deficiencies of the preceding plays. At times this may lead to apparent inconsistencies in analytical perspective, but each new moment of aesthetic experimentation represents an answer to different aesthetic and/or political questions, and the focus of the different readings must at least in part tailor itself to these differing questions.

The outline of Kroetz's career has already noted that he worked at the margins of the theater, continuing as a presence on the West German stage in essence only because of the overwhelming successes of the earliest one-act plays and the slightly modified versions thereof that are *Oberösterreich* and *Das Nest*. And although critics cite him as *the* representative of the new critical *Volksstück*, the latter is too diverse a category to make the label particularly meaningful. Instead Kroetz is an exemplary figure in twentieth-century drama because of his tireless pursuit of a functioning political aesthetic for the theater. He pushes the theatrical model of *Oberösterreich* as far as he can, and expands it to its own limits in works like *Nicht Fisch nicht Fleisch* and *Furcht und Hoffnung der BRD*. He does so at an historical juncture at which socio-political and aesthetic tendencies point in different directions. In this context even his seeming abandonment of a political theater in the late eighties and early nineties allows for the concluding questions: How far can a political aesthetic go before it runs afoul of itself or its time? Was the critical rejection of many Kroetz plays in the eighties only a result of his pursuing a political aesthetic at a time when the notion of political activism in Germany had long since begun to waver, if not to evaporate, or did his own aesthetic methodological choices create certain productive dead-ends in his work that led to his waning popularity? For instance, what might Kroetz's work for the theater tell us about the possibilities for a realist aesthetic in German literature from the late sixties to the late eighties?

Related questions form additional concerns for the analyses that follow. Does the thematic focus of his plays from *Oberösterreich* to *Bauern sterben* reflect preoccupations that the majority of theater-goers in the Federal Republic did not share? Do the plays generate a depiction of German society in the seventies and eighties that does not adequately address the specific forms of social differentiation in West Germany? Finally, do his specific attempts to engage the theater in a struggle against oppression (however formulated) represent an overestimation of the theater's potential? Ultimately, although the answers to such questions pertain explicitly only to Kroetz, the analysis of the individual plays will reach conclusions that can help to shape a more general study of political aesthetics in post-war German theater.

Notes

1. See Rolf-Peter Carl, *Franz Xaver Kroetz* (Munich: C.H. Beck, 1978), pp. 7–18; Otto Riewoldt (ed.), *Franz Xaver Kroetz* (Frankfurt/M.: Suhrkamp Verlag, 1985), particularly pp. 60 and 321; Ursula Reinhold, *Tendenzen und Autoren: Zur Literatur der siebziger Jahre in der BRD* (Berlin: Dietz Verlag, 1982), p. 342.
2. It was in particular *Heimarbeit* that caused the public outrage. In this piece there is both the on-stage attempt at a home-abortion as well as infanticide. Reports on the play's contents, which naturally preceded the play's actual premier, caused such public outrage, that demonstrators decided to storm the premier performances.
3. The so-called renaissance of the critical *Volksstück* and its relationship to *Volksstücke* of contemporary authors such as Kroetz will be the subject of further explication later in this chapter.

4. I say *seemed* because Otto Riewoldt has convincingly demonstrated that Kroetz's literary production has always been characterized by wide-ranging formal and thematic experimentation. See Otto Riewoldt, "Franz Xaver Kroetz. Der lange Weg zum Volksstück," in *Studien zur Ästhetik des Gegenwartstheaters*, ed. Christian Thomsen (Heidelberg: Carl Winter Universitätsverlag, 1985), pp. 268–291. The discussion will return to the scope of these experiments in the section on realism as an aesthetic strategy.

5. For a description of these pieces see both Riewoldt, "Franz Xaver Kroetz. Der lange Weg zum Volksstück," p. 281 and Carl, *Franz Xaver Kroetz*, p. 75.

6. See for instance the interview with the *Spiegel* from 1986: "Ich glaub', daß ich ausgeschrieben bin. Es erscheinen jetzt nicht umsonst in Kürze meine 40 Stücke gesammelt, ich glaub', daß das 40. Stück das letzte ist." *Der Spiegel* 40, no. 52 (22 Dec. 1986): p 132.

7. The reason this appears so unusual pertains to the long-standing leftist commitment to combat the kind of sensationalistic and inflammatory journalism the *Bild-Zeitung* represented for the student movement and its successors. It was, after all, the target of a widespread and vigorous (not to mention violent) critique during the so-called *Osterunruhen* following upon the attempted assassination of Rudi Dutschke, one of the most prominent leaders of the student movement.

8. "Der liebe Gott ist noch viel rücksichtsloser," an interview with Lothar Schmidt-Mühlisch und Horst Stein, *Die Welt*, 5 Oct. 1987.

9. Franz Xaver Kroetz, *Stücke*, vol. 4 (Frankfurt/M.: Suhrkamp Verlag, 1989), p. 137. Unless otherwise noted, all further references to this work will be followed by *FH* and the appropriate page number from this edition.

10. See Gerhard Preußen, "Portrait des Künstlers als alte Sau," *Theater heute*, no. 6 (1991): p. 26.

11. Ibid.

12. See for instance the following comment from 1972: "Theater hat in der Bundesrepublik nur einen Sinn, wenn es sich bemüht, die Ungerechtigkeiten unseres Systems herauszufinden und aufzuzeigen. Wenn es sich in den elitären Pfühlen der oberen Zehntausend rekelt, ist es verwerfenswert und macht sich mitschuldig am Gegenwärtigen." rpt. in *Weitere Aussichten . . . Ein Lesebuch . . . Neue Texte* (Berlin: Henschel Verlag, 1976), p. 558. All further citations from this volume will be followed by WA and the appropriate page number.

13. Franz Wille, "Der Ruf der Liebe: 'Hätt-i-di-dulliöh'," *Theater heute*, no. 7, (1994): pp. 4–9.
14. Kroetz's own reference to Hauptmann as a literary model for his own work does not necessarily do justice either to his theater plays or to the numerous other influences on his development. In fact, Kroetz's brand of naturalism has very little to do with Hauptmann, but comes rather through Ödön von Horváth and Marieluise Fleißer, as filtered through other post-war developments in European theater. Any number of direct and indirect influences could be cited: for instance Beckett's absurdist theater, Artaud and the theater of cruelty, and the work of such playwrights as Jean Genet and Edward Bond. Contemporary developments in acting and in literary form, such as the so-called "Happenings," also affected Kroetz's early developments in the theater. Rainer Werner Fassbinder and his "antiteater" constituted another profound impact on Kroetz's turn away from the highly abstract, essentially purely formal theater work he was engaged in at the Büchner-Theater in Munich, to which Fassbinder's ensemble took refuge when they were evicted from their own theater. In fact, Kroetz acted in Fassbinder's *Zum Beispiel Ingolstadt* (a loose version of Fleißer's *Pioniere in Ingolstadt*). According to Fassbinder, Kroetz at first resisted the realism of the Fleißer work, but eventually warmed to the piece. Clearly, this experience constitutes one of his earliest exposures to the Fleißer/Horváth renaissance. In order to secure the participation of the Büchner-Theater group in his production, Fassbinder made concessions in the area of language, agreeing to employ a highly stylized form of Bavarian dialect. He claims they would otherwise not have been interested in the realist portrayal of events in a small town. This combination of linguistic stylization and largely realist narrative focus marked Kroetz's work from the first one-act plays onward. See Riewoldt, *Franz Xaver Kroetz*, pp. 22–25.
15. Reprinted in excerpt form in ibid. pp. 115–116.
16. Susan Cocalis, "'Mitleid' and 'Engagement'. Compassion and/or Political Commitment in the Dramatic Works of Franz Xaver Kroetz," *Colloquia Germanica* 14, no. 3 (1981): particularly pp. 210 and 216. Cocalis seems to base her claims here primarily on what the author says of himself, which is often a risky thing to do with Kroetz, since he has made so many contradictory and inflammatory statements throughout his career. Although Kroetz does talk of his fears of losing favour with his audience (see WA, 596), such an admission only tells part of the story. In another passage from the very same interview, Kroetz claims that any time

a director finds his material good, he feels he has not been *radical* enough: "So lange mir kein Intendent sagt, das Stück ist so links, daß man es nicht aufführen kann, werfe ich mir immer vor, daß ich zu brav schreibe" (WA, 596f).

17. Carl, *Franz Xaver Kroetz*, p. 111.
18. For a particularly helpful discussion of post-war German drama, see Wolfram Buddecke and Helmut Fuhrmann, *Das deutschsprachige Drama seit 1945* (Munich: Winkler Verlag, 1981). Here in particular pp. 63–89.
19. C.D. Innes, *Modern German Drama. A Study in Form* (Cambridge: Cambridge University Press, 1979), p. 92.
20. Peter Weiss, *Die Ermittlung*, in *Stücke* I (Frankfurt/M.: Suhrkamp Verlag, 1976), p. 259.
21. W.G. Sebald (ed.), *A Radical Stage* (Oxford: Berg Publishers, 1988), p. 2. See also Günther Rühle, "Von der Politik zur Rolle. Rückblick auf ein Jahrzehnt (1965–1975)," in *Positionen des Dramas: Analysen und Theorien zur deutschen Gegenwartsliteratur*, ed. Heinz Ludwig Arnold (Munich: C.H. Beck, 1977), p. 171.
22. To reduce the number of important dramatists in the seventies to four is an oversimplification and an almost unanswerable dismissal of the many other creative, productive and outstanding playwrights of the period. Virtually all of the documentarists continued to earn and get the attention of the theater world, as well as figures such as Martin Walser, Günter Grass and Martin Sperr. Even the influence of the four dramatists I cite did not remain constant: Handke's importance as a dramatist waned into the seventies and is only now resurging, while Botho Strauß's work did not really come into public attention until the mid-seventies. Nonetheless, these four authors, all from roughly the same generation, were at the center of the theater's critical attention for most of the decade. Furthermore, the issues they raise with their work are representative of broader literary trends in the Federal Republic within this time frame.
23. Rühle, p. 188.
24. Buddecke, Fuhrmann, p. 216.
25. Dieter Kafitz, "Die Problematisierung des individualistischen Menschenbildes im deutschsprachigen Drama der Gegenwart (Franz Xaver Kroetz, Thomas Bernhard, Botho Strauß)," *Basis* 10 (1980): p. 114.
26. See for example Buddecke, Fuhrmann, p. 170 and Kafitz, pp. 96f.
27. Buddecke, Fuhrmann, pp. 170f.
28. Both Susanne's fight to keep Moritz away from a relationship with another woman, despite their chronic inability to *find* each other, as

well as Moritz's decision to stage at least a personal protest against a reconfigurement of his exhibition because of the disgruntlement of one board member are signs, albeit very modest ones, that these characters are prepared to combat the alienation, isolation and sense of powerlessness they feel. Susanne's description of her frustrated and frustrating relationship to Moritz does include a moment of hope: "Sie wissen nicht, wie oft wir voreinander umgekehrt sind, im letzten Augenblick. Er ist gegangen oder ich bin gegangen. Unsere einzige Hoffnung: der gleiche Lauf der Wiederholung. . . . Am Anfang ist immer der Abschied . . . dann kommt ein Wiedersehen. . . . Zwischen Kommen und Gehen die Wende, dort treffen wir uns," in Botho Strauß, *Trilogie des Wiedersehens/Groß und Klein. Zwei Theaterstücke* (Munich: Deutscher Taschenbuchverlag, 1980), pp. 117f. See also, Kafitz, p. 118.

29. Strauß, p. 260.

30. Handke's work has changed substantially in form over the years, as has that of Botho Strauß. However, since the primary purpose of this all too sketchy overview is to illuminate the dramatic landscape in Germany from the time Kroetz entered the theater until he had essentially cemented his own position *vis-à-vis* his contemporaries, following the careers of these other individuals further into the seventies and eighties goes beyond the present need.

31. Buddecke, Furhmann, p. 173.

32. See e.g. Rühle's description of the major focus of the decade: "zu erkennen was Sprache ist, was sie mit uns macht, was allein dadurch mit uns geschieht, daß wir in einen vorgeprägten Sprachraum hineingeboren werden, in dem eine Sprache als Material zur Verfügung steht," p. 187. C.D. Innes calls "the relationship between political exploitation and linguistic manipulation, individual and social expectations" the "keynote of post-war German drama," one that links "various stylistic approaches," p. 267 and also p. 259. Innes also points out the other common feature of post-war German drama: the absence of the individual: p. 265.

33. For two studies that stress the similarities in German drama of the seventies, see Kafitz and Ingeborg Walther, *The Theater of Franz Xaver Kroetz* (New York Berne, Frankfurt/M. and Paris: Peter Lang, 1990), particularly pp. 15–34.

34. In an interview with *die taz*, Kroetz explains his relationship to the events of 1967–1969 as follows: "So hat beispielsweise das Jahr 1968 und die entsprechende Bewegung für mich gar nicht stattgefunden. Ich hatte mich zu dieser Zeit ganz dem Theater verschrieben. Die APO, die Studentenbewegung überhaupt, gab es

für mich nicht. Leute meines Bildungsweges haben gegenüber Studenten ja sowieso einen starken Neidkomplex, weil man eigentlich laut elterlicher Voraussicht selbst hätte studieren sollen. Von daher hatte ich bereits keinen Bezug zu dieser Bewegung." rpt. in Riewoldt, *Franz Xaver Kroetz*, p. 23

35. Other major representatives of the so-called new critical *Volksstück* are Martin Sperr, a Bavarian, Peter Turrini, and Wolfgang Bauer, both Austrians. I will give a more detailed description of Sperr's *Bayrische Trilogie* shortly. Both Turrini and Bauer's works were obviously familiar to Kroetz. I cannot, however, gauge the extent of their mutual influence. Bauer's pieces such as *Change, Magic Afternoon* and *Film und Frau (Shakespear, ein Sadist)* seem sufficiently different from Kroetz's plays to question the extent of their commonalities. Bauer's early works focus not on the underprivileged, inarticulate members of society, but rather on a class of well-off, well-educated and bored young people, for whom physical violence has become something of a game. Violence in Kroetz's one-acts, in contrast, generally stems from the characters' inability to see alternative behavior choices.

36. Horváth's *Kasimir und Karoline* (1931) was staged by Peter Palitzsch in 1964 and by Hans Hollmann in 1968. Hollmann also directed *Geschichten aus dem Wienerwald* (1930) in 1966 and 1971. The renewed interest in Marieluise Fleißer's work began in 1966 when the *Schaubühne am Halleschen Ufer* staged *Der starke Stamm*. Rühle claims that this early production did not have the impact that the 1971 Wuppertal staging of *Fegefeuer in Ingolstadt* had, but it was through the Berlin performance that Martin Sperr became acquainted with Fleißer's work. See Rühle, p. 180.

37. Rühle, p. 179

38. See Wend Kässens and Michael Töteberg, "Fortschritt im Realismus? Zur Erneuerung des kritischen Volksstücks seit 1966," *Basis* 6 (1976): pp. 33–37 and Wend Kässens, "Wer durchs Laub geht, kommt darin um. Zur Sprachbehandlung und zu einigen Motiven in den Dramen von Franz Xaver Kroetz," in Riewoldt, *Franz Xaver Kroetz*, p. 262.

39. Helmut Karasek, "Die Sprache der Sprachlosen," rpt. in Riewoldt, *Franz Xaver Kroetz*, p. 79.

40. Martin Sperr, "Was erwarte ich vom Theater?" in Helmut Kreuzer (ed.), *Deutsche Dramaturgie der Sechziger Jahre* (Tübingen: Martin Niemeyer Verlag, 1974), p. 66. See also Ursula Schregel, "The Theater of Franz Xaver Kroetz," trans. Peter Harris and Pia Kleber, in *Modern Drama* 23, no. 4 (Jan. 1981): p. 473.

41. See for instance Calvin Jones, *Negation and Utopia. The German*

Volksstück from Raimund to Kroetz (New York: Peter Lang, 1993); Hugo Aust, Peter Haida and Jürgen Hein, *Volksstück. Vom Hanswurstspiel zum sozialen Drama der Gegenwart* (Munich: Beck, 1989); Jean-Marie Valentin (ed.), *Volk – Volksstück – Volkstheater im deutschen Sprachraum des 18.–20. Jahrhunderts* (New York: Peter Lang, 1986); Thorsten Bügner, *Annäherungen an die Wirklichkeit. Gattung und Autoren des neuen Volksstückes* (New York: Peter Lang, 1986); and Gerd Müller, *Das Volksstück von Raimund bis Kroetz* (Munich: Oldenbourg, 1979).

42. Helmut Motekat, *Das zeitgenössische deutsche Drama* (Stuttgart: Kohlhammer, 1977), p. 106.

43. Only such early works as *Katzelmacher, Zum Beispiel Ingolstadt* (loosely based on Fleißer's *Pioniere in Ingolstadt*), and *Bremer Freiheit* mark Fassbinder's brief association with the *Volksstück*. Although Kroetz and Fassbinder did work together for one production, their creative relationship quickly became very problematic. Fassbinder created a film version of Kroetz's *Wildwechsel* in 1973 that Kroetz denounced as totally foreign to his own understanding of the piece.

44. Buddecke, Fuhrmann, p. 145.

45. Here I would agree with Gerd Müller's assessment of the term. He argues that any definition of the label *Volksstück* must base itself on the historical period in which it appears. Müller, p. 10.

46. See for example Kässens and Töteberg, "Fortschritt im Realismus?" p. 30.

47. Motekat, p. 112.

48. See Kässens and Töteberg in Riewoldt, *Franz Xaver Kroetz*, pp. 36f.

49. Innes, p. 230.

50. Rühle, p. 182.

51. Buddecke and Fuhrmann point out that the use of the term "realism" or "realist" to describe such playwrights as Sperr, Kroetz and Fassbinder risks blurring the very substantial differences both formally and thematically between them and between prose authors who have also assumed the label. Buddecke, Fuhrmann, p. 144.

52. Moray McGowan, "Subject, Politics, Theatre – Reflections on Franz Xaver Kroetz," in Sebald, p. 81.

53. Kässens and Töteberg, "Fortschritt im Realismus?" p. 30.

54. Karl Markus Michel, "Ein Kranz für die Literatur," *Kursbuch*, no. 15 (1968): pp. 169–186.

55. The following discussion will problematize both this term and its implications as the various positions come under closer scrutiny.

56. This is not to say that art is not a commodity. Once the work of art

hits the market, i.e. after it passes out of the production stage, it is subject to the same conditions as any other product to be sold. However, the conditions of aesthetic production have remained, according to Adorno, distinct from the prevailing means of production. See also Ernst Grohotolsky, *Ästhetik der Negation – Tendenzen des deutschen Gegenwartsdramas: Versuch über die Aktualität der "Ästhetischen Theorie" Theodor W. Adornos* (Königstein/Ts.: Athenäum, Hain, Hanstein, 1984), p. 26.

57. Max Horkheimer and Theodor W. Adorno, *Dialektik der Aufklärung* in Theodor W. Adorno, *Gesammelte Schriften*, vol. 3 (Frankfurt/M.: Suhrkamp Verlag, 1981), p. 177.

58. Ibid., p. 144.

59. The process of bureaucratization, alienation and atomization within society has received exhaustive treatment. See e.g. Herbert Marcuse, *Eros and Civilization* (Boston: Beacon Press, 1974) and *The One Dimensional Man* (Boston: Beacon Press, 1964), and Jürgen Habermas, *Strukturwandel der Öffentlichkeit* (Darmstadt and Neuwied: Hermann Luchterhand Verlag, 1962).

60. Horkheimer, Adorno, *Dialektik der Aufklärung*, p. 168.

61. Adorno, *Ästhetische Theorie*, in *Gesammelte Schriften*, vol. 7 (Frankfurt/M.: Suhrkamp Verlag, 1970), pp. 336f, see also p. 373.

62. Adorno, "Engagement," in *Gesammelte Schriften*, vol. 11 (Frankfurt/M.: Suhrkamp Verlag, 1974), p. 425. See also *Ästhetische Theorie*, p. 335.

63. See also Russell Berman, "Adorno, Marxism and Art," *Telos*, no. 34 (Winter 1977–1978): pp. 157–166, particularly p. 163.

64. Adorno, *Ästhetische Theorie*, p. 337.

65. Ibid., p. 337.

66. Ibid., p. 10.

67. Ibid., p. 229.

68. Ibid., see p. 15: "Die Kommunikation der Kunstwerke mit dem Auswendigen . . . geschieht durch Nicht-Kommunikation."

69. Ibid., p. 218.

70. Although the term "blooming" can conjure up images of spring flowers, Adorno seems more to have uncontrollable weeds in mind.

71. Adorno, "Engagement," p. 416.

72. Ibid., p. 417.

73. Ibid., p. 418. There is a key aspect of the aesthetic process missing here, which could at least partially redeem Brechtian dramatics from this insightful assault. This element is reception. Despite Brecht's insistence that pre-epic theater did not estrange reality from the spectator, all art represents mitigated social reality, that is to say any element within any aesthetic product is in some form or

another estranged. In Brechtian theater this is a very conscious and intentional process. The idea was that the spectator in daily life may indeed know that a person cannot be absolutely good in capitalist society. However, this knowledge may not be active, reflected or even conscious. It is the task, so to speak, of the play to bring this recognition to the fore, to locate if possible the source of the problem and, finally, to turn passive knowledge into working knowledge. In this light it is not necessarily a case of stating the obvious, but rather of doing so in a different, as yet novel manner.

74. Adorno, "Der Artist als Statthalter," in *Gesammelte Schriften*, vol. 11, p. 125.

75. Adorno, "Erpreßte Versöhnung," in *Gesammelte Schriften*, vol. 11, p. 261. See also the following passage from the same essay: "So rechtmäßig auch Lukács in der Tradition der großen Philosophie Kunst als Gestalt von Erkenntnis begreift, nicht als schlechthin Irrationales der Wissenschaft kontrastiert, er verfängt sich dabei in eben der bloßen Unmittelbarkeit, deren er kurzsichtig die avantgardistische Produktion zeiht: der der Feststellung. Kunst erkennt nicht dadurch die Wirklichkeit, daß sie sie, photographisch oder 'perspektivish', abbildet, sondern dadurch, daß sie vermöge ihrer autonomen Konstitution ausspricht, was von der empirischen Gestalt der Wirklichkeit verschleiert wird." p. 264. See also pp. 268 and 270.

76. Adorno, "Standort des Erzählers im zeitgenössischen Roman," in *Gesammelte Schriften*, vol. 11, p. 43. Referring specifically to Hochhuth's *Der Stellvertreter* and its realist form, Adorno adds: "Keine traditionalistische Dramaturgie von Hauptakteuren leistet es mehr. Die Absurdität des Realen drängt auf eine Form, welche die realistische Fassung zerschlägt." In "Offener Brief an Rolf Hochhuth," vol. 11, p. 595.

77. Bertolt Brecht, *Gesammelte Werke* (Frankfurt/M.: Suhrkamp Verlag, 1967), vol. 19, p. 322. See also his *Arbeitsjournal* (ed. Werner Hecht) (Frankfurt/M.: Suhrkamp Verlag, 1973), vol. 1, p. 270. In future all citations from the collected works will be followed by "GW", the volume and page number.

78. Where language was ineffective Brecht would have been more likely to see its inappropriate application. See e.g. GW14,1409.

79. I am not using the word "language" in any heightened sense, such as was the case in, for instance, *fin de siècle* Vienna, but rather as the vehicle for certain aesthetic products, such as drama and the novel.

80. Brecht uses this metaphor on several occasions. See e.g.: GW 19, 332.

81. It would, however, be incorrect to assert that Brecht was a pioneer in this attempt to include under the rubric of art areas of human production generally regarded as extra-aesthetic.
82. GW 9,774.
83. The term "perversion" indicates here only the fact that the fascist movement harnessed the momentum within the labor movement, including the dissatisfaction of the working class with its political and economic situation.
84. See Walter Benjamin, *Das Kunstwerk im Zeitalter seiner technischen Reproduzierbarkeit* (Frankfurt/M.: Suhrkamp Verlag, 1966), pp. 42ff.
85. GW15,260.
86. Brecht, *Arbeitsjournal*, vol. 1, p. 236.
87. GW15,193 and GW16,520.
88. Brecht stresses this idea in various comments about the work of sociologists. See e.g. GW14,1420.
89. Walter Benjamin, "Der Autor als Produzent," in *Versuche über Brecht*, ed. Rolf Tiedemann (Frankfurt/M.: Suhrkamp Verlag, 1966), p. 110.
90. GW15,222.
91. GW16,515 and 517.
92. Brecht, *Arbeitsjournal*, vol. 2, p. 637.
93. This is not a prudish condemnation of the ornate, but rather a critique of techniques that obscure or make overly difficult the process of understanding and, ultimately, changing reality.
94. See for instance Brecht, *Arbeitsjournal*, vol. 2, p. 780.
95. Keith Bullivant, *Realism Today* (Leamington Spa: Berg Publishers, 1987), p. 34.
96. Josef Haslinger, "Der proletarische Selbst-Zerstörungsroman — Über den Wirklichkeitsverlust der neueren österreichischen Literatur," *Wespennest*, no. 76 (1989): p. 55.
97. Bullivant, p. 34.
98. Dieter Wellershoff, *Literatur und Veränderung* (Cologne: Kiepenheuer & Witsch, 1969), pp. 85f.
99. Drews implicitly calls attention in the following passage to a probable link between the new realists and communism simply by bringing it up. That he goes on apparently to deny such a link is more a rhetorical gesture than a serious rejection. He writes, "Daß in Abständen der Ruf nach einem neuen literarischen Realismus auch in der Bundesrepublik oder in Österreich ertönt, angestimmt von linksbürgerlichen oder DKP-nahen Schiftstellergruppierungen, ist wohl weniger einer kulturpolitischen Hörigkeit dieser Schriftsteller gegenüber dem Osten zuzuschreiben als vielmehr der

eingestandenen oder uneingestandenen traurigen Einsicht, daß Literatur von Rang sich in einer arbeitsteiligen Welt ... so hochspezialisert hat, daß sie nur noch ein schmales Publikum erreicht." in "Wider einen neuen Realismus," Peter Laemmle (ed.), *Realismus – welcher?* (Munich: Edition text + kritik, 1976), p. 152.

100. See Bullivant, p. 28.

101. Stephan Kohl, *Realismus: Theorie und Geschichte* (Munich: Wilhelm Fink Verlag, 1977), p. 166

102. Otto Riewoldt, "Franz Xaver Kroetz. Der lange Weg zum Volksstück," p. 269.

103. Peter Laemmle (ed.), *Realismus – welcher?* (Munich: Edition text + kritik, 1976).

104. Clearly this applies to Kroetz as well. See for instance the passage cited in note 12.

105. Kohl writes: "Neben diese meist unbewußte Verbreitung bürgerlicher Werte und Normen tritt in realistischen Werken die bewußte Vermittlung einer moralischen Vorstellung. Eingebracht werden die präskriptiven Absichten der Autoren ins realistische Werk genau dort, wo die künstlerische Gestaltung zwischen dem Partikularen/Individuellen und dem allgemein Exemplarischen vermittelt. Auf die moralisch-didaktische Konzeption des 'Typischen' nach marxistischer Definition sei hier als Beispiel verwiesen." He goes on, however, to a make a crucial distinction: "Wird in einem literarischen Werk... die zeitgenössische Wirklichkeit so 'ernst genommen', daß ihre Darstellung Bedingung und Grundlage für alle moralischen Intentionen und Versuche der Ideologievermittlung eines Autors abgibt, läßt sich sinnvollerweise von 'Realismus' sprechen. Treten dagegen die Bestandteile der Realität – so naturalistisch sie gezeichnet sein mögen – nur in der Funktion auf, ideologische Inhalte zu 'beglaubigen', spricht man besser von 'Illusionismus'." p. 212.

106. Laemmle, p. 7.

107. Uwe Timm, "Von den Schwierigkeiten eines Anti-Realisten," in Laemmle, pp. 169f.

108. Ibid., p. 174.

109. Jörg Drews, "Wider einen neuen Realismus," in Laemmle, p. 157.

110. Timm, "Realismus und Utopie," in Laemmle, p. 145.

111. Ibid., p. 142.

112. Drews, "Wider einen neuen Realismus," p. 156.

113. Timm, "Von den Schwierigkeiten eines Anti-Realisten," p. 173.

114. Kroetz's Marxist philosophy and its relevance to his aesthetic project are the subject of extensive analysis in chapter two.

115. Wellershoff, *Literatur und Veränderung*, p. 39.
116. It does seem, however, appropriate to note that one could easily read Balzac's own *Père Goriot* in a similar fashion.
117. Interview with Donna Hoffmeister from 1978 "Ich kann nur schreiben, von dem, was ich sehe, nicht von dem, was ich sehen möchte," in *Modern Language Studies*, vol. 11, no. 1 (Winter 1980–1981): p. 44.
118. Timm, "Realismus und Utopie," p. 143.
119. See Drews "Wider einen neuen Realismus?" p. 159.
120. Timm, "Von den Schwierigkeiten eines Anti-Realisten," p. 174.
121. Kohl, p. 202.
122. See e.g. Schregel, p. 473.
123. Franz Xaver Kroetz, "Kirchberger Notizen," in Riewoldt, *Franz Xaver Kroetz*, p. 173.
124. Kroetz writes of the theater: "Es ist in den Dornröschenschlaf zurückgesunken, aus dem es um 1970 aufgeweckt wurde, durch die Wiederentdeckung von Horváth und Fleißer, durch realistische junge Theaterautoren, die bundesrepublikanische Wirklichkeit in den Mittelpunkt ihres Schaffens stellten, durch Schauspieler und Regisseure, die sich dem Realismus verschrieben hatten." in "Kirchberger Notizen," p. 172.
125. The *Concise Oxford Dictionary of Literary Terms* defines socialist realism as "a slogan adopted by the Soviel cultural authorities in 1934 to summarize the requirements of Stalinist dogma in literature: the established techniques of 19th-century realism were to be used to represent the struggle for socialism in a positive, optimistic light, while the allegedly 'decadent' techniques of modernism were to be avoided as bourgeois deviations. The approved model was Maxim Gorki's novel *The Mother* (1907)." Chris Baldick, *The Concise Oxford Dictionary of Literary Terms* (Oxford: Oxford University Press, 1990), pp. 206f. A description of socialist realism's basic aesthetic theoretical tenets follows.
126. Carl, *Franz Xaver Kroetz*, p. 27.
127. Ernst W.B. Hess-Lüttich, "Neorealismus und sprachliche Wirklichkeit. Zur Kommunikationskritik von Franz Xaver Kroetz," in Riewoldt, *Franz Xaver Kroetz*, pp. 299f.
128. Hans Koch, Klaus Jarmatz, Hermann Kähler, Werner Mittenzwei et al. (eds), *Zur Theorie des sozialistischen Realismus* (Berlin, GDR: Dietz Verlag, 1974), p. 537.
129. See Claus Träger, *Studien zur Realismustheorie und Methodologie der Literaturwissenschaft* (Leipzig: Reclam, 1972), p. 101: "Indessen wird die *Widerspiegelung*, die künstlerische wie die wissenschaftlich-theoretische, als *Bewußtseinstätigkeit* gesetzmäßig

zu einer die Wirklichkeit unmittelbar mitschaffenden Kraft und damit zu einem unentbehrlichen Element der gesellschaftlichen Entwicklung: Sie kann darum auch als eine Form der *Produktivität* begriffen werden."

130. Koch et al., pp. 377, 382 and 386.
131. Träger, pp. 76f.
132. Koch et al., p. 611.
133. Franz Xaver Kroetz, "Form ist der Teller von dem man ißt," in Riewoldt, *Franz Xaver Kroetz*, p. 91.
134. Kohl, p. 150.
135. Carl, *Franz Xaver Kroetz*, p. 26
136. Koch et al., pp. 634f. See also p. 381.

–2–

Oberösterreich and *Das Nest*

The Margins of Society

It would not be an exaggeration to say that Franz Xaver Kroetz's early plays met with astonishing success. Written mostly in the mid- to late sixties, they did not premier until 1971 with the staging of *Heimarbeit* and *Hartnäckig*. These two plays caused a tremendous uproar within the German theater-going public. Word that the plays contained not only illicit language and explicit sexual behavior, but also in *Heimarbeit* the onstage attempt of an at-home abortion, created a public scandal in the conservative theater audiences in Munich. However, despite heated demonstrations against their performance on the grounds of moral turpitude, these short pieces launched the career of the man who would be one of the most influential German dramatists of the seventies.

Kroetz earned his reputation as an up-and-coming dramatist with a series of short or one-act plays. These early works, for which both *Heimarbeit* and *Hartnäckig* are exemplary, have a fairly stable basic structure. Of the pieces up to and including *Oberösterreich* (1972) none have more than four major figures. Most of them revolve around a conflict within one small family: in *Wildwechsel* it is a teenage pregnancy that leads to patricide; in *Heimarbeit* it is the birth and subsequent murder of an illegitimate child; in *Stallerhof* and *Geisterbahn* it is the rape, seduction and pregnancy of a mildly learning-disabled girl and the death of her infant son at her own hands.

A general overview of reviews and of academic literature on these early works reveals that attention centers on the marginal social position of the characters portrayed and on the inability of these individuals to express themselves in a fashion adequate to their emotional and social needs.[1] One critic described Kroetz's characters as follows:

> Kroetzens Ausgepowerte – die weder ihrer sozialen noch ihrer damit ver-
> wickelten psychischen Lage Herr sind, auch nicht zu werden vermögen und
> keine Chance mehr dazu kriegen werden – sie sprechen kaum noch: zwischen
> langen Pausen versickern ihre kurzen Sätze; wenn sie schweigen, vor sich

hinsinnieren, in ihrer Isoliertheit sich einpressen, beweisen sie sich noch am ehesten als lebend; redend zeigen sie vornehmlich die ihnen zugefügten Risse und Beulen vor, die sozialen Defekte, das traurige Unvermögen, sich zu befreien – und sei es in Hoffnung.[2]

Out-powered and powerless, dramatic action in a play like *Heimarbeit* is dumb. Silence descends on the stage and marks even those few utterances the characters make. Instead of communication, the language of the figures reveals only defects and damage. Kroetz himself accepted the description of his characters as speechless. In the program to the premiers of *Heimarbeit* and *Hartnäckig* Kroetz writes: "Die Sprache funktioniert bei meinen Figuren nicht. Sie haben auch keinen guten Willen. Ihre Probleme liegen so weit zurück und sie sind soweit fortgeschritten, daß sie nicht mehr in der Lage sind, sie wörtlich auszudrücken." Although he later tried to differentiate this characterization, it did little to change public perception of the figures in his plays.

One reason that language and the apparent marginality of his characters received such attention by academic and journalistic critics alike is that the world his dramatic figures inhabit in the plays up to *Oberösterreich* is governed by physical brutality. In it communication is reduced to verbal grunts. The truncation of communication helps to explain why this is so. A typical example of dialogue would be the following selection from *Stallerhof*, an early work that premiered not long after *Heimarbeit* and *Hartnäckig*:

Staller: Magst ein Geheimnis hörn: schwanger is.
Sepp: Warum.
Staller: Ebn.
Sepp: Nix wahr is. Alles glogn.
Staller: Mir ham Beweise.
Sepp: Das geht net.
Staller: Genau.[3]

Obviously this interchange is peppered with verbal particles that are in no way pertinent to the statements Staller and Sepp make. Instead these seeming irrelevancies serve only as defense mechanisms. Words like *genau* or *ebn* take on a quasi-physical character, similar to a hand gesture to brush off accusations.

As time passed, both the author and his critics came to modify their positions on the linguistic capacities and the demographic positioning of these first figures. Indeed, the characterization of Kroetz's characters as "Randgruppen," or marginal social figures is probably largely attributable to the fact that Kroetz's rise as a dramatist occurred against the background of the Ödön von Horváth and Marieluise Fleißer renaissance in the late sixties and the concomitant development of the new critical *Volksstück*. Both Horváth and Fleißer depicted individuals who, although not underrepresented in society – the petty bourgeoisie (*Geschichten aus dem Wienerwald*), soldiers, young, uneducated women (*Pioniere in Ingolstadt*) – were not the stuff of high culture. Kroetz may have, once the connection was made between his work and that of Horváth and Fleißer (particularly the latter), intentionally read his own plays as portraying characters outside of society's mainstream, or outside of what was traditionally considered proper material for the theater. Closer analysis, however, does not bear this out, and Kroetz himself later came to assert that these figures were in no way at all marginal to society, but rather that society consists of innumerable *Randgruppen*: "Wenn man unsere 60 Millionen genau unter die Lupe nimmt, dann zerfallen sie zuletzt alle in Randerscheinungen. Die fette Mitte gibt es nicht, sie existiert nur in den Köpfen einiger denkfaulen Politiker" (WA, 555).

The labels "marginal" or "Randgruppen" stem from Kroetz's inclusion in his cast of characters teenagers (*Wildwechsel*), the physically and mentally disabled (*Hartnäckig* and *Stallerhof/Geisterbahn* respectively), the elderly (*Weitere Aussichten* and *Heimat*) and a petty sexual offender (*Lieber Fritz*). However, as pointed out above, a careful reading of these early works reveals that the figures in them are in truth not particularly marginal in economic terms. In *Stallerhof* the father owns a rather large farm. In *Hartnäckig* the two families are each proprietors of relatively successful restaurants. In *Männersache* Martha inherited a butcher shop from her parents. Certain characters in these pieces have, indeed, been marginalized by society: again, not according to actual class status, but rather according to potential economic productivity. For instance, the son in *Hartnäckig* is cast aside by both his fiancée and essentially by his parents, because, having lost a leg in a military exercise maneuver, they think he is no longer able to function as a "Wirt" in either his own family's restaurant or in that of his fiancée. Another example is both Sepp and Beppi in *Stallerhof*. Sepp, an aging farm hand, is of no socio-economic value to either the Staller couple or the labor market in general because he is both unskilled and old. Beppi, the Staller's moderately mentally handicapped daughter, does not have her parents' full esteem not only because of her learning disability, but also because she is a girl, and as such neither as much help to her father on the farm, nor an appropriate heir for his property.

Since the subject of this chapter is not the early plays themselves, but rather how Kroetz's later perception of them led him to change the fairly stable aesthetic strategy they represent, it is not of immense importance here to pin down the precise social status of these characters. Where this is, however, crucial is in determining why Kroetz's repeated attempts to modify his politico-aesthetic program fail to achieve the goals he himself sets for them. This question will be addressed later in this chapter. The general view on his work was that it portrayed characters outside of society's mainstream and definitely in the lowest of economic strata. And for the present, it is the public's and the dramatist's own perception of these works that provide clues to why Kroetz breaks with a dramatic strategy that garnered him such great success.

Certainly one of the main reasons this break occurs is because of Kroetz's decision to join the German Communist Party (DKP) in 1972, the year in which *Oberösterreich* was written and premiered. It is worth re-emphasizing that it was within this organization that his interests in politics developed and not in the context of the student movement of the late sixties and early seventies. By the time Kroetz joined the DKP, the student movement had already begun to fragment and to dissipate. The students who did not turn away from the politics of the public sphere to the politics of the self then turned to the communist party, which attracted the authoritarian, orthodox wing of the student movement. It was then the orthodoxy of the DKP that helped to crystallize Kroetz's understanding of Marxism and his interpretation both of German society during the late sixties and throughout the seventies as well as of the character of cultural political activism. I use the terms "orthodox" here for the following reasons. The party maintained: 1) that society is stratified by economically determined classes; 2) that economic structures and processes play a major role in the constitution of social reality; 3) that the proletariat is the agent of historical change in society; and 4) that the role of the communist party in class struggle is that of an avant garde.

The last two are the particular points that separate Kroetz most clearly from neo-marxists or other "left-liberal" groups. The concept of the proletariat as the agent of historical change had a tremendous impact on the content of his plays, beginning at the very latest with *Oberösterreich* and *Das Nest*. Both the first and the second tenets of orthodox Marxism listed above influenced his ideas about the reception of his work. Given the historical roles of the proletariat and the party as its avant garde, the former was necessarily the targeted audience of Kroetz's work in the seventies. On the other hand, the preemptory concept of an avant garde determined the position the author assumed *vis-à-vis* that audience, i.e. a position of superior knowledge. Such positioning can easily entail a short-circuiting of the learning process in which the audience is simply told what to believe and do. This, in turn, can threaten the enlightenment intentions of a democratic political aesthetic.

In any case, his commitment to the party was so strong that, in addition to modifications to the aesthetic strategy of the early plays, Kroetz in fact wrote two overtly political pieces at the behest of the party: *Globales Interesse* and *Münchner Kindl*. Why his relationship to the DKP plays such a crucial role in the character of his aesthetic development, and how this relationship becomes problematic for that development will become clearer as this discussion progresses. Kroetz quickly abandoned the experimentation with agit-prop work, apparently encouraged to do so even by fellow party members. Nonetheless, despite the radical departure of *Globales Interesse* and *Münchner Kindl* from plays like *Heimarbeit* or *Oberösterreich*, they represent a broader pattern of aesthetic experimentation.

Throughout the years 1971 and 1972, but especially after his entry into the DKP, Kroetz began to express dissatisfaction with his previous works. Both he and the critics questioned the actual ability of his characters to respond to the world external to them in any other fashion than he had already demonstrated, namely in an outburst of violent aggression. In addition to the Wendt passage cited above, the following excerpt from Helmut Motekat's book *Das zeitgenössische deutsche Drama* illustrates very well the perceptions Kroetz hoped to avoid with the revisions to his aesthetic project:

> Ihr Verhalten ist unvorhersehbar. Ihre Taten werden durch momentane Anstöße ausgelöst. Sie sind blindbewußtseinslose Ausbrüche von meist grausamer Brutalität aus einem chaotischen Gemisch von Auflehnung, Verstörung, Hilflosigkeit und Apathie. Solche Handlungen geschehen nicht im Zusammenhang eines in sich folgerichtigen Vorgangs oder als dessen Ergebnis. Und sie artikulieren und begründen sich nicht im logischen Fortschreiten einer Auseinandersetzung. Sie sind ihrem Wesen nach undramatisch, da sie nicht Ausdruck der Absichten oder des individuellen Willens der handelnden Personen, sondern des bewußtseinslosen, apathischen Befolgens von gültigen Normen oder Prinzipien der Gesellschaft oder des hilf- und ziellosen Protests gegen diese sind.[4]

The description of Kroetz's characters as blind, apathetic and essentially unconscious beings, whose actions are not rooted in any logic (and Motekat's voice is only one of many) set off alarm bells in the mind of Kroetz, the political activist.

Critics perceived these figures as irremediably damaged at the hands of nature, primarily, and society, secondarily. Again, one of the major areas of cultivated deprivation is language capacity: cultivated by those interested in maintaining the status quo. Within Kroetz's communist framework that implies the so-called "Groß-Kapitalisten," specific individuals who control the means of production: for example Siemens and Thyssen. These powerful figures of modern capitalism have, according to Kroetz, an economic interest in perpetuating the intellectual slavery of their workers.

In retrospect Kroetz, with the help of some journalistic and academic critics, constructed a theory of linguistic exploitation unique to capitalism, a theory that would explain how such intellectual and economic slavery is maintained. Although linguistic manipulation was, naturally, only part of the overall exploitation of the proletariat within the capitalist mode of production and distribution, it did offer a plausible account for the type of dialogue Kroetz employed in his first plays. The dialogue of these works is a collection of clichés and conversational particles that serve essentially only to mark time in the conversation rather than to express emotion or opinion. In addition to the passage already quoted from *Stallerhof*, the following passage from *Michis Blut* offers a prime example of the stunted language of Kroetz's characters:

Karl:	Was redst dann und mischt dich ein?
Marie:	Hab auch ein Recht.
Karl:	Nix hast du.
Marie:	Versoffn bist.
Karl:	Genau.
Marie:	Asozial bist.
Karl:	Schiach bist.
Marie:	Ein Hamperer bist.
Karl:	Eine Flitschn bist.
Marie:	Bin ich nicht.
Karl:	Bist. (I,228)

Michis Blut represents an extreme manifestation of an already extreme dramaturgy. Gone from this passage are subject pronouns and present only the hint of complete sentences. Instead the two characters pass to each other one vicious slur after another. Kroetz maintains that this stunted language preserves class relations, upholding the dominant position of the bourgeoisie. Conversely, those individuals who have command of the language have command of their situation in life – or can wrest it from those who do: "Menschen, die gelernt haben zu reden, können sich verständigen, oder, was wichtiger ist, sie können sich wehren" (WA, 520).

Kroetz goes beyond this to assert that the inability of these individuals to express themselves is the direct result of an intentional act on the part of capitalists to render the proletariat speechless: "Ja, denn niemand anderer als der Kapitalismus hat die Monopolisierung von Sprache zum Zweck der Ausbeutung erfunden" (WA, 526). This linguistic incapacity, or calculated decapacitation, merely reflects on one level the gradual, but perpetual process of enslavement. It is not sufficient in capitalism simply to exploit the worker as a worker. The enslavement must be complete. Kroetz, echoing others, maintains that to this end there developed a culture and – to a certain extent – a consciousness industry, within which the needs, thoughts and activities of individuals are fashioned and administered.[5] The intention of this administration is to reinforce the established relations of subservience, in part by instilling in the members of the proletariat values and desires that lead them only to wish to be a part of the system that in reality forges their chains.

The theory of a culture or consciousness industry, although of great explanatory and analytical insight, creates problems for Kroetz's particular political/aesthetic strategy. To understand why this is so, it will be helpful to take a brief look at the character of the individual subject as constructed within Theodor W. Adorno's ideas about the culture industry and, subsequently, the impact such a theory has for his aesthetic theory. In their *Dialektik der Aufklärung*, a very influential book during the cultural and political debates of the sixties and seventies, Theodor Adorno and Max Horkheimer trace the growing dominance of instrumental rationality in the struggle of human beings against nature. Gradually, as human beings, in their battle for survival, begin to employ their powers of rational thinking, the preeminence of the dictates of reason begins to overwhelm elements outside of the course prescribed by reason. Certain behavioral and intellectual patterns become dominant, excluding alternative responses to situations. This process forces a flattening out of the possible, reducing "the wealthy multiplicity of concrete qualities to the abstract identity of formal homogeneity."[6] Of particular importance to this study is the very destructive implication of this process that culminates in the anonymity of power. The demands of reason govern actions, policy decisions, the rights of individuals, and ultimately the scope of their intellectual and emotional choices.

That is to say, instrumental rationality extends its control in this way to human consciousness itself. Instead of acting as the tool for the exploration of the possible, consciousness becomes the vehicle of social integration, thereby acting to ensure the smooth functioning of society. It delimits the boundaries of the acceptable and renders the individual happy and harmless. In his *One Dimensional Man*, Herbert Marcuse, another representative of Frankfurt School critical theory, and a tremendous intellectual influence on socio-cultural theory of the late sixties and seventies, examines the state of consciousness in modern society. His term for this state is "happy consciousness," which is the product of the dialectic of enlightenment. Marcuse describes this phenomenon as follows:

> It reflects the belief that the real is rational, and that the established system . . . delivers the goods. The people are led to find in the productive apparatus the effective agent of thought and action to which their personal thought and action can and must be surrendered. And in this transfer, the apparatus also assumes the role of a moral agent. Conscience is absolved by reification, by the general necessity of things.[7]

Individuals no longer really exist in a system to which they have conceded their individuality, and which they believe to be the instantiation of the moral. Yes, the individual is free, but only to recognize the necessity of the status quo. Once successfully integrated into society, the individual is just as free to choose from any number of options, but that choice does not extend beyond a preestablished array of goods and lifestyles. The choices an individual has close in around him or her. What on the systemic level came under the dictates of reason, becomes on the individual level the dictates of the market.

Nowhere do the powers of integration stand out more clearly than in the machinations of the culture industry. Adorno never tired of exposing the immense, indeed overpowering, integrative capacity of this phenomenon. For every consumer there is a pre-determined pattern of consumption. Individuals are sorted into types; no one is left out. Those who stray are marginalized or eliminated, "Was widersteht, darf überleben nur, indem es sich eingliedert."[8] The culture industry functions to standardize the individual, to guarantee that each member of society perpetuates the system. The individual is in a sense an illusion of our collective memory. It can no longer act as the (semi-)autonomous instigator of political change. The dialectic of enlightenment has so crippled the political subject so as to render it meaningless.

Adorno does in a sense preserve the individual in its absence. The violence to which instrumental rationality has subjected the individual has left its mark on the body and bears witness to oppression, and with that to the negation of oppression.[9] In *Modern Culture and Critical Theory* Russell Berman argues that Adorno remains faithful to the political project of self-determination, that "'education for autonomy' can be a serious political goal."[10] Yet, the current status of the individual would seem to dampen even such a modestly optimistic assessment. Adorno maintains that human beings have been so mutilated by the culture industry as to leave them thoroughly manipulated.

A project of education for autonomy becomes even more questionable when one takes into account Adorno's conviction that communication itself has been perverted by instrumental rationality. He implicitly states that political discourse actually serves oppression.[11] Participation in the political process is equal to sanction, and praxis itself is inherently violent. He writes, "Praxis tendiert ihrer schieren Form nach zu dem hin, was abzuschaffen ihre Konsequenz wäre; Gewalt ist ihr immanent."[12] Adorno has effectively closed off any practical venues for protest. The individual is reduced to being the dumb witness of the crimes against it. The mask human identity has donned in society "is the form that identity must assume in order to appear in repressive society, and it bears the marks of the repression while denouncing them mutely."[13] The protest remains symbolic, a noble tribute to human potential.

Although Kroetz may not at this time agree with Adorno's assessment of the status of the individual, the characters of his early pieces clearly resemble the emptied vessels Adorno describes so eloquently. However, individuals, completely manipulated by external sources and virtually incapable of autonomous action in a dialectically tempered sense, simply cannot act as the conscious vehicles of political change, let alone of revolutionary upheaval. Regardless of the process that led to such crippled individuals, they can no longer serve Kroetz's political aesthetic once he began to construct one. Kroetz himself comes to recognize this. He writes:

> In einem Dutzend Stücke habe ich die Ränder der Gesellschaft der Bundesrepublik ganz klar porträtiert. Das reicht mir. Ich bin bei der DKP. Ich bin politisch tätig; deshalb reizt es mich auch, jetzt Modelle zu liefern, Wege zu zeigen, die weiter führen. Es müssen positive Gestalten auftreten, und die müssen reden können. Wenn sie nicht reden können, ist es schwer andere zu verlocken, daß sie ihnen folgen. Das ist mein spezielles literarisches Problem, und unser Realismus-Problem. (WA, 601)[14]

Within the framework of a political strategy intent on mobilizing the working class against those in possession of the means of production, any aesthetic product that could not, even theoretically, further that goal had to appear as a failure. This naturally reveals very little about these early pieces themselves, since Kroetz wrote them before he had any direct interest in communist class politics. It would, therefore, be a mistake to view them, as Kroetz occasionally did, as failures. However, in terms of his desire to develop a revolutionary political aesthetic, his own dismissal of these works does provide a key to the play that forms the major focus of this chapter: *Oberösterreich*.

Oberösterreich

This work garnered for Kroetz a prestigious literary prize, and, through its broadcast as a television play, exactly the national exposure he sought, but the circumstances of the latter also in a sense predicted how the audience would receive the play. Originally Kroetz had planned a televized discussion to follow the initial broadcast. When the network found out that he intended to include fellow communist party members, it declined to air the program. With the opportunity lost to discuss publicly the political implications of the piece, the audience was faced with a play about a young couple, an unplanned pregnancy and the wife's determination to complete the pregnancy. The ramifications of such restrictions will become clearer as the following analysis proceeds.

In *Oberösterreich* Kroetz presents Anni and Heinz, both of whom work for the company that produces "Milka" chocolate. Anni works in a clerical position and Heinz drives a delivery truck. The crisis this Kroetzian couple confronts is the unplanned pregnancy mentioned above. Anni responds very optimistically to the pregnancy, but for Heinz it is a shock. At first, though surprised, he tries to react positively to the idea of having a baby, but slowly he begins to express his doubts and anxieties about the impact a baby will have on their lives, in particular on his life. He insists they cannot afford a child and suggests they draw up a monthly budget to see if they can support a third person. They find they really cannot and Heinz makes an appointment for an abortion, although at the last minute Anni decides she cannot go through with it. Shortly after that Heinz is caught driving intoxicated by the police and loses his license. The company keeps Heinz on, but transfers him to a much lower-paying position until his driver's license is reinstated. Although this will create additional financial difficulties, the couple has resolved to have the child.

This play, written in 1972, clearly initiates a new phase in Kroetz's work, although it does not as yet represent the solidification of his new dramatic tactics as they work themselves out in *Das Nest*, *Mensch Meier* and *Der stramme Max*, a series of three plays, all of which depict the moment at which an otherwise obedient and deferent worker takes the first step toward independent and class-conscious behavior. *Oberösterreich* does not go that far, but in it Anni and Heinz make no attempts at senseless personal violence. Heinz, as a character, has gained a measure of linguistic and intellectual independence, and the play guides the two characters through a personal crisis without that crisis ending in catastrophe.[15] Overall, the characters come closer to being the positive models Kroetz claims he seeks.

The Average Citizen

Seit etwa Herbst 1971 stört mich das Extreme an meinen Stücken. Mir scheint, es verhindert, daß die Dinge, die der "junge Kroetz" richtig gesehen hat, voll verstanden werden können, weil die Beispiele, an denen allgemeingesellschaftliche Mängel angeprangert werden, immer an Extremen abgehandelt werden. So habe ich also begonnen, um der größeren Verständlichkeit willen, mich mit dem Durchschnitt zu befassen. (WA, 587)[16]

In order for his new characters to fulfill their exemplary function, they could no longer be limited to being the virtually mute and passive recipients of structural violence. They had to have the verbal and intellectual facilities with which to explain their actions. The modest changes in the Kroetzian character were to denote a greater quantum of individual autonomy. It is clear, however, that *Oberösterreich* failed to fulfill all of the dramatist's goals on these points. An analysis of the figures of Heinz and Anni reveals some of the intrinsic limitations operative in the piece.

Although a great deal of dialogue in this play still resembles earlier works, Kroetz has bestowed his characters with a measure of greater verbal competency. This greater verbal proficiency creates adequate space for Kroetz to let at least one dramatic character make actual statements about his state of consciousness. When Heinz's doubts about his readiness and willingness to be a father become irrepressible, he attempts to explain to Anni how he feels about his work and about his life more generally. In the following passage Heinz expresses the profound sense of alienation he feels in his job with more eloquence than any Kroetzian character before him:

Mir is manchmal, wenn ich am Steuer sitz, oder auch im direktn Verkehr mit die Kundn, der ja persönlich sein muß, wie es heißt, als wär das gar ned ich, als wär das irgendeiner, der keine Bedeutung hat. Ich.

and

Man macht etwas, irgendeiner der zufällig man selber is, sozusagen, und das ham schon Millionen vorher gemacht, ganz genauso.
Pause.
Keine Persönlichkeit dahinter. (II,107)

Heinz articulates, without stating it in Marxist terms, the alienation of the worker in a capitalist economy, in which he has no say as to how, when or where he spends his productive labor time. He also describes the sense of being a replaceable unit, an interchangeable part, without any perceived personal autonomy, and without any real way of achieving a measure of independence.[17]

Heinz, however, is alone in his ability to give expression to the conflicts within himself.[18] When his wife, Anni, decides she cannot go through with the abortion, she cannot explain to Heinz why she feels the way she does.

Heinz: Ich will dir nix einredn, was ich ned selber glaub, aber ein Kind is ein Faktor, wo kein Mensch überschaut. Da, ich hilf dir in den Mantel.
(*Pause.*)

Anni: Weilst feig bist, Heinz.
(*Heinz schweigt.*)
Weilst von einem Kind Angst hast, das dein eigenes is. Weilst es nicht habn willst, wost es nicht einmal gsehn hast. Vielleicht tät es dir gfalln. Das kann man doch ned wissen, im vorhinein.

Heinz: Gehn mir jetz?
(*Pause.*)
Redn mir unterwegs weiter. Im Auto. Sonst kommen mir zu spät.

Anni: Ich fahr nicht, weil ich dableib.
(*Pause.*)

Heinz: Was man ausgmacht hat, muß man einhaltn.

Anni: Ich hab nix ausgmacht.
. . .

Heinz: Was man ausmacht muß man einhaltn.

Anni: Ich nicht. Weil ich da keinen Wert drauf leg. Nachdem ich alles weiß.

Heinz: Weils alles besser weißt und dir nix sagn laßt. Das is es.

Anni: Nein, aber Wissn macht stark. (II,119f)

Anni neither responds to the quasi-existential questions and concerns Heinz has raised in the course of the play, nor can she explain her determination to carry the baby to term in any way intelligible to him. Her defense of her decision is reduced to tautology ("Ich fahr nicht, weil ich dableib") and to a vague reference to some knowledge that strengthens her will to resist Heinz's urgings. The "Wissn" to which she refers could be anything, ranging from insight into her husband's general inability to impose his will on her to a religious surety that a fetus is human life from the moment of conception onward. She does not in any case have the linguistic arsenal with which to clarify her decision.[19] This passage will be key again when the discussion moves to an analysis of implicit political and social norms portrayed in the play; here it serves merely to re-emphasize the expressive constraints within which these two figures function. Linguistic limitation (as opposed to expanded conversational skills) is by far the more dominant factor in the couple's relationship to one another. This obvious deficiency helps to illustrate other ways in which the couple are manipulated.

For instance, Kroetz used moderate, stylized dialect extensively in this play and in his other works. The fact that most of the dialogue is written in a mild dialect form (to be spoken according to the actors' geographic origin and/or ability to create the dialect as a "Kunstsprache") gives those sections in the text where the characters switch to standardized German a descriptive purpose they would not otherwise have. Indeed, virtually all instances of standardized German in *Oberösterreich* occur when either Heinz or Anni are parroting things they have heard or seen in the media. The occasions when they fall out of their more natural dialect then function to reveal to what extent the two have been inculcated by such factors as media advertising and television programing.

Unable to manipulate their own language well enough to create an individualized response to any given moment, they borrow from a pool of reusable, essentially meaningless phrases, conceived, prepared and distributed to them by marketing specialists – whether those be actual advertising specialists or other figures bent on selling something to the general public, such as weather forecasters.[20] On Easter Sunday Heinz and Anni make an excursion to Starnberger See. After dinner they contemplate taking a boat ride around the lake. Anni says: "Aber schön könnt es schon sein, so eine Dampferfahrt. Vielleicht ein unvergeßlicher Eindruck, wo ein Ostern mit strahlender Wärme und Frühlings-sonnenschein is" (II,96). The second sentence in this passage clearly plays on tourist brochures and weather reports, both of which, but particularly the former, try to create for the consumer a purchasable moment of happiness. Images of Heinz and Anni relying on marketers to contextualize their own lives merely reinforce the verbal dependence of the characters on others to provide them with a usable language.

The play demonstrates this phenomenon again when Anni prepares to tell Heinz about the pregnancy. In celebration of her announcement that they are to be parents, she prepares for him Curd Jürgens's (a popular movie and television personality) favorite salad. And at an earlier point in the play, Heinz laments the fact that their car is only a Kadett, "ein Massnauto" (II,94), as if an automobile could elevate both their internal and external worth – just as automobile manufacturers would have the customer believe.

The repeated employment of the cliché, as a moment of everyday language, only cements the portrait of the couple as thoroughly instructed in the type of behavior that will keep them in subordinate positions.[21] Their dialogue is peppered with *Volksweisheiten*, some of which are patently intended to content the economically disadvantaged with their lot in life and to make them proud of those "small accomplishments" that distinguish the individual within his or her restricted world. "Die Großn hams auch ned leicht" is a typical example of a phrase that works to draw attention away from the unequal distribution of resources in the world, to convince the poorer that they would have little to gain but money, were they able to share in that wealth or even displace the wealthy. Anni's response to Heinz's compliment on her skills as a cook, "Eine gute Köchin spart der Familie Geld und beschert ihr höchste Genüsse" is another instance of a cliché that functions to stimulate the poor to be happy and content with their lot in life and to take pride in the challenges it presents them (II,107 and 93).

Again, the intended enhanced verbal capacity of the characters in *Oberösterreich* reveals itself to be minimal at the most. For Kroetz, however, these small changes literally made the difference between life and death. Alluding to the brutality of his earlier works, he has the couple present the audience with what could have happened had Heinz and Anni no escape valve for the pressures building up in them, and with what certainly would have happened in many of the pieces that came before this one. In the last scene Anni reads to Heinz from a newspaper article describing the murder of a pregnant woman and her husband's reasons for committing it: "Ich hab es getan, weil sie schwanger war und einer Abtreibung nicht zustimmte, obwohl es gegen die Vernunft war" (II,112). Heinz is struck by the similarity to their situation, but Anni assures him of the difference between them: "Schmarrn, du bist doch kein Mörder." Heinz: "Das is der Unterschied" (II,112). Although the characters themselves seem comforted by this distinction, the audience has no reason to be this smug.

There is, in fact, little evidence as to why the play comes to the conclusion it does, although an audience familiar with Kroetz's earlier work would certainly have a sense for what the reasons could be. This is a problem peculiar to the kind of self-reflective aesthetic strategy with which he structures his dramas. Kroetz has in *Oberösterreich* created an aesthetic answer to a play such as *Heimarbeit*, at the end of which one of the characters murders an infant whose "illegitimate" existence challenges the very specific intellectual confines of his family. The fact that Heinz does not explode in senseless physical violence at the end of *Oberösterreich*, as both Willi of *Heimarbeit* and the husband in the newspaper did, is a marker for the audience that there is a qualitative difference between a character such as Heinz and one like Willi or Hanni in *Wildwechsel*.[22] Without, however, an acquaintance with such earlier figures, Heinz's "Das is der Unterschied" cannot be very enlightening to a member of the audience. Intended to demonstrate blatantly his move away from what he saw as extreme characters and extreme situations, the conclusion of *Oberösterreich* runs the risk of banality if the theater public is not fairly well versed with Kroetz's previous aesthetic strategies.[23]

Kroetz certainly became aware of the fact that this particular piece did not convincingly portray the incipient stages of socio-political consciousness, and sought to address this deficit with *Das Nest*. Nonetheless, this latter work maintains this self-referentiality in several key points, thus perpetuating the problems inherent to it. This type of critical self-reflection in a work for the theater is problematic since the theater essentially cannot assume any familiarity with previous pieces, and must rely on the ability of the aesthetic moment to convince. Kroetz will continue to refine his methods of character depiction as he experiments with new characters and new character constellations in works to come, but for the purposes of this chapter it is important to note that this type of self-reference and self-reflection in *Oberösterreich* (as well as in *Das Nest*) is one of the factors that hampers a successful implementation of his own reconceived political aesthetic model.

Another instance of self-referentiality and yet another way in which Kroetz employs language is dialect. In addition to being a useful contrastive tool (the counterpositioning of standardized and dialectal German described above), the use of a stylized form of southern German dialect is both a conscious effort at authenticity and, in the particular way Kroetz uses it, a statement about the actual linguistic capacity of the characters in his plays who are to perform as representatives of a real social class of individuals. The inability of the dramatic figures to utilize standard German in any original or creative fashion underscores their lack of access to the public sphere, and therewith to any means of effective political expression. Wend Kässens and Michael Töteberg both underscore that Kroetz at this point views dialect negatively, i.e. as a handicap. Kässens writes:

> Der Ideologie, der Kroetz aufsitzt, die gleichwohl nichts von der Gültigkeit seiner Analysemodelle nimmt, ist, daß er den Dialekt grundsätzlich als eine

Reduktion der Hochsprache begreift – als ob die Fähigkeit zur Hochsprache generell die Sprach-Gewalt und den durch sie verursachten
Unterdrückungszusammenhang aufhebe und als ob die Dialekte den Vorrat
an Sprachmaterial nicht auch erweitern können.[24]

Even though *Oberösterreich* marks Kroetz's first steps away from the
aphasic characters in the earlier plays, the terms reduction and reduced
still aptly describe the language Heinz and Anni speak. He does come
later to revise his understanding and use of dialect, but at this point it is
still a liability.

In direct opposition to Brecht, Kroetz felt that instilling his
characters with a language not truly accessible to them was both a
fiction and, in a sense, a betrayal of those he hoped to help through his
work. In an article about the plays of Marieluise Fleißer Kroetz writes:

Brutalität wird sichtbar gemacht durch den Ausstellungscharakter der
Fleißerschen Sprache. Mit Brecht hat diese Sprache nichts zu tun. Haben die
Proletarier Brechts immer einen Sprachfundus zur Verfügung, der ihnen de
facto nicht zugestanden wird von den Herrschenden, also als Fiktion einer
utopischen Zukunft verstanden werden muß, so kleben die Figuren der
Fleißer an einer Sprache, die ihnen nichts nützt, weil sie nicht die ihre ist.
(WA, 525)

Despite the constraints it imposes on its speakers, the choice of dialect
is also an act of political solidarity on the author's part. Through dialect
the author takes the part of those who are made to suffer. To give them
language was to smooth over the marks of their oppression.

Kroetz adheres here to what is basically a naturalist concept of
theatrical language and ignores the potentially productive view of
drama as theoretical or "pictoral" model – in other words as a tool for
abstraction. Since naturalist methods seek to cover over any gaps
between the work of art and the slice of empirical reality to be
conveyed, Kroetz's own naturalist tendencies in characterization
contradict his stated desire to lay bare the exploitive structures of
contemporary society.[25]

Although one could question just how true Kroetz's particular use of
dialogue is to the social reality he wishes to portray, it is of greater
importance here to examine, again, what ramifications this has for his
own aesthetic strategy. The intention, as seen in the above quote, is not
to intervene extensively in reality as Brecht supposedly does by
bestowing his figures with essentially unrestricted language ability.
However, given that the reconstruction of a portion of social reality in
an aesthetic product is always one of intervention, the care Kroetz takes
not to commit an injustice against that reality is moot. What it instead

effects is a severe limitation of representation: the audience must be able to relocate this particular section of society back into society as a whole and from there pinpoint the mechanisms of oppression and control to which these individuals mutely gesture.

The following passages illustrates this problem quite well. The first shows the couple browsing through advertising circulars and dreaming of future acquisitions:

Heinz: Es gibt sogar einen Springbrunnen. Schau!
   (*Er blättert um.*)
Anni: Ein schwimming-pool wär mir aber lieber.
Heinz: Nur als Beweis, was es alles gibt. *Liest.* Heißner-Springbrunnen die Zierde jedes Gartens. Ente aufrecht, einundvierzig Zentimeter siebenunddreißig Mark. Ente gebückt, zweiundvierzig Zentimeter auch siebenunddreißig Mark. Seehund dreiundvierzig mal vierunddreißig Zentimeter dreiundneunzig Mark.
Anni: Einen Seehund tät man vielleicht wolln, aber eine Ente nicht.
Heinz: Nein. (*Lacht.*) Keine Ente. (II,92f)

Although on one level they recognize how ridiculous such items are, they nonetheless feel compelled to choose between them. During their Easter excursion, they also stop for dinner, where they react with amazement at the flambéed dish one of the guests has ordered:

Anni: (*schaut auf den Nachbartisch:*) Das nennt man Flambiern, gell?
Heinz: Ned so laut, sonst hört man es, daß mir es ned wissn.
Anni: Aber man nennt es Flambiern.
Heinz: Freilich. Aber wenn man es weiß, braucht man es ned erwähnen, sonst merken die andern, daß man es nicht gewohnt is, weil man so hinschaut. (II,95)

They do not want to show the other restaurant guests that they themselves have never seen anything like it before, let alone eaten anything so sophisticated. Both their survey of advertising supplements and Heinz's apparent shame at his cultural unsophistication can be read as a demonstration of how the culture industry has programmed the individual to want the items it sells, how those items then become associated with personal identity (a duck would be considered tacky, whereas a sea lion approaches the realm of the acceptable), how such a conceptualization of identity perpetuates the virtual enslavement of individuals to the market and how it maintains the viability of the market itself. However, unless audience members are familiar with theories of a culture or consciousness industry, they are likely to see in such a scene simply a gross example either of cultural naiveté or very bad taste.[26]

It would be ridiculous to imply that an audience cannot make the connection between the reality presented on the stage and the social structures to which they are to refer, but it is appropriate to point out that Kroetz himself does not give the audience the tools to accomplish the task he sets before it. This is especially striking when one considers the fact that Kroetz's dramatic and political project at the time of *Oberösterreich* included as members of an ideal audience precisely those sectors of society he portrays as having been made incapable of such intellectual abstraction. If there existed in society individuals very similar to Heinz and Anni, would they not be unable to read themselves into the characters on the stage? Would they be any more likely to see the market indoctrination in Anni's decision to make Curd Jürgens's favorite salad for her husband as an anniversary surprise or in the couple's shame that they have never seen or eaten a flambéed dish? It seems unlikely. Here Kroetz's work creates a contradiction between the stylistic method chosen and the perceived intellectual capabilities and training of the target audience. A look now at the structure of the work reveals how it compounds these difficulties and resurrects an aesthetic crisis to which *Oberösterreich* was the preliminary solution.

As a style of presentation that tries to create a facsimile of the world external to the theater corresponding most closely to general perceptions of that reality, realism places certain constraints on subject within the context of a relatively short dramatic piece. One cannot easily parade a cast of characters across the stage that would be truly representative of the diversity in contemporary society. On the other hand, one must question whether the microcosm of the Kroetzian three to four person family can adequately disclose the broader societal structures of domination and submission, which are at least partially reflected within the structure of the family. Kroetz addresses this issue in the following passage:

Ich will meinen Stücken die Durchschaubarkeit von Machtverhältnissen mit auf den Weg geben – von Machtverhältnissen in der Familie, in der Gesellschaft, von Druckverhältnissen und Angstverhältnissen. Und immer will ich zeigen, durch wen sie kommen und warum, aus welchen Gründen einer etwas in einem anderen erzeugt und wie es wirkt. Das ist meine Intention. (WA, 599)

A review of elements in *Oberösterreich* that function to expose *Machtverhältnisse* would again include the above-mentioned citations from the mass media that demonstrate the pervasiveness of the culture industry's suggestive powers and its ability to engender customers at every possible purchase level, and the scene at the lake, in which Heinz and Anni try to conceal their astonishment at a flambéed dish. The episode illustrates how ingrained social status symbols are and how strong the desire of wage laborers is to find themselves in the socio-economic category where flambéed dishes and swimming pools are the norm.

A final example of the ways in which the broader societal context is mediated through the play is the section in the fourth scene in which Heinz and Anni are trying to make love. Heinz is preoccupied with the story of one particular office supervisor who had reportedly made sexual advances to a young Yugoslavian cleaning woman. He is concerned about the likelihood that his own wife could fall prey to such behavior (II,97f). Anni thinks she is immune from such harassment because she has a slightly better position in the company than the cleaning woman. Heinz responds by citing the man's salary:

Heinz: Man redt ja bloß. Den hams mit dreitausend brutto eingestellt, heißt es.
Anni: Ein Abteilungsleiter is ein Abteilungsleiter.
Heinz: Ebn, das mein ich ja. (II,98)

The implication, although a somewhat shaky one, is that the man's position in the firm's hierarchy and his gross income create for him the privilege of abusing those below him. In order for this scene to be read as part of an implicit critique of capitalism, one must essentially see it as an illustration that wage laborers are not only alienated from the means of production, mere tools in the capitalist market economy, but also that their very bodies are not their own. The office supervisor stands in symbolically for the entire class of individuals who control the means of production. The young Yugoslavian cleaning woman in turn represents, as a woman and a foreigner, the most disempowered group in Germany society. Thus Heinz's fears that the supervisor could set his sights on Anni next reflects his own fears of powerlessness, of the possibility that they too are nothing other than the object of someone else's power. If Heinz's function is to be a model for the average wage earner in German society, the scene illustrates that a workable sense of self is systematically and systemically denied to individuals like him.

Although these points are plausible and relatively clear to see once they have been uncovered, they are surely fairly subtle for an audience not looking specifically for, or one particularly resistant to, an anti-capitalist critique. There are no scenes of interaction between Heinz and/or Anni and one of the executives of the firm in which they both work, nor would such an appearance serve any enlightening purpose. However, the ability of an absent character to function as a surrogate for the "capitalist," or even to point to exploitive structures within capitalist production, is limited at best. Positioning a lone capitalist on the stage with these people and singling him or her out as the origin of social misery would either have a comic effect or could simply be brushed aside by the audience as one bad apple on an otherwise healthy tree.

A Brechtian reading of this play would note that Kroetz's strategy here does not in fact adequately reveal the underlying structures that have largely determined the nature of Heinz and Anni's existence.[27] The dramatist's realist techniques do not facilitate an interpretation of the work that would go beyond the specific to the general, i.e. from the office supervisor who sexually harasses a young foreign cleaning woman to the capitalist who successfully exploits the wage laborer by virtue of his or her position within the production process. Heinz's identification and sympathy with the plight of the cleaning woman parallels the audience's identification with and compassion for Heinz's fears, but does it spawn a recognition in either the character or the audience of the underlying structural causes of the situation? There is, of course, every reason to ask whether a realist aesthetic strategy is the source of the theoretical unclarity of this scene or whether it was simply a poor thematic choice on the dramatist's part.

This problem of generalization from the micro to the macro is one that surfaces in every one of the pieces examined in this study. An analysis of this question must try to separate the accidental from the structural problems in Kroetz's aesthetic strategy. In his attempt to approximate as closely as possible the so-called real world, Kroetz confines himself to the small sphere of the family. He does not have his cast confront directly the world outside of the kitchen. If he were to allow them to describe that world in more detail, such a description might circumvent this difficulty. However, because his subject is the essentially uneducated, unskilled laborer and because he refuses to imbue characters at this stage in his career with explanatory powers they would not normally have, they cannot function to depict adequately the larger societal mechanisms that govern their behavior in the home, nor can they act expressly to revive a dusty sense of class consciousness as he had hoped, let alone to help develop such a class consciousness in his ideal audience.[28]

This brings up again the very real problems created by Kroetz's "ultrarealism."[29] He understood realism to be a method or a set of techniques with which to render the portrayal of an aesthetic subject as close to empirical reality as possible. The audience should be able to find, so to speak, the reality presented on the stage again outside the theater walls. Critics, who have argued that the dramatist's work is not fundamentally naturalist, have often stressed the exaggeration of the Kroetzian staged world. Ingeborg Walther writes, for instance, that Kroetz's works are not "milieu plays" in the traditional sense. She argues that the apparent naturalism of these plays is is in fact "illusory."[30] She asserts further: "The ultrarealistic quality of Kroetz's plays lies in the extent to which traditional forms of realism are subverted. ... They are ... highly concentrated 'models' which condense elements of reality much in the manner of the 'test-tube' image ."[31] There is a moment of intensification, almost of exaggeration, but essentially what the viewer sees on the stage is an accurate rendition of the external world. The brutality and obscenity of that world was to shake the audience awake from its ignorance and force it to confront the exploitation and oppression of the lower classes.[32] In other words, the audience members' confrontation with reality was to act as a catalyst for a change in their socio-political consciousness.

Kroetz's aesthetic at this point relied on a theory of reception that assumed an audience would be able to abstract from the particular example of social behavior on the stage to larger societal structures. It is an aesthetic that has been controversial since at least the turn of the century. Hence the question: does Kroetz's ultrarealism provide more than just a view into the living rooms of the small families he puts on the stage? The analysis of *Oberösterreich* has been somewhat ambivalent on this point and will remain so. Adorno's rejection (not to mention that of numerous Kroetz contemporaries) of such an aesthetic has already been the focus of discussion. Furthermore, whether or not a work such as the one in question here conveys the kind of structural look at society as Brecht envisioned is less important than the fact that the problem continued to nag at Kroetz's production and led him to seek new methods.

In time Kroetz came to reassess his initial dismissal of Brecht and began to appreciate the earlier dramatist's position. As seen above, he recognized the need to expose social structures and even attempted to employ certain Brechtian devices in a few of his works (notably *Dolomitenstadt Lienz* and *Sterntaler*), but he never managed to appropriate those techniques in a manner suitable to his own style. They remained awkward experiments and were quickly abandoned. Indeed, throughout the seventies Kroetz generally maintained the technique of realism.

As we have seen, Adorno felt that realist techniques and attempts to offer quasi-photographic representations of reality are implicated in the highly oppressive societal structures generated by instrumental rationality. Communication itself being little more than a vehicle for such oppression, any artwork which endeavors to engage its audience in the act of communication is necessarily sullied. Instead, as has been said before, only the artwork's denial of manifest meaning allows it to function, in a sense, as a critique of social reality.

Such works are not, however, immune from cooptation. Their very refusal to engage in rational discourse allows them to be neutralized and absorbed into corporate culture, where they serve as adornments of capitalist conquests: "Im Zeitalter totaler Neutralisierung freilich bahnt falsche Versöhnung ebenfalls sich an: Ungegenständliches eignet sich zum Wandschmuck des neuen Wohlstands."[33] This neutralization, on the other hand, befalls all aesthetic products: it is the cost of aesthetic autonomy in a thoroughly administered world.[34] If Adorno is correct in this position, there is little point to discussing the relative merits of certain aesthetic strategies over others.

A blanket statement such as this one is, however, not dialectical and deserves a somewhat reserved reception. Perhaps the key to pursuing an examination of this sort is the term "relative merit", a term that would assume different criteria in any given instance. Clearly, there is scant hope that the issue will find resolve in this chapter, but it can guide the analysis of the use of realist techniques in Kroetz's work.

Relative merit is certainly a factor in the decision to apply realist strategy to the detriment of a less elitist perspective. Terry Eagleton comments on the issue of perspective in the following passage of *Criticism & Ideology*: "For realism ... presupposes a privileged epistemological standpoint from which precise moral judgement may be effected, a fine transparent intelligence outside which there is nothing, which can be transfixed by no critical gaze from beyond the limits of its discourse."[35] There are those who have argued that among Kroetz's strengths as an author is his ability to present his characters in a non-condescending manner, to portray them from within.[36] Yet there is a sense in which authors cannot truly do this. A moment of separation is always present in any artistic endeavor in which an author creates something distinct from him- or herself. Realist techniques must blur that separation since their claim is to represent reality as it is and not reality as seen through the eyes of the writer. Such a perspective logically entails a "privileged epistemological standpoint" without acknowledging it. Interpretation thus becomes fact and remains unchallenged. This is of consequence here because it indicates both the surety with which Kroetz delimits the content of his works and how that surety erects barriers to hinder a recognition of the historical limitations and/or flaws in that content.

Before we pursue this argument, it will be helpful to take a brief look at *Das Nest*, Kroetz's response to the difficulties he encountered in *Oberösterreich*. As outlined above, *Oberösterreich* neither offered an adequate explanation of why Heinz and Anni did not turn to violence in the situation with which they had to cope, nor did it provide Kroetz with characters capable of acting as a medium for a clearly discernible political message. For various reasons the play could not show the moment at which the individual develops a (political) consciousness of his or her situation.

Das Nest

Baby Steps

In *Das Nest* (1974) Kroetz sought to construct a model of just that moment. Kroetz reconstructs his interest in doing so in an interview from 1978:

> Das Faszinierende ist: Wo beginnt das Sich-Wehren, wo beginnt das Denken? Alles andere geht dann seinen Weg leichter. Aber es ist wichtig zu zeigen: Wann kommt ein Mensch, der eben überhaupt nichts mitbringt, der keine Voraussetzungen hat, an den Punkt, wo er sagt, im Kopf und im Herzen: Jetzt fange ich an. Wie und wann findet dieser allerallererste Schritt statt? Das ist der wichtigste Schritt, und der muß dargestellt werden, denn das hat historische Bedeutung.[37]

The theory of socialist realism helps to clarify the supposed historic import of such a moment, to which Kroetz here refers. The pedagogical character of the dramatized conflict in the socialist realist work contains in its typicality the intellectual and emotional spectrum of the historical process. The work of art confronts the audience with this process, and outlines possible venues of behavior appropriate to the historical tasks at hand.[38] Claus Träger refers to this property of socialist realism as "aktivierende Widerspiegelung,"[39] a concept that echoes Benjamin's definition of an aesthetic model. This aspect of socialist realist aesthetic theory pertains directly to the importance Kroetz attributes to dramatizing this "first step."

Kroetz apparently feels that human reproduction is the most productive area in which to explore the origins of political consciousness. And *Das Nest* once again confronts the audience with a couple expecting a baby. In fact, it begins with Kurt and Martha watching a televized version of *Oberösterreich*. Immediately, Kroetz sets out to distinguish between the two couples. Neither Kurt nor Martha found Heinz and Anni's situation similar to theirs. Kurt goes so far as to assert that Heinz's behavior was abnormal: "Der hat ja überhaupts ned gewußt, was er will. Ein Mann muß wissen, was er will, dann geht es. Und einer, der vor seinem Kind Angst hat, das is sogar unnormal" (III,51). Another reference to *Oberösterreich* in this work is the scene in which Kurt and Martha run through a list of items Martha believes they will have to purchase for the baby. Heinz and Anni had also compiled a list, a list to determine whether or not they could afford a child. For Heinz and Anni the answer was no, but Kurt proudly approves each item his wife reads off to him (III,54–58).

This financial security proves to be shaky. Kurt's ability to provide certain luxuries for his family depends on the availability of overtime hours. If there are special loads to transport, Kurt is usually the one the boss calls on because he has never been a troublemaker:

Martha: Und wenn alle entlassn werdn, dich halt der Chef.
Kurt: Weil er mich mag, genau. *Kleine Pause*. Weil ich mich aus allem heraushalt und bloß an die Arbeit denk. (III,66)

His willingness to do only what he is told and not to ask any questions almost costs him the life of his newborn son and his marriage. After a relatively long period of time during which there have been no overtime hours to be had the boss offers Kurt a special job. He is to take several barrels supposedly containing soured wine and dispose of them in an out-of-the way spot. Kurt takes the load to a lake where he and his family have often gone bathing, dumps the barrels and drives off. Shortly after he leaves, his wife arrives with their young son and dips him in the water. The child starts to scream and turns blue. When Kurt reveals to Martha what he has done, she flies into a rage and accuses him of being little more than a trained animal: "Du bist ja überhaupts kein Mensch, daß muß mir immer entgangen sein, sondern höchstens ein dressierter Aff!" (III,71). This indictment acts a catalyst for a change of consciousness in Kurt, but once it becomes clear that the baby will pull through, Martha is willing to forgive Kurt. Her comment was only a product of her fear for her son's life. She returns home with the news of their son's recovery to find Kurt putting away the tools for a suicide attempt he could not carry out. Although some critics[40] insist that Martha too has realized the fragility of an existence overdetermined by obedient consumption, I would argue that she does not understand at all the change her husband has undergone.

When Kurt tries to explain to Martha that one cannot go through life blindly following directives, Martha can only respond that Kurt should just look around him to see all he has provided his family with and recognize the personal accomplishment such items represent:

Kurt: Wie weit tät das gehn, bis da drin einmal etwas "nein" sagt? Was kann man alles befehln, einem wie mir? . . .

Martha: Schau dich lieber einmal um, was du alles ermöglicht hast, weilst ein anständiger Mensch bist. . . . Der modernste Kinderwagen, den es gibt, Paidibett, Wäsche (*nickt*), für die Geburt einen Pelzmantel, Persianer – Klaue mit Nerzkragen, kürzlich die neue Waschmaschin, und nicht lang wird es dauern, dann is der Farbfernseher auch da . . .

Kurt: (*brüllt*) Nein! (III,77)

Although he was truly unaware of what was in the barrels, Kurt is conscious of his complicity in a crime. Despite the potential for losing his job, he decides to go to the police and turn himself and his boss in. Martha, however, does not want Kurt to go to the police. She can only see the problems it will cause for her family, she cannot place this one incident into a larger framework. Kurt tries to explain:

Kurt: Martha, niemand kann uns einen Vorwurf machn, weil mir so waren, du und ich, wie mir warn. Die wo über uns sind, die sorgn schon dafür, daß unsereins gar ned zum Lebn erwacht, wie man so sagt. Das können mir jederzeit beweisen. Aber, Martha, wenn mir es jetz, an dieser Stell, ned ändern, und den Kopf wieder in Sand steckn, dann sind mir doch diesmal selber schuld, und man kann es auf niemand schiebn. Das is es. (III,79)

Here Kurt outlines *in nuce* exactly that moment when an incipient political consciousness forms. Although he has always kept himself out of any union activity, a representative of the union contacts him to offer union support and to help insure Kurt's job. He recognizes the advantages, both emotional and political, of group solidarity and the play ends on a positive, all-is-well note.

This conclusion, albeit a reasonably credible (dramatic) decision, brings up one problem inherent to both *Oberösterreich* and *Das Nest*. The focus on the resolution of familial conflict and the characters' obvious love for and desire to protect their families allowed critics and audiences to see and emphasize in the plays a wealth of individual psychological issues that had very little to do with any form of political behavior. Benjamin Henrichs, for instance, writes of *Das Nest* and Kurt: "Seine Revolte gegen den Chef ist auch so etwas wie ein später Mannbarkeitsbeweis. Das Glück, die Zärtlichkeit zueinander, am Anfang noch unsicher gemimt: sie sind am Ende ein Stück wirklicher geworden. Eine Romanze also, nicht nur ein politisches Traktat." He goes on about Kroetz's work in general: "Noch immer teilt er über Liebe viel Genaueres mit als über Politik."[41] Henrichs clearly wishes to redeem Kroetz from communism, over-personalizing the dramatic conflict at hand in the process.

On the other hand, the relatively large number of critical voices who agree with similar readings of Kroetz would indicate that there lies an awkward truth therein. Moray McGowan, from the relatively privileged position of hindsight, comments:

> *Das Nest* contains a plea for social solidarity, insofar as it is suggested that with trade-union support behind him, Kurt will be stronger, but it is also a restatement of the role of individual integrity, since it implies that individual moral fortitude, though it will not overthrow the system or usher in utopia, can at least produce a modestly optimistic conclusion. This may seem a surprising verdict from the playwright who was a communist at the time; here as elsewhere Kroetz seems to combine a Marxist social critique with a Christian-humanist concern for the individual and his moral integrity – his soul, indeed.[42]

It was not only a "surprising," but also a vexing verdict for Kroetz, who was trying to avoid just such limited liberal-humanist readings of his work. The apparent inability of the playwright to write plays that audiences would read the way he hoped they would will be the subject for further discussion later. Here the audience response to the individual psychological problems of the main characters in *Oberösterreich* and *Das Nest* can serve to illustrate the ways in which Kroetz's reliance on the realist portrayal of the nuclear family thwarts a more social, political reading.

Nonetheless, *Das Nest* represents a tremendous step forward in terms of the author's own intentions. Kroetz has created a feasible conflict situation and a character capable of responding to that situation and of learning from it. The average man in this case has gained a heightened ability to express himself and a measure of intellectual independence. Although Kroetz worried that the majority of citizens in the Federal Republic were not in such a position, he opted to portray a character capable of instigating protest to serve as a model for those who had not as yet crossed that barrier.[43]

Two other problems immanent to the play further call into question the progress Kroetz seems to have made. Within the context of an overall critique of capitalism, the dumping of toxic waste has limited value as a model conflict. Although one can place the illegal disposal of toxic products into the larger framework of capitalist production-at-all-costs, the portrayal of one employer ordering an unsuspecting employee to get rid of poisonous materials hardly constitutes a frontal attack on the structure of capitalist society. It is far easier to brand this one individual a criminal than to untangle the intricate chain of events, production relations and power structures that make toxic waste such an immense problem in industrial societies. Once again, Adorno's critique of engaged literature as reductionist would seem to hold true. Kroetz has to reduce the conflict substantially in order to stage it. There is a risk here that an audience will go no further in its interpretation of the work than to condemn this particular act by this particular capitalist. On the other hand this type of incident does lend itself well to dramatization and offers Kroetz the opportunity to test his character's new-found independence.

What distinguishes Kurt from Heinz? What is it that makes the one fight back and the other sit back? Kroetz may actually have set himself a trap in his use of self-reference. Both men drive trucks, but Kurt and Martha are clearly better off financially than Heinz and Anni. The difference is not a great one, and yet it is the only area in which the lives of the two couples differ tangibly. To aver that such a minor disparity would effect such an enormous change in the ability of an individual to respond to problems adequately would suggest an over-simplified view of society.[44] However, if the many comparisons to *Oberösterreich* were not part of *Das Nest*, one could simply assume that Kroetz had refined his notion of the common man, that he had realized the limitations of the first prototype and had adjusted it both to fill his dramatic needs better and to reflect more closely the genuine character of that common man. Unfortunately, *Das Nest* explicitly elicits the comparison of the two pieces and, in doing so, weakens its own arguments.

It is now time to return to the discussion of realism as an aesthetic strategy. As we have seen, Kroetz's realism purportedly offers an accurate rendition of empirical reality. Is this really the case? In his *Ästhetische Theorie* Adorno writes of the naturalists: .

der soziale, kritische Gehalt ihrer Stücke und Gedichte ist stets fast oberflächlich, hinter der zu ihrer Zeit bereits voll ausgebildeten und von ihnen kaum ernsthaft rezipierten Theorie der Gesellschaft zurückgeblieben. ... weil sie die Gesellschaft künstlerisch beredeten, fühlten sie sich zu vulgärem Idealismus verpflichtet, etwa in der imago des Arbeiters, dem etwas Höheres vorschwebe, was immer das sein mag, und der durchs Schicksal seiner Klassenzugehörigkeit daran verhindert wurde, es zu erreichen. Die Frage nach der Legitimation seines gutbürgerlichen Aufstiegsideals bleibt draußen.[45]

There is a very real sense in which this passage applies to all of Kroetz's work up to *Nicht Fisch nicht Fleisch*, written in 1980. In an examination of politically committed literature and in particular of the way it responds to inherent and external challenges it would be impossible to avoid dealing in some depth with one of the central facets of the work or works in question. In the case of Kroetz, one of the key elements of *Oberösterreich*, *Das Nest*, *Mensch Meier*, *Der stramme Max*, *Nicht Fisch nicht Fleich* and, to a certain extent, even *Bauern sterben* is his evocation of the proletariat. The working class is the subject of his plays, in general his targeted audience, and a repeated referent in his programmatic statements. Because this is truly fundamental to his work, a brief discussion of the working class today is in order.

The Proletariat?

Das Nest is a decidedly overt call for the solidarity of workers within the protective circle of the unions. Although unionism is not integral to Marx's thought, it did develop in the last years of the nineteenth century and the early years of this century into an effective tool for the proletariat to secure itself certain betterments. Unions, in fact, became an important mechanism in the formation of class consciousness.[46] If, however, one looks at the role of the unions – at least in West Germany – since the end of the Second World War, quite a different picture emerges. Despite certain real gains, the unions have become little more than an extended arm of the Social Democratic Party, a fact which severely restricted their efficacy during the social-liberal coalition after 1969. They no longer represent a radical tool for communist class struggles. Although Kroetz's call to the unions could be interpreted as an effort on his part to reawaken trade unionism among the German working class, it is also the first indication of an overly simplistic, or perhaps romanticized view of current societal structures.

There may indeed have been a relatively cohesive working class culture in Germany in the twenties. There were neighborhoods of exclusively proletarian families; there were newspapers directed solely at the proletarian community; and there was a wealth of cultural production targeted at the working class. If one were, however, to extend the view back further into history or to look at the years since the rise of National Socialism, the picture of the working classes is much more fragmented in character. In the nineteenth century there was decided opposition within the proletariat between, for example, the skilled and non-skilled laborers, between unionists and non-unionists, and between the various wage levels.[47] The gradual revolution in the factories — Taylorism, automation, scientific management and the slow dissolution of trades and skilled labor — further atomized the worker, separating him or her from a sense of solidarity. Once isolated from that community, the individual is easily made amenable to integration into the bourgeoisie.[48]

In addition to doubts about the actual existence of a working class consciousness, there are also serious issues to consider about the desirability of a society formed around the concept of class structures.[49] The proletariat, as envisaged by Marx, represented in a way the culmination of instrumental rationality. Although the formation of class consciousness allows for the development of a common interest, it is achieved at the price of the individual as he or she had been known: the proletariat consists of interchangeable parts.[50] Jean Cohen argues that there is also little reason to believe that the working class, socialized and trained within capitalist relations of production, should it ascend to power, would wield that power in a manner different than did its predecessors. Cohen writes on this subject:

> if classes and class struggles are constituted by the reproductive logic of capital, if the proletariat is fused, homogenized, posited by capital itself as a moment of its own valorization process, if this logic together with the market imposes an interest structure onto the needs of individuals who participate as agents of production, on what basis can one argue that the self-constitution of these agents of production into a class opposed to capital can be anything more than the subjective affirmation of the logic of capital itself?[51]

While this critique of Marxist class theory has its merits, it also has some flaws. To discuss these would truly go beyond the aims of this chapter. The purpose of the above was to call into question two items: the emphasis in Kroetz's work on a conceptualization of the working class that is antiquated at best and sheer myth at its worst; and the implications of such a class theory.

There are alternative approaches to socialist strategy in the late twentieth-century which merit consideration. As the character of the working place has changed in contemporary society, so have the theories created to respond to the particular demands of that society. The increasing automation of manufacturing has had enormous impact on the actual size of the proletariat. In fact, the majority of the workforce today has moved into the service sector. Such occupations do not lend themselves well to the Marxist concept of labor and praxis. There have been calls for a modification of the emphasis on labor in Marxist thinking. In *Farewell to the Working Class* André Gorz suggests that it is dogmatic to force the issue of finding fulfillment within one's job. Instead he envisions more free time from work to engage in creative activities.[52] Jean Cohen, however, maintains that this is simply a perpetuation of the overemphasis on labor in the determinations of man's being. She writes, "To root the potential 'praxis subject' in the performance of unalienated labor . . . is to reveal an unrecontructed *ouvrier*-ism that glorifies yet again the worker qua worker."[53]

Cohen and others instead call for a new theory of social structures that can account for the stratification of civil society. Such theories call attention to the increasing role of the new social movements as political forces different from the Marxist tradition of class struggles. They discard the notion of a unified, homogeneous working class (or of any unified socio-political agent) and turn to an analysis of social plurality.[54]

This rather lengthy excursus into the character of today's working populace demonstrates certain limitations Kroetz's early work faced and indicates the direction his later pieces took. The changes in the modern workplace and the rise of the social movements will return as central issues in the following two chapters. Here the discussion must go on to consider in greater detail the social norms implicit in *Oberösterreich* and *Das Nest* and their relationship to Kroetz's political project.

Contradictions in Terms

As a self-proclaimed communist and activist author Kroetz was annoyed and disturbed by the phenomenal popularity his work enjoyed in the otherwise conservative German media. Those pieces which he considered to be prime examples of a western socialist realism in fact cemented his success: in 1972, the year that *Oberösterreich* premiered, he received the Westberliner Kunstpreis; he was awarded the Westberliner Kritikerpreis in 1973; in 1974 he won the Hannoversche Dramatikerpreis for *Sterntaler*; in 1975 the Wilhelmine Lübke-Preis for the television piece *Weitere Aussichten*; and in 1976 the Mülheimer Dramatikerpreis for *Das Nest*.[55] There are various reasons for this reception. Some of them have already surfaced above, while others still need clarification.

Despite Kroetz's socially critical intentions, the plays themselves often offer solutions to problems that fit rather nicely into conservative politics. *Oberösterreich* is a fine example of how the resolution of the conflict actually renders support for the family policies of the West German Christian Democrats. As noted above, Anni refers to some

"Wissen" that strengthens her resolve not to go through with the abortion, despite the obvious financial difficulties a third person would entail.

This decision on her part apparently reflects what the dramatist considered to be primal human values. In the interview with Heinz Ludwig Arnold, Kroetz says:

> Für mich hat eine große Bedeutung die jetzt abgeschlossene Trilogie "Oberösterreich", "Das Nest" und "Mensch Meier". In allen drei Stücken geht es um Durchschnittsmenschen in der Deformation und in der Entfremdung. Es geht darum, wie man sich gegen eine Gesellschaft wehrt, die das Menschliche als nicht profitabel wegrationalisert. In allen drei Stücken geht es intensiv um das Zurückfinden zu menschlichen Werten, um das Zurückfinden zu einer urmenschlichen Position.[56]

Needless to say, Kroetz did not cull these primal values from Marxist theory. Without any intent to overlook the author's actual intentions, the emphasis on the securing of human life at all costs and on the preservation of the traditional family is an integral part of the platforms of virtually all conservative political parties. It is, then, little wonder that a play promoting exactly that should find wide approval in conservative circles. The crude attempts at abortion in the earlier pieces may have incited to scandal, but the quiet resolve of a young woman to keep her baby was sure to garner applause.

We have also seen how the restrictions of Kroetz's realist techniques determine to a certain extent the nature of the overt political conflicts he can bring on to the stage. *Das Nest* involved a conflict that could be seen as one between an honest and a dishonest individual. The broader societal structures generated by capitalist modes of production can lead to the crass abuse of the environment. These structures are, however, extremely complex and would be very difficult to discern from the antagonisms the piece presents. In fact, the conflict in *Das Nest* lends itself to an overly schematic interpretation. What was conceived as a blatant critique of capitalist exploitation – both of human and of natural resources – could amount to nothing more than an affirmation of the very traditional value of honesty, a value seldom disputed by either left or right.[57] Problems of both content and form in these plays thus contribute to their integration and acceptance by the already pervasive and efficient powers of neutralization within the culture industry.

There is one further factor worthy of comment in this section and it is an external one. The constant pressures from the culture industry on the consumer to reject objects with overtly political or socially critical content made it difficult for an author who professed his desire to be both the most popular playwright of his time and the one farthest to the left to continue his work on an expressly leftist aesthetic strategy. Kroetz alluded to these pressures in the interview with the Süddeutscher Rundfunk cited in chapter one, note 15: "Das Publikum hat mehr reagiert auf eine Schreibweise wie 'Oberösterreich', der extreme politische Anspruch wurde nicht angenommen. Es wurde immer der moderate, menschliche Anspruch angenommen. Und ich habe dem einfach nachgegeben."[58] The need to accommodate the audience, to tend to its cultivated tastes, surely played a role in Kroetz's dramatic strategy as it developed through the seventies: without an audience there can be no theater, politically committed or otherwise. It would, however, be rather silly to exaggerate this aspect. It is merely one of the forces acting to shape the character of the pieces Kroetz wrote after he met with his initial success.

Oberösterreich represented a response to Kroetz's desire to overcome the marginal, to make a more generally valid commentary on today's lower classes. It constructed anew certain barriers to that goal: the still inadequate linguistic capacity of the characters portrayed, the lack of a clearly political commentary, and a conflict resolved in a manner easily accepted by a conservative audience. An additional question was whether the characters in the piece were not so thoroughly manipulated – trained, in a sense, to respond to their environment in a preordained manner – that they were unable to recognize either the sources of their own behavior or the obstacles to such a recognition.

Das Nest was, in turn, another effort to present the average man and to crystallize the first moment in the development of political consciousness. Kurt is the first Kroetzian character who can identify the structures of exploitation in his life. Although the conflict situation functioned well to incite this individual development, it did not lend itself well to a general critique of capitalism. This was in part attributable to the nature of the conflict itself, but also to the restrictions of presentation imposed by the dramatist's preferred aesthetic strategy.

Finally, the examination of Kroetz's work of this period revealed an anachronism of subject. The author's training in orthodox Marxism contributed substantially to his views on the role and character of the working class in contemporary society. The mission of the proletariat has, however, been challenged by the changes in the means of production. These historical changes have altered the very constitution of this socio-economic class and subjected it to a process of atomization and dispersion. Given the results of this process, it is highly unlikely that the working class can assume a leading role in the struggle for social progress.

This recognition necessitates a more differentiated picture of the agent of social and political change and with that of the characters in

Kroetz's own works. It should be clear that the issues in chapter one constitute the central focus in the analysis of this author's work. Kroetz has rejected implicitly a representation of the political subject as completely autonomous and yet he cannot accept a conceptualization of that subject as thoroughly incapable of responding to its own destruction within the mechanics of the culture industry. Kroetz's construction of the political subject approximates that of Brecht, but he does not on the other hand share Brecht's aesthetic strategy. In *Oberösterreich* and *Das Nest* he attempts to move the individual from an entirely subjected situation to a more autonomous one. He does so, however, with an aesthetic strategy that at least partially thwarts his efforts.

A relatively stable dramatic model gives way in *Oberösterreich* to accommodate a new social and political perspective. Kroetz alters it again slightly in *Das Nest*, but it and the central plays that follow, *Mensch Meier* and *Der stramme Max*, represent a reasonably consistent series, the elements of which do not differ from each other considerably. Nonetheless, all of the difficulties Kroetz's political and aesthetic strategies confront in *Oberösterreich* and *Das Nest* continue to be problems up through *Nicht Fisch nicht Fleisch*.

Notes

1. Given the excellent bibliographies available on Kroetz, it would be redundant to list here all of the works that treat these aspects of Kroetz's early production. Instead I shall recommend Michael Töteberg's bibliography in Riewoldt, *Franz Xaver Kroetz*, pp. 325–373 and also my own bibliography.
2. Ernst Wendt, "Kroetz, ein Realist," in *Wie es euch gefällt geht nicht mehr* (Munich: Carl Hanser Verlag, 1985), p. 188.
3. Franz Xaver Kroetz, *Stücke*, vol. I–IV (Frankfurt/M.: Suhrkamp Verlag, 1989). All future quotes from Kroetz's works will be followed by the volume number and the appropriate page number.
4. Motekat, pp. 117f.
5. For the theory of a culture industry, see Adorno/Horkheimer, *Dialektik der Aufklärung*. For a description of the consciousness industry, see Hans Magnus Enzensberger, "Die Bewußtseins-Industrie," in *Einzelheiten I* (Frankfurt/M.: Suhrkamp Verlag, 1962), pp. 7–17.

6. Russell Berman, *Modern Culture and Critical Theory* (Madison: University of Wisconsin Press, 1989), p. 14.
7. Herbert Marcuse, *One Dimensional Man. Studies in the Ideology of Advanced Industrial Society* (Boston: Beacon Press, 1964), p. 79.
8. Horkheimer/Adorno, *Dialektik der Aufklärung*, p. 153.
9. For a more detailed analysis of this aspect of Adorno's thinking, see chapter one on Foucault and Adorno in Berman, *Modern Culture and Critical Theory*, pp. 12–26.
10. Ibid., p. 15.
11. Adorno, *Ästhetische Theorie*, p. 218
12. Ibid., p. 359.
13. Berman, *Modern Culture and Critical Theory*, p. 18.
14. This passage hearkens back to the theoretical demand within a socialist realist aesthetic that a committed work of art illustrate not only what society looks like now, but also how it *will* look in the future.
15. The purported increase in the characters' verbal capacity is much disputed. The discussion will return to this below.
16. Kroetz runs the risk here of confusing the average with the "typical," the second required component of good socialist realist art as outlined in the introduction. However, a close reading of the passage allows room for the interpretation that Kroetz found it impossible to portray the "typical" using society's extremes, and turned therefore instead toward what he perceived as a richer source for characterization.
17. This is at least partially in contradiction to the Marxist-Leninist notion of the collective subject, a reconceptualization of political subjectivity based on the idea that a class of individuals and not specific individuals will bring about the revolution of class structures. It indicates that Kroetz's own notions of society and politics already here contain potential ares of conflict between his own position and that of the DKP.
18. There are critics who disagree with this reading of Heinz. Gerd Müller, for instance, emphasizes exactly the opposite, namely Heinz's inability to express himself in any meaningful form: "Er gibt sich Mühe, sich verständlich und klar auszudrücken, bringt aber trotz dieser Anstrengung nur Formulierungen zustande, die seine Aussage wiederholen, ohne ihren Informationsgehalt zu vergrößern. . . ja viele seiner auf diese Weise gewonnenen Formulierungen haben geradezu tautologischen Charakter." p. 140. Whereas Wend Kässens maintains that generally language *functions* again in *Oberösterreich*. See Kässens, "Wer durchs Laub geht kommt darin um. Zur Sprachbehandlung und zu einigen Motiven

in den Dramen von Franz Xaver Kroetz," in Riewoldt, *Franz Xaver Kroetz*, p. 274.

19. Actually, pregnancy was perhaps an inappropriate choice for a dramatic conflict, given the author's political intentions. On almost every count Anni's decision merely perpetuates their position of exploitation within a capitalist context. The defiance – one cannot let economics determine human reproduction – is totally moot. For a more extended treatment of pregnancy and abortion in Kroetz's work, see my article "Franz Xaver Kroetz: The Use and Abuse of the Unborn Child," in *seminar* 29, no. 4 (Nov. 1993): pp. 382–397.

20. See also Kafitz, pp. 100, 103.

21. Ingeborg Walther has a slightly different interpretation of the cliché. She writes: "In the double employment of 'Sprichwörter' both as counterpoint and harmony we see the harsh reality of the situation as well as the potential for positive development." It is the last part of this claim that I cannot find in Kroetz's works up through *Oberösterreich*. Here p. 55.

Peter Handke also uses clichés and formulaic linguistic constructions in some of his works (see for instance *Kaspar Hauser* or *Innenwelt der Außenwelt der Innenwelt*). However, he does so as a means to explore the nature and construction of human language itself. He does not use the cliché as a means of characterization as does Kroetz. The clichéd language of Kroetz's characters, highly stylized and only in a limited sense naturalistic as it is, does not constitute an intense and extensive abstract exploration of the relationship between language and subjectivity (although one could certainly argue that it is necessarily pertinent to such an exploration); rather for Kroetz's plays, language – in its various forms – appears bound to particular socio-economic classes and geographical regions.

22. Although one could argue that the violence in a play such as *Heimarbeit* is in no way senseless, but rather structurally overdetermined, i.e. a formal gesture rather than just a point of the plot, I am using the word here to underscore that Willi's infanticide will in no way alter the contours of the couple's existence. By murdering the child, he does not remove the threat to his existence that he senses emotionally, or even subconsciously. The death will not help him locate the threat on a systemic level, nor give him the means with which to combat the pressures such systemic inequities create in his life.

23. Both Rolf-Peter Carl and Ursula Reinhold have also noted how reliant an interpretation of Kroetz must be on a familiarity with the dramatist's earlier work. Carl attributes this to Kroetz's relative

isolation in the West German theater world, but recognizes that such a strategy can have profound implications for his reception. See Carl, *Franz Xaver Kroetz*, p. 82. Ursula Reinhold argues that the socially critical insights of Kroetz's works cannot come from the dialogue of the characters themselves, but can result from the context of the various plays taken together: "Durch den Zusammenhang der Stücke allerdings gibt es eine Ausweitung, die die Einschichtigkeit durchbricht: Der Autor setzt beim gleichen Vorgang immer wieder neu an, und das Ergebnis geht über das vorherige hinaus. ... Dieser Zusammenhang ist aber bei der Aufführung des einzelnen Stückes nicht immer präsent." See Reinhold, p. 368.

24. Kässens, "Wer durchs Laub geht," p. 268f and Kässens and Töteberg, "Fortschritt im Realismus?" p. 44.

25. There is a fair amount of disagreement about whether Kroetz's work up to this point is in fact naturalist, realist or something else entirely. Where the individual critics stand on this issue seems to relate primarily to how much they like or appreciate the playwright's aesthetic project. For instance, Carl, "Zur Theatertheorie des Stückeschreibers Franz Xaver Kroetz," in *text + kritik* no. 57 (Jan 1978), p. 3, Michael Töteberg, "Der Kleinbürger auf der Bühne. Die Entwicklung des Dramatikers Franz Xaver Kroetz und das realistische Volksstück," *Akzente* 23, no. 2 (1976): p. 169, and Kässens, "Wer durchs Laub geht," p. 270 all see his work as naturalist in character, whereas Donna Hoffmeister refers to his aesthetic as "petty bourgeois realism." Donna Hoffmeister, *The Theater of Confinement: Language and Survival in the Milieu Plays of Marieluise Fleißer and Franz Xaver Kroetz* (Columbia, S. Carolina: Camden House, 1983), p. 74. Ingeborg Walther acknowledges the temptation to call them naturalist, but declines to do so because of the deterministic overtones of the term. See pp. 12, 40, 61, 65, and 202. She indicates that the problems inherent to naturalism were also problematic for the pieces preceding *Oberösterreich*, but argues that Kroetz had resolved some of these by the time he writes *Oberösterreich*, p. 71.

26. Yet another reaction is possible. They could identify themselves with the characters on the stage and be either insulted or uplifted. In *Paare und Passanten* Botho Strauß offers a fictionalized version of the former: "Der Busfahrer, der eine Ladung Theaterfreunde vor einem Zirkuszelt abgesetzt hat, in dem ein kritisches Zeitstück aufgeführt wird, der sich selbst mit dazu setzt, aber nur für eine Weile, dann erregt, doch ohne ein Wort zu verlieren, das Zelt verläßt... Warum? Weil in diesem Stück von Beginn an der

'übliche Kleinbürgermief' Ziel des Spottes war, weil *sein* Zuhaus, *seine* Einrichtung, seine Kleidung, seine Ansichten und seine Familie der Lächerlichkeit preisgegeben wurden, weil er selbst öffentlich beleidigt worden war." *Paare und Passanten* (Munich: Carl Hanser Verlag, 1981): p. 110. Donna Hoffmeister, on the other hand, sees in such possible identification the key to the play's success: "I suspect that the appeal of this play lies not so much in its ability to evoke a condescending attitude about the petty bourgeois mentality and limited linguistic and intellectual ability of the two characters of this play; rather, the play expresses the quotidian experience of contemporary man in such a way that the spectator is struck by the familiarity of this average life and by his own participation in it." *Theater of Confinement*, p. 113.

27. Again, as with the naturalism/realism problem, there are differing views about how well Kroetz's plays work to uncover social structures. Both Hoffmeister, *Theater of Confinement*, p. 131 and Reinhold believe that his realist techniques do dissect social reality clearly enough for the audience. Reinhold argues: "Bei Kroetz findet der Klassengegensatz nicht Ausdruck in der Konfrontation zweier Protagonisten, sondern ist gewissermaßen in die Figuren hineinverlegt. Er wird auf diese Weise nicht nur als sozialer Antagonismus konstatiert, sondern es werden die Mechanismen freigelegt, die sozial und psychologisch Manipulation bewirken." p. 365. Carl, *Franz Xaver Kroetz*, p. 37 and Töteberg, "Der Kleinbürger" tend to dismiss such claims. Töteberg writes: "Kroetz zwingt uns nicht, die Dumpfheit, mit der seine Figuren handeln, als systembedingt zu erkennen; er führt uns die Dumpfheit nur minuziös vor und macht uns bestenfalls betroffen." p. 169.

28. As late as 1978 Kroetz claims: "Meine Stücke versuchen, sozusagen, verschüttetes Klassenbewußtsein zu entwickeln und aufzudecken, wenn es möglich ist." in Hoffmeister, "'Ich kann nur schreiben, von dem, was ich sehe, nicht von dem, was ich sehen möchte,'" p.45.

29. I have adopted this term from an article by Cocalis, p. 206. I will try, however, to use it only in reference to Kroetz's pre-*Oberösterreich* works.

30. Walther, p. 33.

31. Walther, p. 39. There are others, though, who would suggest, as I do, that whatever distinctions there are between Kroetz's aesthetic and that of the naturalists are so minimal as to be inconsequential. See e.g. Carl, *Franz Xaver Kroetz*, p. 28.

32. See also Cocalis, pp. 204f.

33. Adorno, *Ästhetische Theorie*, p. 340.

34. Ibid., p. 339.
35. Terry Eagleton, *Criticism & Ideology* (London: Verso, 1975), p. 144.
36. A critic in the communist newspaper *Unsere Zeit* from 24 November 1972 wrote of Kroetz: "Die Milieu- und Personenkenntnis schlägt sich in seinen Stücken nieder: Er zeigt seine Helden nicht aus einer überlegenen oder skeptischen Distanz, sondern setzt alle Mittel ein, um sie dem Zuschauer 'von innen' vorzuführen." Reprinted in: Evalouise Panzner, *Franz Xaver Kroetz und seine Rezeption. Die Intentionen eines Stückeschreibers und seine Aufnahme durch die Kritik* (Stuttgart: Ernst Klett, 1976), p. 82.
37. See the interview with Kroetz in Heinz Ludwig Arnold (ed.), *Als Schriftsteller Leben* (Reinbeck bei Hamburg: Rowohlt Verlag, 1979), p. 57
38. Koch et al., pp. 634f.
39. Träger, p. 81
40. See e.g. Walther, p. 130.
41. Benjamin Henrichs, "Bayerischer Kommunismus, nestwarm," in *Beruf Kritiker* (Munich: Carl Hanser Verlag, 1978), p. 119.
42. Moray McGowan, "Botho Strauß and Franz Xaver Kroetz: Two Contemporary Views of the Subject," *Strathclyde Modern Language Studies*, no. 5 (1985): p. 70. Kroetz's return to his upbringing as a catholic and his thematization of the role religion plays in people's lives in *Bauern sterben* lends certain credence to McGowan's retrospective reading of *Das Nest*.
43. Kroetz speaks of socialist realism and the problems he sees with it in an interview with Manfred Bosch, reprinted in *Weitere Aussichten*: "Dieses Schema, wenn man's mal so bezeichnen will, das Stück also, das mit der positiven Utopie endet und das uns eben Mut gibt, das ist die Forderung. Also ich habe mich dieser Forderung nicht verschlossen, sondern bin der Auffassung, daß da sicher etwas Wahres dran ist. Es ist aber die Frage der Überprüfbarkeit dieser Vorgänge, die mich derzeit noch ein bißchen schwanken läßt. Die meisten Menschen in dieser Gesellschaft, in der zu schreiben ich verpflichtet bin, sind nicht oder noch nicht in der Lage, ihre Geschicke so in die Hand zu nehmen, daß sie positiv enden. Also hab' ich unter Umständen mit dem positiven Helden bereits einen Sprung gemacht, den sehr viele Leute gar nicht mehr nachvollziehen" p. 195.
44. See also Carl, *Franz Xaver Kroetz*, p. 82.
45. Adorno, *Ästhetische Theorie*, p. 369.
46. The role of unions in Warsaw Pact nations has, of course, been

problematic. In fact independent unions were not supported by so-called communist governments after their rise to power.

47. For a discussion of the fragmentation of the working class see Ernesto Laclau and Chantal Mouffe, *Hegemony and Socialist Strategy. Towards a Radical Democratic Politics*, trans. Winston Moore and Paul Caminack (London: Verso, 1985), pp. 17ff, 48.

48. For a brief description of the dispersion of the working class, see: André Gorz, *Farewell to the Working Class: An Essay on Post-industrial Socialism*, trans. Michael Sonenscher (London: Pluto Press, 1982).

49. In this context see also Jean Cohen, *Class and Civil Society: The Limits of Marxian Critical Theory* (Amherst: University of Massachusetts Press, 1982), pp. 106, 155f and 193.

50. Heinz's discomfort with being an interchangeable part could be either the result of the capitalist culture industry's tendency to homogenize the individual or the practical consequences of Marxist social theory.

51. Cohen, p. 163.

52. Gorz, pp. 10, 59.

53. Cohen, p. 8.

54. See e.g. Cohen, pp. 2, 24 and 226 and Laclau/Mouffe, p. 84.

55. For dates and details see Carl, *Franz Xaver Kroetz*, pp. 14ff and Riewoldt, *Franz Xaver Kroetz*, pp. 321ff.

56. Arnold, *Als Schriftsteller leben*, pp. 50f.

57. I refer again to McGowan's and Henrich's comments cited above. See also Karol Sauerland's response to the nature of the political conflict represented in *Das Nest*: "findet die Umweltverschmutzung nicht in einer viel umfassenderen, organisierteren und anonymeren Form statt? Das eigentlich Tragische ist doch, daß man der fast unsichtbaren Industriemächte kaum habhaft wird." *text + kritik*, no. 57 (Jan. 1978): p. 36.

58. Reprinted in Riewoldt, *Franz Xaver Kroetz*, p. 116.

Nicht Fisch nicht Fleisch

The previous chapter revealed a curious paradox in Kroetz's development as a dramatist and public figure: his success and popularity with the press and with the largely conservative West German art public grew tremendously as he moved ever closer to an explicitly political aesthetic practice. This was a disturbing tendency for an author who hoped to see his own work function as a vehicle for the political enlightenment of his contemporaries, in particular for the working-class population of the Federal Republic. Chapter two approached this predicament from a thematic perspective, but this seeming incongruity merits a more thorough examination as the discussion proceeds to *Nicht Fisch nicht Fleisch*, written and premiered in 1980.

Adorno's perceptive analysis of *engagement* discussed in the previous chapter also addresses the seeming ineffectuality of political art. According to him political commitment in the aesthetic product is necessarily indeterminate, unless degraded to mere propaganda. That is to say, if the artist wishes to avoid creating an obviously tendentious work, he or she must fashion the conflict in a very general way. The consequence of the abstraction is, Adorno argues, political vagueness. In Kroetz's case this problem is compounded by the aesthetic strategy of realism.

The dramatist's choice of realist methods was, at least in part, the result of his desire to reach an audience unaccustomed to interpreting non-representational art, namely the working class. Realist artworks offer a (perhaps deceptively) facile representation of empirical reality. The audience or reader is encouraged to believe that there exists essentially a direct correspondence between what is on the stage and what is off the stage. Such works appear to facilitate the receptive process by establishing the correlation between artwork and empirical reality within the work itself. Non-representational art, on the other hand, insists that the reader/audience make that correlation. Adorno maintains that modernist art goes so far as to oppose the notion of an intelligible, or understandable reality, refusing to mimic a closure which no longer exists. Non-representational art thus frustrates a reading which would see in it a world that is not yet riven by the cataclysmic horrors of the twentieth century, i.e. it frustrates a conservative, nostalgic receptive stance. Conversely, the unintended side-effect of Kroetz's preferred aesthetic strategy was that it rendered his work palatable to a much larger audience, one which included the conservative tastes of the traditional art public, a public reluctant to confront the disintegration of a cohesive social reality.[1]

However, the false sense of equation that the realist work offers, and the necessary indeterminacy Adorno sees in the politically engaged artwork, are only two facets of his argument. In a sense, Kroetz could have chosen any aesthetic strategy, including the various techniques of non-representational art, and still have faced the integration of his work into the devitalized, ineffectual world of art. Indeed, no work of art can escape the trap of affirmation. By emphatically separating itself from empirical reality, art has sanctioned the preeminence of that reality. It has in effect disempowered itself, at least in terms of the political machinations of society.[2] Adorno's aesthetic theory offers three explanations for why politically motivated works of art seldom have the impact they would wish to have, and beyond that why they often find support within the public they set out to attack.

His aesthetic theory is comprehensive and powerfully convincing within its own boundaries. From a socio-historical perspective, however, it tells us little about the function or dysfunction of political drama within the specific context of the seventies in West Germany. What impact, if any, a political aesthetic can have, depends to a great degree on the socio-political environment in which it is produced and received or "consumed." Thus, the reception of political art in the Federal Republic during the seventies can only be understood against the backdrop of the social-liberal coalition and the developments which led up to it.

Socio-Political Developments

As noted in the chapter one, the Grand Coalition (1966–1969) of the Christian Democratic Party/Christian Social Union (CDU/CSU) and the Social Democratic Party of Germany (SPD) had created a dangerously anti-parliamentary situation, in which there was little effective opposition to counterbalance the politics of the governing parties. This danger was evident not only to the official opposition party, the Free Democrats (FDP), which did not have enough seats in parliament to play its opposition role effectively, but also to the leaders of the APO ("Außerparlamentarische Opposition"). Despite the public's general resistance to what it perceived as the radical character of the APO and the student movement, the political activities of the latter, various governmental scandals such as the *Spiegel*-Affair, and Willy Brandt's efforts to foster political cooperation and detente between the two German states did create a political climate increasingly disenchanted with the twenty-year political dominance of the conservative Christian Democrats and increasingly amenable to the politics of change proposed by Willy Brandt. The year 1969 marked the (temporary) end of conservative hegemony in West Germany and the beginning of the social-liberal coalition under Brandt and Scheel.

As the only remaining post-war political party with traditional ties to Marxism and the working class, the SPD's rise to power might have created more space in public discourse for works of art aimed at the resuscitation of working-class consciousness.[3] And, in fact, there may have been more tolerance for such works, but the potential for the realization of radical leftist politics did not increase measurably. There are several reasons why this potential did not materialize.

The party struggled in the immediate post-war era to cull enough voter support to act simply as an effective political opposition to the conservative Christian Democrats rallied around the very powerful paternal figure of Konrad Adenauer. The SPD strove in the early fifties for popular endorsement, gradually abandoning its overt bonds to Marxism toward the end of the decade and into the sixties. Intent on moving into the role of governing party, the SPD, in a strategically wise move, made concessions first to the CDU/CSU, and then, with the dissolution of the Grand Coalition and the formation of the social-liberal government in 1969, to the FDP. These concessions included the agreement of the SPD to operate according to economic policies that restricted the control of the state over income and capital distribution, a move that represented a clear departure from a socialist economy. It also entailed the introduction of legislation in the seventies intent on thwarting the efforts of extra-parliamentary oppositional forces. Two examples of this were the "Radikalenerlaß" in 1972 and the "paritätisches Mitbestimmungsrecht" in 1976. The former included civil career restrictions on individuals determined by the government to be potential foes of the constitution, "Verfassungsfeinde," and entailed potentially severe restrictions on the right to free speech. The latter provided middle and upper management with seats on the workers' councils, thereby strengthening management's voice in labor disputes and firm governance to the detriment, obviously, of labor.[4]

These compromises on the part of the SPD contrasted with its continued role as the sole institutionally effective party of the left. To the general public the SPD was *the* representative of liberal politics, a role that traditionally included the protection of workers' interests and the guarantee of free political expression. This was particularly true once the German government had effectively dismantled the Communist Party of Germany (KPD) in 1956.

The SPD's move to the center was not, however, unique, but rather symptomatic of institutionalized leftist politics in parliamentary democracies. Once confronted with the actual realities of governance, left parties have historically tended to move more toward the right. The terminological confusions that can ensue from such a shift are apparent particularly in the case of the SPD, as the party abandoned more and more of its foundational policies and traditional political alliances to create of itself a viable governmental party, while at the same time retaining its leftist label.[5] With one of the traditional proponents of workers' causes in a position of governance, any voices that called attention to apparent inequities in the system were bound to confront a great deal of scepticism and mistrust. In combination with aesthetic restrictions both of topic and of form, this may in fact have further defused the political message of Kroetz's work, drawing attention instead to interpersonal conflict and existential questions, i.e. to preserve or not to preserve the traditional nuclear family, or to accept or not to accept responsibility for one's own life.

The integrative powers of a governing party of so-called leftist orientation would seem to be even more daunting than that of conservative parties when they hold the state. Nonetheless, the ostensibly heightened ability of the SPD to smooth over societal conflict, including traditional class conflict, cannot adequately account for the deaf ears on which Kroetz's radical political aesthetic fell. Another source for the indifference with which his political project was met must also be sought in the socio-economic developments of post-war Germany. With its destruction of so many millions of human lives, the Second World War had virtually obliterated the rigidly hierarchical structures of pre-war German society, breaking down the barriers between socio-economic classes. The struggle to rebuild a country in physical ruin, to provide for basic human needs and to reestablish an economic infrastructure claimed the energies of its people, with little left over for fighting seemingly irrelevant class wars. The economic recovery of West Germany in the fifties served then essentially to extinguish what remained of the overt distinctions between the classes.[6] Once the majority of its citizens had achieved a generally high standard of living, one unknown in its breadth in pre-war Germany, the structural inequities in capitalism were forgotten. As Jürgen Habermas points out, collective memory can be very short:

> Dreißig Tage Jahresurlaub oder das erste Auto bedeuten einmal einen
> eminenten Zuwachs an privater Bewegungsfreiheit und Befriedigung –

waren Ziele, für die wir Anstrengungen, sogar Opfer auf uns genommen haben. Aber das einmal erreichte Niveau der Befriedigung tilgt sozusagen die Spuren seiner eigenen Entstehungsgeschichte.[7]

Fully aware of the grim economic conditions in socialist East Germany and passified by the tangible rewards of participation in a capitalist economy, German workers were no longer as eager to work toward a total restructuring of their own society, nor were they convinced that such a restructuring was necessary.

Although one could argue that labor politics are not explicit components of any of the plays described here, the repeated selection of characters from the working class, the continuous references to the alienation of the wage laborer and particularly the evocation of the power within union solidarity leave little doubt that labor and class conflicts form the central focus of Kroetz's work at the very least from *Oberösterreich* until *Nicht Fisch nicht Fleisch*.[8] The discussion of *Oberösterreich* and *Das Nest* included a rather lengthy analysis of the working class in today's society and this analysis supported the idea that the plays in question represent something of an anachronism in this respect. One way to account, in this light, for the impressive ability of Kroetz's audiences to ignore the leftist political content of his work is to underscore the notion that the conflicts he presented no longer seemed of any real substance: Is West Germany not, after all, a classless society?[9]

The absence of any clearly discernible class structure itself draws attention away from the actual composition of the contemporary capitalist market place. Instead, as was once the case, of having "bourgeois" literally on one side of the table and "proletarian" on the other, today's working populace does not even confront, nor is it likely to comprehend, the extremely complex strata of corporate management and ownership. The cloud of unknowing that seems to enshroud virtually everyone in contemporary society will not be dispelled by the confrontation of one corporate bad guy with one blossoming political consciousness, as we saw in *Das Nest*. This is not to trivialize that particular form of socio-political conflict, but rather to present the myriad of potential obstacles to an active (in the Brechtian sense) understanding of political, economic and social structures.

Nicht Fisch nicht Fleisch: A Catalogue of Contemporary Confusions

This very brief introduction offers a virtual catalogue of the issues that take shape in *Nicht Fisch nicht Fleisch*, as it explores the various socio-political crises that have arisen in the history of the Federal Republic.

The play thematizes the response of traditional labor to post-industrial relations of production and the ever-increasing importance of non-industrial production. It calls into question the ability of orthodox Marxism to offer a comprehensive critique of capitalist society and to construct an effective, transformative political praxis. Through the main characters' confrontation with the changing nature of production it also examines the individual's growing unease with socio-economic and technological developments within this post-industrial society that have called into question the very viability of the human subject. At the same time, Kroetz continues to search for an aesthetic strategy that can adequately capture the diverse thematic concerns he wishes to address here.

Nicht Fisch nicht Fleisch centers on two couples, Edgar and Emmi, and Hermann and Helga. Edgar and Hermann both work in the same printing press as typesetters. Edgar and Emmi have no children and both work outside the home. At the start of the play, Emmi's job causes a limited amount of stress in the couple's relationship. As she begins to be more successful in her work, and eventually assumes the management of her own small supermarket, the strain on their marriage increases. This becomes particularly problematic when, because of technological rationalization at the firm and his own inability to over-come the problems involved in retraining, Edgar faces the loss of his job, which he feels forms a central component of his (masculine) identity. Hermann and Helga have two children and are expecting a third. Hermann is active in union politics and Helga, who quit working outside the home when their first child was born, feels he has repeatedly put the well-being of his family in jeopardy through these union-related activities.

After characterizing the two families, the play moves on to portray the emotional and economic hardships caused when the company for which the two men work is bought out by a competitor and then technologically renovated, i.e. printing operations are shifted from manual to computerized typesetting. The historical background of the plot entails the process of concentration and rationalization of the printing industry that, according to Lothar Schwab, began in West Germany's larger cities in the very early seventies.[10] This led at the end of the seventies to a strike movement in the industry and the DKP's decision to concentrate its political activities within the unions.[11]

Both Hermann and Edgar complete a retraining session, but Edgar quits shortly thereafter because he feels his very identity threatened by the loss of the work that he had learned as a young man and that has shaped him throughout the rest of his life. Hermann, on the other hand, realizing the potential for the dissolution of many jobs, persists in his new occupation, grappling as he does so with the possible benefits and the very real dangers the new technology entails.

The crisis at work affects the men's friendship, threatening to divide them because of their opposing responses to the changes at the press. In the penultimate scene (which will be the focus of closer analysis later in this chapter) the two men meet unexpectedly at the edge of an unspecified body of water. This meeting, which has a rather surreal feel to it, illustrates the limitations of each man's particular position, and it is only after this confrontation that the four major characters of the play can return to a relationship, if not of friendship, then at least of minimal animosity. *Nicht Fisch nicht Fleisch* traces the two families through a work-related crisis that calls into question their attitudes toward their work and their personal lives before and after the crisis.[12]

The nature and ramifications of this particular crisis would seem to indicate that Kroetz has realized in this play that there is an ever-present danger in social theories that claim to understand human life in its totality. That danger is stagnation, and stagnation breeds the inability to rethink originally convincing ideas that once explained so admirably the mechanics of social, economic and political life. Jean-Paul Sartre, both a committed socialist and an author who himself attempted to create a political aesthetic, addresses this phenomenon in *The Problem with Method*:

> A system is an alienated man who wants to go beyond his alienation and who gets entangled in alienated words; it is an achievement of awareness which finds itself deviated by its own instruments and which the culture transforms into a particular *Weltanschauung*.[13]

This applies most aptly also to the character of Hermann in *Nicht Fisch nicht Fleisch*. He is virtually the embodiment of orthodox Marxism as filtered through trade-unionist philosophy. He speaks passionately and persuasively of the successful battles waged by labor to secure the individual worker a better life. When his wife Helga accuses him of seeking election to the workers' council simply to feed an extraordinarily voracious ego, he responds with an inventory of the labor movement's accomplishments:

> *Hermann:* . . . Wenn sich die vor uns ned eingsetzt hätten, täten mir jetzt in einem nassen Kellerloch sitzn, und wenn ich überhaupt eine Arbeit hätt, dann sechs Tag in der Woch zehn Stundn lang mit einer Kündigungsfrist von heut auf morgen, und trotzdem hätten mir nix zum fressen und wenn eins krank is, tät man sich den Doktor ned leistn können. (IV,27)

Certainly Hermann's rendition of the labor movement's successes are accurate, and he proves himself to be a very shrewd analyst of management as it pertains to the technological rationalization of industry. He knows that human labor is rapidly becoming dispensable, and that the answer to mass layoffs as a result of technological innovation is worker solidarity. His futile attempts to keep Edgar from quitting make repeated reference to the power of collective resistance. His belief in the necessity of such solidarity leads him to reject Edgar as a friend once the latter has abandoned the fight to secure some benefit from technological progress.

Edgar defends his action with reference to pride and honesty. He finds the idea of working in a field in which his learned skills have become obsolete unbearable. He realizes that the company has only retrained typesetters like himself because the union ensures that they do so. For him this is nothing more than charity, which is an insult to his sense of self-worth.

Hermann unsuccessfully tries to explain his own position to Edgar. In his lengthy and eloquent explanation, Hermann describes the effects of technological progress on the worker:

Hermann: . . . in Japan gibt es schon ganze Autofabriken, die arbeiten ohne einen einzigen Arbeiter. Aber die Bänder laufen, und Autos kommen heraus! So gehts ned bloß in Japan, so gehts in der ganzen Welt, die Herrn Kapitalisten bauen ihre Zukunft auf den technischen Fortschritt, nicht auf die Menschen. Überall marschiert die Rationalisierung und mir sollen unter die Räder. Mit einer vollautomatischen Fabrik braucht man keine Tarifverhandlungen führen, braucht auf keinen Betriebsrat hören, geschweige denn an die Mitbestimmung denken, man braucht keine Kantine, ja nicht einmal ein Scheißhaus, und wenn man eine Maschine entläßt, braucht man keinen Kündigungsschutz. Und anstatt daß man kämpft, bis aufs Messer, wenn es sein muß, daß der Fortschritt nicht dem Kapitalisten sondern dem Arbeiter gehört, leistet sich dieser Herr Gefühle und fällt die andern in den Rücken. (IV,64f)

There is no doubt that the increasing rationalization of production, made possible by a vast array of new and quickly changing technologies, has had a profound impact on industrial labor. Mass layoffs have often followed the implementation of new production techniques, and yet, despite the accuracy of his analysis, Hermann's speech rings somewhat comical. The evocation of the evil capitalist and the upright, worthy worker have an antiquated air in what seems superficially to be a classless society. It is, however, less the anachronism of his words than the rigidity of his position which alienates both his close friends and his colleagues.

His wife Helga repeatedly underscores the inflexibility of Hermann's attitude towards life. After the long tirade against Edgar, Edgar leaves his friends' apartment crying quietly. Helga admonishes Hermann for his brutal treatment of his best friend:

> Helga: (*hochdeutsch*) Du willst für die Menschheit kämpfen und
>   läßt weinende Freunde aus deiner Wohnung gehen! (*Kleine
>   Pause.*) Du bist wie ein Hund, der sich sein Leben lang
>   jedn Bissn erkämpfen hat müssen und der deshalb jeden
>   beißt, der ihm in die Näh kommt. (IV,65f)

While Helga acknowledges the source of Hermann's reaction to Edgar's behavior as one born of a necessary but years-long struggle, she nonetheless points out what loss that struggle has involved, namely an inability to relate to other people as individuals, that is to say on anything but a structural level.

Hermann's unceasing efforts have made him insensitive to the subtleties of human existence that are not part of his unionist framework. Similarly, one could argue, the Marxism of the DKP with its critique of capitalism as an economy still largely driven by industrial production, is incapable of responding to the changing character of production and the effects those changes have on the individual. Extending Helga's simile even further, both Hermann and the DKP have concentrated on the exploitation of labor in industrial capitalism so long that they have failed to see that post-industrial capitalism of the late twentieth century necessitates other strategies, foci and theories.

In the penultimate scene Edgar and Hermann meet again. Hermann is seen crawling slowly along the water's edge, painfully holding his stomach. The dialogue reveals that Hermann's colleagues actually took a bicycle tire pump and filled his intestines with air. Edgar questions Hermann about the event:

> Edgar: Ham dich die Kollegn aufblasn?
> Hermann: (*nickt.*)
> Edgar: Hast sie (*lacht*) aufghetzt, verkehrt rum?
>   . . .
> Edgar: (*freundlich*) Hast sie fertig gmacht wie mich?

Nicht Fisch nicht Fleisch

. . .

Hermann: *(muß lachen, hält sich den Bauch, schreit.)*

Edgar: Der Teufel fährt aus. *(Lacht.)* Karl Marx persönlich, der durch das Arschloch des Herrn Hermann Zwiebel ausfährt.

. . .

Edgar: Weil du ein Klugscheißer im wahrsten Sinn des Wortes bist, jetz hast den Arsch offen, wo es keiner wert is. (IV,70ff)

In his intimation that it was Hermann's know-it-all attitude that disturbed his colleagues the most, Edgar alludes once more to the obstinate surety with which orthodox Marxist politics (in this instance the politics of the DKP) approaches post-industrial capitalist society.

It is difficult to disagree with Hermann: obviously worker solidarity will be more effective in securing what has already been achieved and what has yet to be accomplished than will the fragmentation of the work force. The Marxist insistence on the identity-forming powers of labor, however, is an inadequate response to the changing character of labor itself. It cannot address the ever-diminishing importance of human beings in production other than to safeguard actual jobs. This often entails individuals performing unnecessary and redundant tasks.

Hermann's inability to understand Edgar's position is itself something of a paradox: the union activist cannot comprehend that there is more at stake in this situation than a job. Edgar tries repeatedly to explain to his friend what the loss of his occupation means to him, but Hermann can only offer logistic responses:

Edgar: Wenn mir erst wieder in der Firma sind braucht man bloß noch möglichst schnell Schreibmaschinen-schreiben können und ein paar übliche Codierungen im Kopf haben. Ich hab drei Jahr für meinen Beruf gelernt, und dann war ich noch nicht perfekt. Jetzt tät ich perfekt sein. Und jetzt stellen sie um, die außerhalb der Kuppel. Jedes siebzehnjährige Mädl, das von einer Handelsschul kommt und Maschinenschreiben glernt hat, das kann in drei Wochen mehr wie ich, weil es einen leeren Kopf und flinke Händ mitbringt. Was mir jetzt lernen, schaut kompliziert aus, aber Beruf ist es keiner mehr, weil es jeder in drei Wochen lernen kann. Und was jeder kann, ist kein Beruf, bloß noch eine Arbeit. Für die neue Tastatur sind spitze lange Fingerl gefragt. *(Hält die Hände hoch.)* Die nicht. Wo hab ich die her?

Hermann:	Blei verformt.
	. . .
Edgar:	Ich habe Schriftsetzer glernt und das bleib ich. Ich laß mich nicht zu einem (*kleine Pause*) Schreibfräulein machen!
Hermann:	Die Gewerkschaft sorgt dafür, daß nirgends ein einziges "Schreibfräulein" an den Bildschirm kommt.
Edgar:	Und warum nicht? Weil es die Gewerkschaft vielleicht durchsetzen kann. Aber der fachliche Grund? Keiner. Ich will kein Reservat haben wie die Indianer, damit ich nicht ausstirb. (IV,42f)

In this passage it is Edgar who insists that the nature of his labor has so shaped his personal identity, that he is at this time in his life virtually incapable of change. Edgar's character as a whole represents in fact a wealth of contradictions: the history of the labor movement confronts in Edgar a host of contemporary societal conflicts. In the above passage he essentially reflects a Marxist emphasis on the centrality of labor in identity-formation. However, his attempts to restabilize his identity in a post-industrial economy, in which the basic conditions for self-construction as described by Marx no longer obtain, cannot succeed. The process no longer functions because the conditions of human existence have changed. Although Edgar never embraced a Marxist critique of capitalism, his own sense of self seems hopelessly determined by it.

Hermann appears oblivious to these issues. He misses the synecdoche of the hands completely, reacting instead to their pure physicality. He recognizes the damage lead has done to Edgar's hands, but he does not understand the broader implications for his friend's sense of self. Hermann's quest to do battle for himself, his family, his colleagues and for future generations is admirable, but his tools are not commensurate to the task at hand. He fails for the same reason that Edgar quits his job: he cannot adapt to changes that have occurred.

In their book *Hegemony and Socialist Strategy*, Ernesto Laclau and Chantal Mouffe reexamine Marxism's emphasis on the ontological centrality of the working class against the backdrop of the advent of the new social movements in the early seventies. They come to the conclusion that contemporary society is not constructed of a few, largely homogeneous groups, but rather of a plethora of subject positions and fluid interest coalitions.[14] Laclau and Mouffe, as have many others, assert that one's identity is not determined by one social context, but rather by a range of social positions the individual assumes. They write, "Unfixity has become the condition of every social identity."[15] As suggested above, the character of Edgar constitutes a focal point for various tensions in contemporary society. Thus it is no surprize to find in him both an opponent and a proponent of traditional Marxist labor philosophy. And yet, the character exemplifies the personal consequences social and individual unfixity can have. His once well-defined world is about to collapse in around him, and he cannot establish a new foothold.

One ominous threat to this character is his wife's growing financial and emotional independence. Women working outside the home have also been a major challenge to the traditional family. The ever-increasing influx of women into the workplace has shaken the foundations of patriarchal society. The hostility and insecurity this has caused reveals itself in the way Edgar describes the person ideally suited to computerized typesetting. In the passage just cited Edgar says: "Ich habe Schriftsetzer glernt und das bleib ich. Ich laß mich nicht zu einem (*kleine Pause*) Schreibfräulein machen!" (IV,42). Edgar's spiteful reference to the empty-headed *Schreibfräulein* does more than infantilize the women who work in such positions; he also explicitly distances himself from any possibility that the retraining might effeminize him and implicitly cast doubts on the masculinity of those men who stay on the job.

His displeasure with his wife's working at all shows itself first as amused irritation. When Emmi refuses his sexual advances in the very first scene of the play because she is tired and has a busy day ahead, Edgar reacts with mock indignation:

Edgar: Deine Scheißfirma! Regiert mir ins Bett hinein, die Firma. (*Kleine Pause, grinst.*) Ich sollt es dir überhaupts nicht gestatten, daß du arbeiten gehst. Ist die Frau nicht mehr am Herd, läuft die Ehe schon verkehrt. (IV,9)

What begins as a modest annoyance becomes an increasingly aggressive resentment. After Emmi assumes the management of her own store, and after Edgar quits his job, his perception of his own emasculation and his animosity towards her intensify. He feels he can no longer assert himself as a man in any other way than through sheer physical strength: his sexual demands become more frequent and more adamant, and at one point he even threatens his wife with rape. When Emmi expresses concern for his situation, Edgar responds: "Meinst, daßd stärker bist. Dich sollt man auf den Tisch setzen und die Füß auseinander! Zeign, wer der Herr im Haus is" (IV,60).

Apparently unsatisfied by this aggression, Edgar even performs a symbolic castration on himself via a teddy bear he had won for Emmi through the manly art of shooting.[16] This trophy of his masculinity becomes its victim. He then seeks to reassert his dominance over his wife in the realm of reproduction. In order to ensure that his wife does not get too far ahead of him, he replaces (far-fetched as this sounds) Emmi's birth-control pills with diet pills, calculates the most propitious time for conception and then at that time insists on his conjugal rights. Through Edgar, Kroetz finally forces his own work to confront the results of the women's movement, an issue glaringly lacking in all of his previous pieces.[17] It is, however, only one of the pressure points present in society.

Another component of Edgar's identity crisis is the continuously renewing process of social atomization. The specialization and separation of workers on the job in industry and the service sector, the increasingly institutional character of socialization (as opposed to what was formerly primarily the task of the family itself), the cultivation of the individual consumer and the stress on the cult of the individual – the rugged frontiersman or flamboyant adventurer – have led to the loss of a sense of community. This personal isolation evidences itself in Edgar's desire to return to a romanticized past. In the retraining center Edgar describes to Hermann his vision of a non-alienated existence, one which would involve killing and preparing one's own food, felling and fashioning one's own furniture and providing for one's family without external aid. In Edgar's utopian fantasy families stay to themselves, providing for all of their own needs, disconnected from the outside world, the world of rationalized society, by vast open spaces, and yet secure in their humanness by the reassuring presence of that other cabin beyond the woods: "in sicherem Abstand sind andere in der Wildnis. Manchmal trifft man sich, freut sich und geht wieder auseinander" (IV,46). It is ironic that Edgar's sense of isolation voices itself in the longing for even greater physical isolation, but it is not the only contradiction that manifests itself in this particular character.

When the play opens, the audience is introduced to an individual whose desire for order borders on the fanatic:

Edgar: Kennst du des?
Emmi: Was?
Edgar: (*lacht, schaut auf den Bettvorleger zu seinen Hausschuhen.*) Wenn die genau in Reih und Glied stehen, dann bringt es ein Glück, und wenn nicht, dann passiert was.
Emmi: (*schaut ihn an.*)
Edgar: (*lacht ertappt*) Stehn eh nicht. (*Kleine Pause.*) Das war, wie ich klein war, daß ich mir das einbildt hab, daß das so is.

> (*Kleine Pause.*) Da bin ich oft eine ganze Stund lang immer wieder außm Bett außer und hab die Schuh gricht, damits auch genau stehn in Reih und Glied, und wieder eini ins Bett und wieder außer, wenn es sein hat müssn, bis ich zittert hab vor Kältn. . . . Das is die Linie, der Scheitel sozusagen, und damit muß sich das Schuhpaar schneiden, das auf den Milimeter genau beieinander steht, bis es den rechten Winkel ergibt. Dann stimmts. (IV,9)

Although Edgar presents this amusing anecdote about his need for perceptible and stable structures as something from his childhood that he has long since overcome, the discussion between him and Hermann about the capitalist system in act one, scene three only reinforces the image of this character as one who needs to believe that the world functions according to a just and immutable order. In this scene Hermann and Edgar are practicing karate throws on each other at the local health club. Hermann complains to Edgar about his financial problems, about his hatred for those individuals in contemporary society who have so much more than anyone could possibly need. Edgar insists that there is a logical explanation for income distribution in capitalism and that people get exactly what they need and earn, no more, no less. Hermann, whose wife does not bring any income to the family, challenges this assumption:

> *Hermann*: Was is, wennst weniger verdienst wie du brauchst?
> *Edgar*: Dann wär ein Wurm im System. (*Betont es.*) Ist aber nicht. (IV,16)

Edgar refuses not only to acknowledge that there could be systemic injustice within capitalism, he also believes that capitalism is only part of a universal order. His steadfast belief in the inherent logic of the universe comes out as he tries to explain to his friend the chain of being among the fish of the sea, and, in particular, of his aquarium:

> *Edgar*: Das ist hier die Frage. Wenn es einer von die Raubfisch war, dann is es kein Problem, der is schnell gefunden. Aber auch bei die andern, wo als absolut friedlich erforscht sind, kann ein Krimineller dabei sein. Die Natur.
> *Hermann*: Wie bei die Menschen.
> *Edgar*: (*lacht*) Ein Kosmos im kleinen, genau. Da muß man dann eine lange Zeit aufwenden und suchen: Wo ist der

Übertäter, der die Ordnung durchbricht? Der aus der Art
geschlagene? Am besten man ertappt ihn auf frischer
Tat. (IV,21f)

Life has a predictable and discernible order to it. The order includes
predators, whose natural function is to dominate others, and there are
those who are alive only to serve the needs of the dominant fish. Those
fish or human beings who do not conform to that order must be
removed. According to Lothar Schwab, the word fish is also a particular
technical term among typesetters, referring to a letter that unexplainedly
ends up where it is not supposed to be. As such it prefigures
Edgar's self-removal from the press when he feels he no longer belongs
there.[18] There is further an ahistorical order to Edgar's vision of the
cosmos: it is not subject to change. He does not sense that the order
is artificial and by no means just until he quits his job and loses his
career.

At this point Edgar becomes the epitome of the alienated laborer. His
sense of loss, his desire to construct something for and by himself reads
like a textbook case study for Marx's *German Ideology*. In the
introduction to this work, Marx argues that capitalism and the division
of labor has constrained the individual, and that in a communist society
human beings would be free to roam from one role to the next, free to
explore their creative potential:

Sowie nämlich die Arbeit verteilt zu werden anfängt, hat Jeder einen
bestimmten ausschließlichen Kreis der Tätigkeit, der ihm aufgedrängt wird,
aus dem er nicht heraus kann; er ist Jäger, Fischer oder Hirt oder kritischer
Kritiker und muß es bleiben, wenn er nicht die Mittel zum Leben verlieren
will – während in der kommunistischen Gesellschaft, wo Jeder nicht einen
ausschließlichen Kreis der Tätigkeit hat, sondern sich in jedem beliebigen
Zweige ausbilden kann ... heute dies, morgen jenes zu tun, morgens zu
jagen, nachmittags zu fischen, abends Viehzucht zu treiben, nach dem Essen
zu kritisieren, wie ich gerade Lust habe, ohne je Jäger, Fischer, Hirt, oder
Kritiker zu werden.[19]

Edgar and Hermann discuss the loss of knowledge in today's world:
their inability to turn a wheel, to build an actual fire, to slaughter a pig
and prepare the meat for winter. Hermann responds to Edgar's longings
by telling him he should have become a carpenter if he really wanted to
build things with his own hands, but Edgar is adamant:

Und dann muß ich meinen Stuhl auch am Fabriktor abgeben und krieg ein
paar Fetzn dafür, wo Geld sind und nicht soviel, daß ich meinen eigenen
Stuhl im nächsten Geschäft wieder kaufen kann! Ich will selber verkaufen,

was ich geschaffen hab. Einmal im Monat mach ich eine lange Reise zum Markt. Dann hol ich das beste heraus, weil ich feilsch und handel für mich und die meinen! So geht es von Jahr zu Jahr. (IV,46)

Edgar wants to control the entire production process, he wants to create a whole, of which he then can dispose as he sees fit. Even if Edgar were, as a carpenter, to make an entire chair or table or whatever, he would still not have the right to profit from the chair itself, but rather from his labor. The rationalization of industrial production has generated a situation in which the individual responds only to single, isolated elements, eventually losing a conceptualization of the self as an integral whole, becoming instead simply another isolated element within the entire production process.

In Edgar's case, technological innovations have made him obsolete as a worker. Technological progress is in a very real sense dialectical, insofar as it has made human existence easier while at the same time making us virtually incapable of existing without an extensive technological support system, a system the individual rarely understands. Technology has both empowered as well as handicapped human beings. Beyond the psychic response to our own obsolescence, technology has also brought us tremendous benefits, but only by bringing us into a situation which is always on the brink of a cataclysmic catastrophe.

One fairly common response to the benefits and dangers technology has brought to human society, and also the one Edgar assumes in this play, is to long for a romanticized version of man's primitive past. In addition to his dream of such a peaceful, self-sufficient life on the frontier, Edgar idealizes the earlier evolutionary stages of various animals and of mankind itself. Already during the retraining course in act two, Edgar declares his empathy for the animal world:

Edgar: Ich bin ein Tier. (*Lächelt, nickt, gibt einen leisen tierischen Laut von sich.*) Genau bin ich ein Tier.
Hermann: Bist nicht.
Edgar: (*Macht den Tierschrei laut und lang.*)
Hermann: Ned so laut, die andern schlafen schon.
Edgar: Brüllen mir wie die Tiger, dann wachen sie auf, rennen zusammen und kriegen eine Angst. (IV,47)

And again in the scene discussed above where Hermann is creeping along the water's edge, Edgar has stripped down and envisions himself as part of the primal waters:

Edgar:	Mir schwimmen, kleinere Rasten halten wir auf Walen und von Delphinen lassen mir uns füttern. Durch mein Aquarium hab ich einen sehr guten Draht.
Hermann:	Das hab ich vergessen.
Edgar:	Mein Aquarium vergiß ich nie. Aber das andere Ufer is nur das eine. Mir schwimmen uns gsund, das garantier ich dir, und wenn mir eine Insel sehn, wo es schön is, gehört sie uns. . . . Niemand kann mich aufhalten.
	. . .
Hermann:	Und warum nackert?
Edgar:	Wo man erkannt werden kann ist man nicht frei. (IV,72)

Whether he is seeking release by mimicking the pre-verbal and pre-rational(ized) behavior of some generic animal (*Tierschrei*), or imagining some mystical (i.e. unbroken), Orphic bond to the dolphins of the sea, Edgar's hope is to strip the trappings of civilization from his identity in order to localize that lost sense of self. Although his response to Hermann's question as to why they must swim naked might be read as an attempt to flee one's established identity, there is also the idea here that only one's assumed identity (clothing) stands in the way of individual health and freedom.

Edgar's affinity to animals is an expression of his belief that technological progress has made human beings lose an intellectually tangible sense of self. We have forfeited self-control for the supposed benefits of technology. Instead of governing our own futures, we are now trained, much as dogs and seals, to perform certain tasks. The performance of these tasks, although not necessarily essential to the further existence of the species, keeps the wheels of technological progress running smoothly. The individual has been swept into that circular motion and can no longer step outside the realm of production to ask what is being produced for whom and why:

Edgar:	Mir arbeiten immer mehr und immer schneller. Am Ende der Kuppel is ein Loch. Das wird bewacht, weil es die einzige Öffnung is. Auf einem Fließband, breiter wie die Autobahn, rollen Tag und Nacht Waren durch das Loch ins Freie. Wohin? Is draußen ein Berg, der jeden Tag größer wird? (IV,41)

Edgar:	Sie wird immer weniger, die Arbeit. Das stimmt. Und schlechter. Bloß produzieren tun mir immer mehr. Für wen?
Hermann:	Für den Berg. (IV,43)

The entirely superfluous character of most market-oriented production (producing a mountain of goods for the mountain of goods) becomes an almost totalitarian force in contemporary society, governing not only the individual's working hours, but also his or her private existence, thus blurring the lines between the two theoretically separate spheres.

This discussion reflects the critique of consumption popularized by the student movement at the end of the sixties, i.e. by the first post-war generation that had come of age in a period of overwhelming abundance. The play explores, albeit not extensively, the increasing threat to the social and private identity of the individual brought about by the homogenization of the consumer in the culture and consciousness industries. Extensive intervention of production into the individual's private world causes the space for personalized expression to dwindle rapidly. Both the homogenization and bureaucratization of society, combined with the physical threat to the life of the individual in a world determined by the power of the atom, have created in certain sectors of society the desire to reflect on and modify the path progress has taken thus far.

As the cohesion of the student movement slackened and visions of an international communist revolution faded in the early seventies, the globally oriented political analyses and strategies of Marxist-Leninist theories became increasingly rigid and isolated from society's mainstream. Gradually they lost most of the popularity they had acquired through the student movement, giving way in the public interest to a number of issue-oriented grassroots movements intent on effecting policy changes in the areas of particular interest to them. Some groups, often lumped together under the term "new social movements," focused on women's rights, the ecological future of the planet and the drive for global peace. Kroetz's own political and artistic career at the end of the seventies reflects the shift in West German political culture from the exclusive dominance of traditional political parties to these issue-specific alliances.

At the same time that he becomes disenchanted with the DKP new issues begin to appear in his work, albeit without yet coming into clear focus. Although the Edgar the audience sees in this play is certainly not a budding political activist, the societal contradictions confronting each other within his character are remarkably similar to the concerns within many of the new social movements. They include, but are not limited to: the disruption of social and personal identity, in part at least a result of the transformation of the workplace in post-industrial capitalism; a rejection of the negative aspects of technological progress and a concomitant romanticization of our pre-technological past;[20] and the struggle with changing gender roles and identities.[21] *Nicht Fisch nicht*

Fleisch maps a range of societal conflict on the canvas of the labor movement, but the major focus of this piece remains the crisis in traditional labor politics. Nonetheless, in its treatment of the worker today the play broaches topics that play a more prominent role in *Bauern sterben* (1985).

Of paramount importance to Kroetz throughout the seventies is the question of when the individual (in particular the worker) comes to self-consciousness, both politically and socially. In his portrayal of the individual, Kroetz confronts him or her (usually him) and the audience with the societal context only in its absence. One can only infer, using previously acquired analytical skills and theoretical constructs, how the society that is the characters' backdrop is structured. The audience rarely sees the *dramatis personae* of a Kroetzian play in interaction with any societal institutions other than the family. For this reason there develops an emphasis (perhaps an overemphasis) on social and interpersonal crises from the perspective of the isolated individual.

Nicht Fisch nicht Fleisch is no exception to this. In it Kroetz examines the confrontation of the individual with a thoroughly bureaucratized environment and the concomitant depersonalization of the interpersonal realm. Between what has been the ever-expanding role of the state in the regulation of human affairs and the external control of the actions of individuals in the workplace, there is little room for self-determination. In the scene at the retraining center Edgar explores not only his romanticized visions of our past, but also how he believes the extensive rationalization of human existence will affect our lives in the not at all so distant future. He offers a compelling, Orwellian depiction of a thoroughly administered world:

> Edgar: Genau, die Wohnung. Wenn mir wieder heim dürfen finden mir nur noch einen Parkplatz vor. Keine Mauern mehr, bloß Vierecke mit unverwischbarer Farb. Dächer auch nicht, damit man heineinschauen kann, weil sowieso über allem eine Kuppel für Klima sorgt. Tag und Nacht sind unabhängig. Ihr Geheimnis der Rhythmus, weil Uhren verboten sind. Vielleicht wegn der Marktlage. Is der Absatz stockend, wird die Nacht erhöht und umgekehrt. Alles is eingezeichnet auf dem Parkplatz. Die Strich sind Grenzn. (IV,40)

The absence of walls allows for the constant surveillance of human acitivity. What remains of a protected space for the individual's private self are only lines, and the boundaries drawn to demarcate the sections of everyday life are indelible. They are not subject to individual modification. Self-determination is no longer even a comforting myth. Supervision is constant and even nature's own rhythm is controlled to coincide with the demands of production. Edgar continues his depiction of life in the future, touching on the intimate relationships between men and women, and how they, too, are governed by the market:

> Die Liebe setzt sich manchmal über die Sperre hinweg. Aber wehe, wenn die Frau schwanger wird und man hat keine Erlaubnis für das Kind, wo man vorweisen kann. Was den Ablauf beeinträchtigen könnt, wird ausgemerzt. (IV,41)

In Edgar's horror-vision, socio-economic demands govern human reproduction just as they do the rest of existence. The individual member of society cannot see beyond the dome that separates the majority from those who steer its course to achieve their own ends. Life at work is regulated and production seems to have developed an overpowering logic of its own, even reaching into the personal lives of those who, although without a voice in the overall decision-making process, actually keep the goods flowing to that mountain of products outside the dome.

This diminishing sense of personal autonomy contributes to the destabilization of the traditional nuclear family. When the boundaries between public and private no longer obtain, the traditional family becomes at best a mere vestige of the past, at worst an inoperative fiction. In an interview with Heinz Ludwig Arnold, Kroetz talks about his intent to portray how capitalist society has rationalized human values and "das Menschliche" itself into extinction.[22] In *Nicht Fisch nicht Fleisch* the audience sees the effects of this rationalization depicted in two different families.

For Hermann and Helga, who already have two children, a third child could represent an enormous financial burden. Their sexual relationship is strained when Hermann finds out that Helga has stopped taking the pill. She, however, is already pregnant. On one level Helga is using the children to secure the only source of income for her family, namely Hermann's job. Hermann has already lost one job because of his union activities, and Helga fears it will happen again.

Children become weapons in interpersonal and economic relationships in many ways. For Helga they are both a means to insure the continued financial stability of her family, and also the justification for her existence. In a conversation with Emmi, Helga describes both of these functions:

Helga: Der Hermann kann sich auch nicht scheiden lassen mit drei Kinder (*lacht*) da tät er soviel zahlen müssen, daß er im Obdachlosenasyl nächtigen muß.

Emmi: Ebn, ich will keine Aneinanderkettung.

Helga: Ich schon. (*Kleine Pause.*) Der Hermann wär schon recht, wenn er seine Veranlagung ned hätt.

. . .

Emmi: (*lacht*) Der Edgar tät weiß der Teufel was für ein Kind geben, weil er weiß, daß ich auf dem Ohr vorerst noch taub bin. (*Kleine Pause.*) Wenn es klappt, übernimm ich eine eigene Filiale.

Helga: (*nickt*) Du hast einen Beruf, der wo dich ausfüllt. Aber ich bin hundertmal lieber Hausfrau, als daß ich wieder zum Lodenfrey als Näherin geh, mit sieben Mark 20 in der Stund.

Emmi: Damals.

Helga: Dann sinds heut zehn Mark. Da schau ich nur einmal in die Augen von meine Kinder und weiß den Unterschied.

. . .

Du hast deine Arbeit und ich meine Kinder. Ich weiß, für wen ich es tu. Für mein eigenes Fleisch und Blut. Und nicht für den Herrn Lodenfrey. (IV,19f)

Helga is willing to reduce the bond between Hermann and herself to one of pure economic exigency. The threat of total impoverishment is her means of disciplining her husband, of forcing him to abandon any behavior that will endanger her family. Having children has freed her from an alienated life as an underpaid seamstress, but in a Marxist interpretation, both Helga and capitalism use her children to keep Hermann in a subordinate position. Once the children are there, they function as a stabilization factor for the labor market. The logic is that Hermann simply cannot afford to pursue his political aspirations. Instead of enhancing his existence as a private citizen, the family highlights his sense of isolation and alienation within the realm of production.

In the case of Edgar and Emmi, their lack of children is the most obvious sign of stress on the traditional family. For Emmi this does not pose a problem; for Edgar it is only one more aspect of his life governed by progress. Edgar hopes that forcing his wife into motherhood will regenerate his ideal world. Human reproduction ideally is a creative act for two people that is subject to no interference or control by external forces. In a sense, a child is the only product that a worker, otherwise alienated from the means of production, creates and over which he or she, at least theoretically, maintains control. In this view children become a substitute for the subject–object relationship in the production process.

The increasing number of women working full time outside of the home has only further strained the credibility of the still dominant vision of the nuclear family. Orthodox Marxist labor philosophy, however, has no answers to questions such as those raised by the changing constitution of the workforce, of labor itself, and the ramifications this has for the individual. Negotiations for better labor conditions no longer satisfy the majority of workers. This would appear, in any case, to be the message Hermann's colleagues wish to bring across to him. His impassioned plea for worker solidarity and union power is to them nothing but hot air.

A Crisis of Commitment

Kroetz would indeed seem to have recognized the limitations of the political philosophy at the heart of the German Communist party (DKP). In 1980, the year this play was written and premiered, Kroetz left the DKP. Retrospectively he relates his sense of being a token cultural figure to the party, a member with a symbolic rather than actual function. In answer to a question about his activities as a party member, Kroetz states: "Ich war in fast allen Kulturgremien, ich war Mitglied der Programmkommission. Allerdings hatte ich nicht sehr viel zu sagen, das hat mich dann auch später geärgert. Ich wurde immer nur als Aushänge-schild benützt."[23] The DKP's interest in cultural production was limited at best. Furthermore, if the artist did not conform to the party's notions of a politically correct aesthetic, his or her work faced marginalization.

On the other hand, internal disagreements over aesthetic questions were not the only areas in which Kroetz became disenchanted. The character of Hermann as the inflexible dogmatic labor activist provides another key to Kroetz's resolve to leave the DKP. In his review of *Nicht Fisch nicht Fleisch* Michael Skasa writes of the metamorphosis the character of Hermann (in the portrayal of Josef Bierbichler) undergoes:

> Je mehr er mit geballter Faust brabbelt vom Arbeiter und vom Kapitalisten, desto mehr gerinnt seine Figur, wird zum tönenden Denkmal, und körperlich spürt man, wie hier ein leerer Kopf nach dessen Fülle sucht. . . Bierbichlers Verwandlung vom Funktionär zum Frankenstein . . . Kroetz's Wandel vom DKP-Mitglied zum Grünen.[24]

It was not, however, only disenchantment with a particular political party which bred the crisis that developed in Kroetz's views on politically committed art. Nor was it, as Skasa seems to imply, simply a question of a new political allegiance on Kroetz's part. With his loss of faith in both the structural interpretations and the solutions to societal inequities that the DKP had to offer came a breakdown in Kroetz's belief in the character and function of engaged art.

Kroetz has never been blind to the difficulties facing political theater. Already in 1972 he noted:

> Das Theater für das Volk sitzt weiterhin zwischen zwei Stühlen: entweder es hat die Massen, dann funktioniert es gegen die Interessen derselben, oder es hat sie nicht, dann funktioniert es, auch wenn es auf dem richtigen Dampfer ist, bloß noch als Insider-Scherz der Intellektuellen. (WA,543)

Either pandering to the tastes of a mass audience not accustomed to artworks that demand rigorous participation from their audiences or accepting that only a small fraction of society will be able to comprehend one's work seem to be the only alternatives obtaining. Aware as he was of the limitations imposed on engaged drama, Kroetz nonetheless exhibited an ideological surety in his work in the early seventies that has since continued to weaken. Reflecting the policy of the DKP to concentrate its efforts on the stabilization and increase of union membership, *Das Nest* emphatically and programmatically calls for workers to join the unions and through them to fight for a better world. The play leaves little doubt that union solidarity was both a key to a heightened individual political consciousness as well as the solution to a whole host of social ills including the exploitation of wage laborers and the problem of toxic-waste dumping.

Although *Mensch Meier* (1977) examines closely and explicitly the feelings of alienation and exploitation its title character experiences as an unskilled auto-factory worker, its focus is on a less Marxist, more humanist problem, namely the process of becoming a "Mensch." When Otto Meier's feelings of frustration and his fears of losing his job erupt in a very physical and destructive outburst, his wife and son leave him, insisting that they will not return until they have all learned to be human(e). This is particularly evident in the scene in which Otto's son Ludwig tries to explain to his father what distinguishes his own life as a mason from his father's life as a factory worker. Otto paints Ludwig a dim picture of life as an alienated worker:

> *Otto*: Irgendwann hast das Gschäft durchschaut und siehst, wer noch aller Maurer is auf der Welt, und daß das gar nix is, und daß es noch ganz andere Dinge gibt auf der Welt! (*Nickt.*) Und dann wirst du genauso wie ich, das garantier ich dir.

Ludwig: Nein.
Otto: (*lächelt.*)
Ludwig: Weil ich nämlich nicht bloß ein Maurer werdn will, sondern auch ein Mensch. (III,393f)

Clearly Ludwig's sense of self goes well beyond his identity as a laborer. It is no longer sufficient to find oneself in relation to one's work. Nonetheless, the project of becoming a human being is still ill-defined. When Otto's wife Martha tells Ludwig that she will no longer be able to devote herself to his care, she makes the play's only reference to what the process of humanization will entail:

Ludwig: Ziehn mir zam, sonst gib ich die neue Adress dem Papa. (*lacht.*)
Martha: Erpresser. (*Pause.*) In ein paar Monat vielleicht, wenn jeder auf die eignen Füß stehn kann. Sonst kann ich mich nicht um dich kümmern, weil ich erst an mich denkn muß, und das bin ich nicht gwohnt.
Ludwig: Und der Papa!?
Martha: (*zuckt die Achseln, ruhig:*) Muß es auch.
Ludwig: Was?
Martha: Was mir tun. Lernen. (III,399)

Just as Anni in *Oberösterreich* gained strength from some vague knowledge, *Mensch Meier*'s Martha also sees the key to the future and the preservation of the self in the nebulous notion of learning. The only thing that is not part of this personal enlightenment is the recognition of one's own alienated status within a capitalist economy. Otto has, after all, a very well-developed sense of how his existence is overdetermined by his work. One can, thus, only conclude that Martha's project goes well beyond that.

The incipient political uncertainty developing in *Mensch Meier* only deepens in the following play, *Der stramme Max* (1978). In this work the main character, who is already a union member, discovers that the company he works for has intentionally selected a group of older employees to work on a toxic chemical project. The firm's directors chose only what they believed were healthy older employees who would either die before they experienced negative physical side-effects or, at the very least, would suffer any ill-effects only after retirement. Max had withheld a previous hepatitis condition from his application in order to ensure that he get a spot on the new project. Because of the chemicals, Max's health deteriorates progressively until he lands in the hospital. As compensation the company offers him a job as a parking attendant, but only if he promises not to sue. The play ends with his mute promise to resist the temptation of secure employment. He refuses to submit to the laws of capitalist production, but his promise is literally only a nod: the course of political action is left to the imagination.

Whatever power *Das Nest* had invested in Germany's unions is explicitly denied here. When rumors begin to circulate that Max's company is going to downsize its operations, the union representatives quickly tell their members not to worry (III,419). The fact that they were so blatantly wrong indicates either that the unions are now conspiring with company officials or are simply out of touch with reality. In any case, they no longer offer any meaningful support to the workers they supposedly represent.

The increasing uncertainty about orthodox leftist political strategies that finds expression in both *Mensch Meier* and *Der stramme Max* leads to a direct confrontation in *Nicht Fisch nicht Fleisch* between a union activist and one of the employees the unions are supposedly protecting. The conflict between Hermann and Edgar ends with Hermann's humiliation at the hands of his co-workers. The final scenes of the play elicit no promises from Hermann to pursue his union activities, or to amend his views on the basis of his colleagues' violent refusal to accept his solutions. Edgar's attempt to flee today for our primal watery past also fails, as it had to. After surviving the crisis at hand, the two families simply return, as best they can, to their lives as they have always been. The work offers no political program, no general positive conclusion and no promise of action, mute or otherwise.

In a speech made in 1980 Kroetz describes his authorial crisis as follows:

> Wenn ich zu wählen habe zwischen dem aufgeblasenen subjektivistischen Tasso mit seinem "ein Gott gab mir sagen, wie ich leide", und der messerscharfen Frage: "Was konkret wollten Sie mit diesem Stück an Wirklichkeit verändern?" merke ich, daß ich schnell mein literarisches Hütchen nehmen und mich durch die Hintertür davon schleichen will.[25]

Kroetz raises at least three distinct issues in this passage. The first is art's sometime claim to autonomy, with God alone to tell it the content and form of its suffering. The second is the explicit political purpose of the work of art. The third is the insinuation that the struggle to find the balance between the two is basically an irrelevant, trivial one given the diminutive role ("mein literarisches Hütchen") of the aesthetic realm within society as a whole. Kroetz has not yet turned completely from attempts to mediate aesthetically pertinent political topics, and he continues to reject an overemphasis on the intrapersonal as regression: "Alles gegen die Strategen der Bourgeoisie, die mit dem Vehikel neue Innerlichkeit die Kunst wieder auf die Darstellung trauriger Künstler und Intellektueller zurückschrauben wollen."[26] Kroetz may be willing at this point to entertain questions about the validity of a political aesthetic project, but he is not interested in exploring the inner quandaries of the artist. His target audience is still the lay public, and not – as yet – a community of aesthetic insiders.

This brings up one of the problems facing politically committed literature: the constitution of the literary public. In his essay on engaged aesthetics, Jean-Paul Sartre maintains that the writer must have a public that has the freedom and the means to change society. To be able to do this, that public must undergo a constant process of reflection and renewal: "In short, literature is, in essence, the subjectivity of a society in permanent revolution."[27] However, despite efforts to expand the scope of the theater public, the constituency has generally remained the same. Kroetz was conscious of the problem of audience already in 1972: "Das Publikum setzt sich aus Linksliberalen und Theater-interessierten zusammen. Zusammen ergeben sie das aktive Bildungsbürgertum, dessen Klassenbewußtsein darin besteht, 'um Gottes willen immer auf dem Laufenden zu sein', – worüber ist ganz egal" (WA, 537). Instead of having an audience that sees itself as co-workers or co-experimenters in the attempt to revolutionize West German society, the theater public seems to Kroetz to be capable only of running after the latest literary trend, of submitting to the aesthetic whims, so to speak, of such aesthetic innovators as Peter Handke, Thomas Bernhard and Botho Strauß.

Theoretically, the West German theater audience may have the power to change societal conditions on a large scale, but several factors work against the potential for this to happen. A largely upper-middle-class public has no real need for a redistribution of societal wealth – be that wealth intellectual or material. It does not experience the lack that Kroetz's characters do. Furthermore, even an educated audience faces enormous difficulties in sifting out the current structuration of today's society, on the whole, leaving it, too, at a loss as to what course of action to assume. Finally, the structural inequalities within contemporary capitalism are carefully couched in a rhetoric of social equality, a rhetoric that only further clouds the problem areas most in need of greater attention.

Sartre's suggestion that the theater public must be in a state of constant renewal in order to complete the literary project is intriguing. It insists on the audience's recognition of its complicity in the aesthetic (political) project: his aesthetic *engagement* is an inclusive project. One must ask, however, both whether the theater audiences in the Federal Republic during the late seventies and early eighties were in anything resembling a state of constant self-reflection and renewal, as well as whether one could reasonably expect them to be. Kroetz's answer to this is an increasingly adamant no; the incipient alienation discernible at this time is only a preview of his intense estrangement from the audience at the time he writes *Bauern sterben.*

His growing separation from the theater public also surfaces at this time in his own redefinition of the content of his work. Kroetz long insisted his work was strictly a socio-political description of contemporary West German society.[28] After his parting from the DKP Kroetz gradually moves towards the admission that his pieces are largely autobiographical depictions of his own suffering and trials. Although this tendency toward an emphasis on the autobiographical character of political realism in the seventies is apparent in other authors as well,[29] it is questionable whether the characteristic "autobiographical" is fruitful here. At times the assertion seems to function as an all too ready explanation of certain aesthetic problems. In the very speech quoted above, he reinterprets his work:

> Ich dürfte nicht sagen: "Da gehts nicht, weil die mit Kunst zu tun haben" – sondern ich müßte sagen: "Da gehts nicht, weil die von mir handeln." Und weil sie von mir handeln, sind sie nicht so gradlinig, eindeutig, zweckorientiert, entschieden, so ohne Verletzungen, Brüche, Verzweiflungen, Depressionen, Einsamkeiten, Demütigungen, Minderwertigkeitskomplexe, Wunden.[30]

Here Kroetz denies that the contradictions and weaknesses he and others have seen in his work have anything to do with aesthetic criteria, but are rather problems inherent to his personality. In other words, they are problems that a reconceptualization of his aesthetic methods cannot solve, that are accessible only on a personal psychological level. He goes on, for instance, to say that he has never been able to portray adequately those individuals who actually wield power in capitalist society because he cannot personally identify with them:

> Ich schreibe – ich hab' das lange nicht zugegeben – ob es über Kinder oder Opas geht, sehr viel von mir. Ich bin mehr diese Figuren als der Manager oder Betriebsleiter A und B oder der Herr von Siemens. Zu diesen Figuren fällt mir absolut nichts ein . . .[31]

Of course, this can only be accepted as the author's own subjective interpretation of his inability to illustrate such figures. On the other hand, his analysis overlooks the difficulties inherent in any attempt to portray the actual power configurations in post-industrial capitalist society. It also sidesteps the issue of aesthetic strategy and the question of whether Kroetz's particular style of realist presentation, even in the modified version of *Nicht Fisch nicht Fleisch*, can respond to these difficulties.

Character and Style

This brings us again to the topic of aesthetic structure, style and method. The discussion here focuses on how Kroetz portrays his characters in this play, including language and socio-economic status. It also looks at structural elements new to *Nicht Fisch nicht Fleisch*, such as competing social philosophies and a departure from the strictly naturalistic realism of the earlier plays. Finally, it will examine the particular mixture of stylistic and thematic conservatism in this work.

Although *Das Nest* offered the audience a character possessed of a greater degree of reflective intelligence and self-confidence, there was no correspondingly pronounced shift in this character's ability to express himself. It is not until *Mensch Meier* that the main protagonist acquires the ability to use language in an astoundingly (for a Kroetzian character) creative manner. In scene four of the first act, the audience watches as Otto envisions himself as a famous model plane pilot being interviewed by a sports reporter:

> Sie hätten, wenn ich hier eine Fachzeitschrift zitieren darf, technisch-fliegerisches Genie. Ist das so? – Na ja, man soll sich ja nicht selber loben, aber eine Begabung muß da natürlich schon dabei sein, weil die gängigen Modelle natürlich bereits mit allen Raffinessen ausgestattet sind und die großen Hersteller alle Möglichkeiten haben. (III,360f)

At another point in the play Otto mimics a television game show in which panelists guess the occupations of the contestants:

> Ich bin ein Arschloch. . . . Sie sind Autobauer? Ja. Autoschraubeneinschrauber, Schraubschrauber, Schrauberling, Schraubologe. . . . (*Spricht jetzt vernünftig zu sich*:) Ich bin ein Arbeiter. A-r-b-e-i-t-e-r! Kein Arzt, kein Rechtsanwalt, kein Steuerberater, kein Minister und kein Fabrikbesitzer. (*Pause.*) Ich kann mich nicht mit mir abfinden. Komisch. Ob ich will oder nicht. (III,388f)

Kroetz does not abandon the stylized dialect of his earlier work completely, nor do his characters suddenly have access to an exaggerated eloquence. Yet the fact that there are several passages in these plays worthy of repeating in this context marks a decided departure from the majority of this dramatist's work in the late sixties and early seventies.[32] In *Mensch Meier, Der stramme Max* and *Nicht Fisch nicht Fleisch* Kroetz has created a language to match his goal of depicting characters capable of reflecting on their own position in life, of actively responding to the situation given, and of explaining both their thoughts and actions to the audience (so to speak). The process of piecing together the portrait of the *dramatis personae* no longer falls quite so heavily on the shoulders of the viewer. The dramatist has definitely closed more of the lacunae for the audience, giving them more tools with which to make their own sense of the play.

Kroetz has also redefined the socio-economic status of the individuals he puts on the stage. In *Mensch Meier* Otto is still an unskilled laborer, but is paid well and enjoys a relatively pleasant standard of living without the overtime hours Kurt had to work in *Das Nest*. In *Der stramme Max* Kroetz turns to a character who has learned a trade; as has already been noted, the two male leads in *Nicht Fisch nicht Fleisch* have both learned typesetting as a skilled trade. As skilled laborers, these three characters represent a shift in the type of worker on which the plays focus. They are clearly designed to function as model workers.

In the case of *Der stramme Max*, it is a model for a possible path of resistance. This path is, nonetheless, essentially undefined. It certainly is not informed by programmatic orthodox communist strategy. Instead the piece shows the strategy of one man, in a sense the heroic individual, who decides to oppose his own abuse at the hand of his employers. Implicitly his decision assumes a Marxist analysis of labor's exploitation within capitalism, but the play never makes this explicit, as had *Das Nest* with its call for union solidarity. In fact, as noted above, the play expresses at least one negative aspect of the mediatory success West Germany's unions have had since the war: they have become so much a part of the bureaucracy of capitalist production that they no longer have a profile distinct enough from management to act as effective opposition. The play does not end with an evocation of worker solidarity, but with the promise of one worker (who is, incidentally, a union member) to combat the system of quiet exploitation. Kroetz is apparently no longer able to portray the right political decision for a worker in such a situation. The political surety of his earlier work is beginning to falter. On the other hand, although he cannot create a convincing, explicitly Marxist oppositional strategy, he still uses Marxist philosophy to construct the socio-economic analysis on which the play rests. It is not until *Nicht Fisch nicht Fleisch* that Marxism as an analytical tool comes under fire.

It is worth repeating that the way these individuals view themselves is markedly opposed to the sense of self Heinz in *Oberösterreich* and Otto in *Mensch Meier* demonstrated. The fact that they are workers is not a source of shame or self-chastisement. They see themselves shaped by their work and are relatively satisfied in their jobs. Kroetz needed generally valid ("allgemeingültig") figures in order to paint a more generally valid picture of contemporary society as he saw it. Whether or not one wishes to concede that Kroetz has effectively depicted "the average man," or a "generally valid" individual, he has moved his characters considerably closer to the center of the societal spectrum. They are no longer the helpless, disoriented and disenfranchized figures of the early plays, who could not function as political agents.

However, on a structural level other changes were still necessary before he could extend the limited confines of his kitchen-stove realism and offer a broader abstract of social reality. One of the problems in Kroetz's preceding works is that they offered essentially a lone perspective, i.e. that of the particular family in that particular play. In *Nicht Fisch nicht Fleisch* the audience is offered at the very least four different socio-economic perspectives which run from an insistence on the innately social character of human existence to economic individualism and opportunism.

In the figure of Hermann, as has already been discussed to a certain degree, the audience finds a proponent of the adamant assertion that human beings are inherently social beings and that any deviation from their natural constitution must result in a weakening of the self, in heightened inefficiency and in a loss of purpose. He is an exemplary activist, who simply cannot understand those who do not fight for their rights. In fact, he equates an unwillingness to do so with stupidity. As they argue about Hermann's union activities in scene seven of act one, Helga points out to him that she at least never caused any trouble when she worked at Lodenfrey as a seamstress. Hermann snaps back at her: "Ja, weilst zu blöd dazu warst" (IV,26). His response to Helga is typical for a model of rational thought that brands those who do not conform to its particular propositions as either intellectually incompetent or intentionally destructive. Thus Helga is "zu blöd," while Edgar is a "Verräter." Hermann's logic is compelling, but it is also unyielding. It excludes any and all who are unwilling to recognize its legitimacy.

Edgar, on the other hand, espouses several views throughout the play. Initially, he purports a perception of capitalist society as an order-maintenance system, a system capable of providing each person with those items necessary for a reasonably satisfying existence. This belief rests on a concept of individualism promulgated by the culture industry and widely accepted in society: the cult of the self-sufficient individual, generally a white male. When the order of Edgar's own cosmos is disturbed, he does abandon his previously staunch conviction in the equity of technological progress and of capitalist relations of production, but he does not disavow his faith in the rugged individualism of both the frontier and pre-civilization.

The character of Emmi is an amalgam of features grouped together under the rubric of the working woman. The ambiguity of her role in the play will be the topic for an analysis further on in the chapter. In this context she represents economic opportunism and the logic of consumerism. She is a perfect model for how individuals socialized as consumers continuously regenerate the mechanics of the market. In the following passage, Emmi describes how she intends to configure her new store from the perspective of the buyer:

> *Emmi:* Ich hab als Kunde die Vorteile in der Hand: Großmarktpreise, individuelle Bedienung soweit erforderlich, und das Wohlgefühl einer nicht repressiven –
> *Edgar:* (*schaut bei dem Wort.*)
> *Emmi:* Einkaufsumwelt, die mir unauffällig entgegenkommt.
> . . .
> *Emmi:* Als erstes will ich durch kluge Warenauswahl dafür sorgen, daß der Kunde merkt, dieses Geschäft entspricht mir. Das gehobene Sortiment, durchgehend, in einem Rahmen, der niemand abschreckt.
> (*Pause.*)
> (*Sie schnauft.*) Personelle Konsequenzen hat es auch. Die nämlich jetzt hinter dem Wurschtstand is, verkauft meine Wurscht in Zukunft nicht, entweder sie verändert ihr Erscheinungsbild, oder sie geht. Die am Gemüse und Obst ist in Ordnung. Die paßt in die neue Konzeption. (IV,50)

This excerpt illustrates not only the ways in which the consumer is manipulated into buying, but also the costs to the individual who does not fit into the concept. It is an ideal example of what Horkheimer and Adorno describe in the *Dialektik der Aufklärung*:

> Für alle ist etwas vorgesehen, damit keiner ausweichen kann, die Unterschiede werden eingeschliffen und propagiert. Die Belieferung des Publikums mit einer Hierarchie von Serienqualitäten dient nur der um so lückenloseren Quantifizierung. Jeder soll sich gleichsam spontan seinem vorweg durch Indizien bestimmten "level" gemäß verhalten und nach der Kategorie des Massenprodukts greifen, die für seinen Typ fabriziert ist.[33]

In their narrative, retail actively produces the myth of individuality. Subtle differentiation between individuals is exposed as nothing more than various reshufflings of a predetermined deck. In other words, Horkheimer and Adorno maintain that the culture industry tolerates the individual only to the extent that it becomes identical with the dominant concept of the individual, i.e. only insofar as it coincides with the product to be sold.[34] In the spirit of true egalitarianism, this applies to those on both sides of the retail counter. Edgar's reaction to his wife's comments makes it perfectly clear that the language his wife is speaking is not her own: she has been indoctrinated in the jargon of business. The career woman of *Nicht Fisch nicht Fleisch* is successful because she has sold herself.

Helga is an intentionally emphatic contrast to Emmi. She has tried to escape the alienation of the market by retreating to the intimate world of the family. She is a vigorous proponent of the family and the almost spiritual bond between parent and child. She acts as the mediator in conflict and the guide to compromise. She has no political consciousness. In a comparison to Emmi, Helga demonstrates that the supposed emancipation of women has only freed them to the same alienated existence as the men in the workforce. As Elizabeth Boa writes, the goal of a woman's labor then becomes nothing other than "to increase another's profit" or it is "redundant in the name of rationalization."[35]

Given that Helga exhibits little sense of self, other than as defined by her position within the family, she is basically only the empty shell of a character. Nonetheless, her positional function as the fulcrum in the void is crucial as a social cohesive. In a sense, she cannot be a distinct character if she is to play her role as the personification of the family, to which all of the characters return in the final scene of the play. In this scene she spoons out soup to the others from her throne, the kitchen stove. Emmi and Hermann have already sought refuge, when Edgar knocks at the door.

Helga: (*stellt ihm einen Suppenteller auf den Tisch*:) Iß. (*Wendet sich wieder zu ihrem Herd.*)
Edgar: (*schaut, setzt sich.*)
  (*Pause.*)
  (*Alle sind beschäftigt.*) (IV,73)

She dishes out physical and spiritual nourishment to the others, who have been bruised by the viciousness of capitalist society. Given the relative absence here of the spoken word, her solace seems to come from the soup kettle; perhaps the very primordial brew that Edgar sought out unsuccessfully at the water's edge. It is not, however, Helga, who resuscitates the sagging spirits of the others, but rather the *mater familias*. The holy, if inarticulate, mother is all that is left of the tightly knit nuclear family, but she is also clearly still a figure of both power and hope.

The characters in this work offer a variety of reactions to current social crises, but they also represent a structural response to the limitations of the singular perspective in Kroetz's preceding pieces. Here we have not only one couple, but two, we have the crisis of not only one character, but essentially of four, and we have four vastly different perspectives on the play's thematic concentrations. There is, however, an aspect of *Nicht Fisch nicht Fleisch* that goes even further in Kroetz's attempts to cross the narrow boundaries of his previous realist strategy. In addition to the heavily symbolic act Hermann's colleagues commit on him, the scene at the water's edge delves deeper into the surreal than anything in Kroetz's earlier works.

The penultimate scene of the play departs sharply from the strictly defined contours of the kitchen or the bedroom. The stage description reads: "irgendwo Wasser" (p. 75). Is it a lake, a river, the ocean or, as Edgar intimates, the primordial soup out of which human beings emerged? It is a body of water that contains a variety of mythological elements: Orphic dolphins and whales that carry individuals to safety and that offer them amusement and pleasure; uninhabited, virgin islands where one can both escape the restrictions of life in society as well as rule supreme; and the power to purge the soul, to strip the individual of all the debilitating effects of civilized society. After having shed his civilized skin (his clothes), Edgar plunges into this water in the hope of emerging a cleansed, revitalized man. Empirical reality does not resurface until Edgar recognizes that the water has no magic power.

As do all the others, Edgar must realize that regeneration is not out there "irgendwo," but rather back within the confines of the family, although now the family is no longer the triadic or quadratic grouping of concrete individuals, but rather the spiritual focal point from which human society radiates.[36] In other words, the play does not return us to the mundane reality of just another Kroetzian kitchen, but rather to a quasi-metaphysical kitchen.

Kroetz had struggled throughout the late seventies to break down the four walls of the kitchens he himself constructed. He explains the need for a departure from the largely realist style of socialist realism in the following manner: "Der revolutionäre Weltprozeß wird immer komplizierter. Die Kunst kann ihn nur begleiten, wenn ihr adäquat komplizierte Darstellungsmethoden zur Verfügung stehen. Deshalb brauchen wir das radikale Formerlebnis in der sozialistischen Ästhetik."[37] The dramatist clearly did extend or strain his previous realist techniques in *Nicht Fisch nicht Fleisch*, but the play does not represent a major stylistic break. The kitchen to which everyone returns in the final scene may be a symbolic one, but it is still a typical Kroetzian kitchen. He may have added new stylistic elements, but he did not abandon the kitchen stove.

The program to a performance of the work aptly describes its tenor as "phantastischer Realismus."[38] The piece generally follows a traditional dramatic structure: exposition, climax, denouement. The text is also easily accessible from the standpoint of an audience or a reader. In contrast to earlier and later works by Kroetz, *Nicht Fisch nicht Fleisch* does not contain a significant amount of or extreme forms of dialectal speech. Sentences are patterned after everyday language, and the language of the play does not draw on heavily symbolic figures to make its point. These stylistic items combine with certain thematic elements to create, alongside its decidedly leftist orientation, a more conservative complexion for the work.

This mixture causes varying degrees of confusion in the portrayal of different characters and plot lines. The picture *Nicht Fisch nicht Fleisch* offers of women is a particularly good example of the way the various components of the play work together – or maybe against each other to propagate politically conservative values. As noted above, Emmi is the first female character in a Kroetzian play who works outside of the home because she wants to do so. Unfortunately, that makes this particular female character something of a test case. What a director or an actress decides to emphasize about Emmi plays an admittedly significant role in how the audience will perceive her. On the other hand, unless a theater group engages in some rather extensive editing, Kroetz's dialogue has largely predetermined the interpretation. The ruthlessness of Emmi's climb up the business ladder, as evidenced by the passage quoted above, reflects on both the system that engenders such attitudes and on the individual that espouses them. Emmi is the epitome of the hard-driving, sacrifice all (husband, children, employees, friends – if need be) business person. She is also a woman. Where does the one begin and the other end? This may be a falsely formulated question, but it is one that *Nicht Fisch nicht Fleisch* asks. The play certainly does intimate that she would not be as harsh, if she, as does Helga, were to devote her attentions to her home and her family.

After the audience sees Emmi as the shrewd, calculating businesswoman, even Edgar's crazed ravings might seem credible. In scene one of act three he accuses her of deliberately squashing him:

Edgar: Eine Frau hält zu ihrem Mann.
Emmi: Ja, wenn er ihr die Chans laßt, aber wenn ich dir die Hand gebn will, schlagst sie weg.
Edgar: Du gibst mir nicht die Hand, du druckst mich weiter hinein mit deinem Wesen. Mir hättn nicht heiraten sollen. Will kein Mannweib, das der Meister is. (IV,60f)

Emmi claims that Edgar refuses to accept the help she offers him. He counters this with the assertion that her help (metaphorically the outstretched hand) is tainted by her own perversion of her gender identity. A woman who cannot play the role of woman cannot offer solace to a man, who can only play the role of a man. Given that the loss of his job has already challenged his sense of who he is as a man, he cannot cope with the destabilization of the gender economy in their relationship. Everything she does will contribute to his increasing sense of self-alienation unless she reestablishes herself as the weaker and manifestly dependent member of the family. Because there is no one to contradict Edgar's misogynist views, the last word remains his:

Edgar: Ein Mann, der wo keine Arbeit hat, sondern auf das angewiesen is, was die Frau verdient, der is im eigentlichen Sinn kein Mann, der is ein Weib. Schlimmer!
Emmi: Was is denn schlimmer als eine Frau sein?
Edgar: Nix. (*Kleine Pause.*) Will kein Weib sein, du bist das Weib. (IV,58)

Although Edgar maintains that there is nothing worse or of less value than a woman, it is clear that there is something even more horrific. And that is a *business*-woman. Emmi's redomestication thus becomes the prerequisite for the play's conclusion.

In his review of the performances in Düsseldorf and Berlin Henning Rischbieter recounts that at the end both Helga and Emmi are visibly pregnant.[39] It is unclear if this was the case in both stagings or just in one. It is also worthy of note that this is not part of the text. However, the reintegration of errant woman would conform nicely to the characters' return to the normalcy of the family kitchen. Instead of expanding his standard set of characters to include a self-confident and competent professional woman, Kroetz has actually only portrayed yet another catastrophe that could arise as a result of the traditional family's destabilization. He thus misses the opportunity to portray positively the effect the women's movement has had on society, leaving the audience instead with an ambiguous example of deviant gender behavior.[40]

The core of conservative arguments against the changing role of women in society is that it threatens the stability of the traditional family, which in turn leads to a whole host of other social ills: illiteracy, drug use and violent crime. In 1985 Kroetz recounts the following story:

> Am meisten hat mich die Geschichte vom Jumbo fasziniert. Der kleine Elephant Jumbo, der entführt wird. Das war mein liebstes Buch. Der mit seiner Familie und einem Zirkus reist; die Eltern waren nicht da, und der kleine läuft davon und wird von einem Bösen gequält, und zum Schluß kommt er mit einem Flugzeug angeflogen, zu seinen Eltern zurück. . . . Der Kern meiner ganzen Literatur.[41]

It would be foolish to assign too much significance to this story. It is, however, of interest in this context in that it is a story of a family that has been torn apart. Once the child is separated from its parents, it is subject to evil. As soon as the baby is returned to its family, the world is restored to order. Kroetz goes so far as to call this idea the essence of all his works. This is questionable at best, but the nuclear family as the bullwark against the assaults of capitalist society is truly a central aspect of his work. It is also one of the more conservative facets in this and in other plays. Michael Töteberg writes: "Das traditionelle Bild von der Familie als Nest, bei Kroetz als Widerstandshort gegen die Ansprüche der (kapitalistischen) Gesellschaft gezeichnet, hat konservative und patriarchalische Untertöne."[42]

This image of the family is a vehicle for unnecessary stress on the male characters of Kroetzian plays. In *Der stramme Max*, when Max is faced with losing his job and being forced to look for another, Anna reminds him of his duty to provide for his family:

Anna: Du mußt wieder eine Arbeit finden, wennst entlassen wirst, unbedingt, sonst geht es nicht.
Max: Ja.
Anna: Du bist der Ernährer und darfst uns nicht der Schande preisgebn.
Max: Tu ich eh nicht. (III,423f)

If the structure of the family in one of these plays were to change as a result of a crisis, and if this change were recognized as positive, one could interpret such passages as the one quoted as a subtle critique of coercive and inflexible familial roles. Kroetz, however, continues to portray the family in this manner (even in *Bauern sterben*), i.e. with the husband as breadwinner and protector and the mother and children as his responsibility, existing solely to complete the man's world.

The last scene in *Nicht Fisch nicht Fleisch* has already been the focus of attention in this chapter. In the context of the overall conceptualization of women and the family the reintegrative function of this particular scene becomes even more distinct. Whether the author saw the return of all four characters to Helga's kitchen as a positive or negative outcome to the crises they have faced, the play's resolution is a reaffirmation of the status quo. To a certain degree, this, perhaps unintentional, validation of the status quo stems from an absence of perspective, or rather of prospective possibilities for change. Töteberg describes this lack of perspective in Kroetz's work (here *Oberösterreich*) as follows:

> So führt bei Kroetz die Erkenntnis seiner Perspektivelosigkeit selbst in Stücken wie *Oberösterreich* noch nicht zu Alternativen. Zwar hat hier der "Durchschnitt" mehr Möglichkeiten, Probleme zu artikulieren und zu diskutieren, wodurch der bereits beschriebene Affektstau verhindert wird, aber als Perspektive bleibt nach Durchrechnung aller Möglichkeiten das Sich-Arrangieren mit der Gesellschaft.[43]

The characters in *Nicht Fisch nicht Fleisch* explore various solutions to the crises they face: Marxism and political activism (Hermann), careerism (Emmi) and spiritualism (Edgar), and yet none of them is successful. The only one in the play who does seem to have accomplished what she set out to do is Helga, the staunch and devoted upholder of traditional family values. What remains for the others is only an "arrangement" with society's status quo. This is true not only of *Nicht Fisch nicht Fleisch*, but also of every play since *Oberösterreich*. Perhaps it is, as Töteberg suggests, only a vestige of Kroetz's move away from the violent conclusions of the early one-acts, but the return to normalcy ultimately constitutes the major characteristic of Kroetz's plays.

A credible objection to Töteberg's critique of Kroetz would pose the following questions. Must politically committed literature offer society plausible, constructive ways out of a given set of structural inequalities? Should – no, can – political drama do more than just outline the situation at hand? Should it provide artificial solutions when true answers are not manifest? These questions will resurface in the analysis of *Bauern sterben* as well.

Nicht Fisch nicht Fleisch represents, in a sense, another experimental response to difficulties Kroetz had encountered in previous works. It addresses the problems of character limitations, both the ability to articulate societal structures, even indirectly, as well as the generalizability of the experience. The composition of the piece also attempts to extend the boundaries of the dramatist's earlier realist style and, thus, to broaden the scope of the play. In addition, the drama works in new subject matter, such as the effect of the women's movement on the traditional family and the changing character of the workforce in a post-industrial age. Some of the elements that shape the contours of *Nicht Fisch nicht Fleisch* will reappear in *Bauern sterben*, a piece that pushes the struggle to find adequate aesthetic expression for political themata at least one step further.

Notes

1. Adorno, *Ästhetische Theorie*, pp. 11, 54.
2. Ibid., p. 239.
3. Formally, the SPD abandoned its specific alliance with labor movement politics in the late fifties (in the so-called "Godesberger Programm"), but this could not completely obliterate its past relationship to working-class causes.
4. Detlef Lehnert, *Sozialdemokratie zwischen Protestbewegung und Regierungspartei 1848-1983* (Frankfurt/M.: Suhrkamp Verlag, 1983). See chapter 5, pp. 175–222.
5. E.H. Carr, for instance, writes of the left in 1939: "History everywhere shows that, when left parties or politicians are brought into contact with reality through the assumption of political office, they tend to abandon their 'doctrinaire' utopianism and move towards the right, often retaining their Left labels and adding to the confusion of political terminology," in *The Twenty Years Crisis: 1919–1939* (New York: Harper and Row Publishers, 1964, first edition, London: Macmillan, 1939), p. 20. Carr's claims about the changes in leftist politics, once invested with institutional political power, are not original to him, and had, in fact, already been the focus of communist critiques of the SPD during the Weimar period, but what is of specific interest in this context is the confusion of political terminology and political alliances.
6. See e.g. Lehnert, p. 179.
7. Jürgen Habermas, *Die neue Unübersichtlichkeit* (Frankfurt/M.: Suhrkamp Verlag, 1985), p. 68.
8. These issues also represent the political focus of the DKP after the party's founding in 1968.

9. This is, of course, a rhetorical question. The distinctions between socio-economic classes in the Federal Republic have by no means vanished. They have, however, become considerably more subtle. Whereas once personal property was a good gauge for socio-economic status, now the differences between the classes largely has to do with educational opportunities and economic mobility.

10. Lothar Schwab, "'Wildnis der Meere': Zum Genrewechsel in 'Nicht Fisch nicht Fleich' von Franz Xaver Kroetz," in *Deutsches Drama der 80er Jahre*, ed. Richard Weber (Frankfurt/M.: Suhrkamp Verlag, 1992), p. 54.

11. See e.g. Siegfried Hermann, "Deutsche Kommunistische Partei," in *Parteien Handbuch: die Parteien der Bundesrepublik Deutschland 1945–1980*, ed. Richard Stöss (Opladen: Westdeutscher Verlag, 1983), p. 923. A more extensive study of the history of printing and unions in relationship to *Nicht Fisch nicht Fleisch* would undoubtedly yield interesting new insights to the interpretation of the play, but exceeded the scope of this particular work.

12. This is the structural pattern for the majority of Kroetz's work, although earlier dramas generally restricted their focus to a single family.

13. Jean-Paul Sartre, *The Problem of Method*, trans. Hazel E. Barnes (London: Methuen, 1963), p. 115.

14. Laclau/Mouffe, pp. 2, 4, 84.

15. Ibid., p. 85. Needless to say, they are not the first authors to theorize the disintegration of an integral individual. What makes their work important for this study is the fact that they do so from within an explicit leftist political philosophy.

16. This scene indicates a rather clichéd understanding on Kroetz's part of Freudian psychoanalysis, which for this reader fits in well with the latent misogyny in this play as well as other Kroetz works.

17. The role of women and their portrayal in this play will return again later as a topic unto itself.

18. Schwab, pp. 57f. He also lists two other symbolic levels for fish: 1) Edgar's affinity as a character to fish symbolism relates to the Christian use of the fish symbol to refer to Christ and his passion; and 2) fish as a traditional Freudian symbol for male fertility. Schwab bases his reading of the fish symbol as a reference to Christ on an early version of the play, and admits that the published version does not offer much support for such a relationship.

19. Karl Marx, *Die Deutsche Ideologie*, in *Karl Marx, Friedrich Engels Werke* (Berlin: Dietz Verlag, 1983), p. 33.

20. One of the reasons Kroetz lists in his press release for his withdrawal from the DKP is a sensitization about the relationship

of human beings to nature: "Ich bin alles in allem eher heute fortschrittsskeptisch, was sich schwer mit dem Bild des herkömmlichen marxistischen Fortschrittsglauben vereinbaren läßt. Das hat speziell in meinem Schreiben zu schmerzlichen Widersprüchen geführt." rpt. in Riewoldt, *Franz Xaver Kroetz*, p. 178.

21. For analyses of new social movements, see: Joachim Raschke, *Soziale Bewegungen. Ein historisch-systematischer Grundriß* (Frankfurt/M.: Campus Verlag, 1985); Roland Roth, "Neue soziale Bewegungen in der politischen Kultur der Bundesrepublik – eine vorläufige Skizze," in *Neue soziale Bewegungen in Westeuropa und den USA. Ein internationaler Vergleich*, ed. Karl-Werner Brand (Frankfurt/M.: Campus Verlag, 1985), pp. 20–82; and Elim Papadakis, *The Green Movement in West Germany* (London: Croom Helm, 1984).

22. Arnold, *Als Schriftsteller leben*, pp. 50f.

23. From an interview in the program to the Hamburg performance of *Bauern sterben*. See Peter Zadek (ed.), *Franz Xaver Kroetz. Bauern sterben: Materialien zum Stück* (Reinbek bei Hamburg: Rowohlt, 1985), p. 156.

24. Michael Skasa, "Alltag im Kopfstand: Kroetz inszeniert Kroetz' 'Nicht Fisch nicht Fleisch'," *Theater heute* (Dec. 1983) p. 14.

25. Franz Xaver Kroetz, "Engagierte Literatur," *Wespennest*, no. 40 (1980), p. 91.

26. Franz Xaver Kroetz, "Die Richtung des Zuges wird nicht verändert," *Der Sonntag*, 14 Aug. 1979.

27. Jean-Paul Sartre, *What is Literature?*, trans. Bernard Frechtman (New York: Philosophical Library, 1949), p. 159.

28. See e.g. "Meine MÄNNERSACHE" (WA, 553–558) and "Die Schwierigkeiten des einfachen Mannes" (WA, 605–608).

29. See e.g. Gustav Ernst, "Literatur und Leben. Zum (neueren) literarischen Realismus," *Wespennest*, no. 74 (1989): pp. 3–39.

30. Kroetz, "Engagierte Literatur," p. 92.

31. Franz Xaver Kroetz, "Ich schreibe nicht über Dinge, die ich verachte. Ich bin für mich sehr interessant," *Theater heute* (July 1980): p. 18.

32. Astrid von Kotze has a very different interpretation of Otto's linguistic capabilities, but her reading relies on programmatic statements Kroetz made about his earliest plays and not about the post-*Oberösterreich* works. This is a potent illustration of how risky it is to trust an author's own statements about his or her own production. Astrid von Kotze, "Monopolisierung von Sprache in *Mensch Meier* von Franz Xaver Kroetz," *Acta Germanica* 13 (1980): pp. 165–174.

33. Horkheimer/Adorno, *Dialektik der Aufklärung*, p. 144.
34. Ibid., p. 177.
35. Elizabeth Boa, "Kroetz's *Nicht Fisch nicht Fleisch*: A Good Red Herring?" *German Life and Letters* 38, no. 4 (1985): p. 318.
36. See also Schwab, p. 609.
37. Kroetz in Riewoldt, *Franz Xaver Kroetz*, p. 171.
38. Quoted in Michael Töteberg, "Ein konservativer Autor: Familie, Kind, Technikfeindlichkeit, Heimat: traditionsgebundene Werte in den Dramen des Franz Xaver Kroetz," in Riewoldt, *Franz Xaver Kroetz*, p. 292.
39. Rischbieter, "Vom Druck auf den Durchschnitt und vom Drang, auszubrechen." *Theater heute* (July 1981), p. 4.
40. Both *Mensch Meier* and *Der stramme Max* offer two positive women characters. However, both of them insist that the appropriate role for the wife and mother is to tend the home and the family. Martha in *Mensch Meier* leaves her home to find a job. She does not do so by choice, but rather is forced out into the workforce by her husband's erratic, domineering and abusive behavior (III,384). Anna in *Der stramme Max* is as self-confident as Emmi, but she always emphasizes that her place is in the home, she is not the doer – that role belongs to her "strammer Max" (see e.g. III,423f,427).
41. Franz Xaver Kroetz in Zadek, *Franz Xaver Kroetz. Bauern sterben*, p. 146.
42. Töteberg in Riewoldt, *Franz Xaver Kroetz*, p. 288.
43. Ibid., p. 40.

—4—

Bauern sterben

Kroetz's *Tendenzwende*

By 1985, the year in which Kroetz wrote *Bauern sterben*, he claims to have resolved for himself the crisis of politically committed literature. He now maintains that politics no longer play much of a role in his life anymore. As he says to Günter Gaus in an interview televized in 1986: "Bin wieder Schriftsteller. Hauptberuf Kunst. Basta. Das ist auch gut."[1] He has also publicly distanced himself from those people who were once the central characters of his work. In an interview for the program to the Hamburg production of *Bauern sterben* Kroetz says: "Mich hat niemals das Volk interessiert! Ich habe nur mich und meine Familie und meine Frau gesehen. Ich habe mein Leben lang nur von mir geschrieben. Es interessiert mich dabei überhaupt nicht, was das Volk denkt."[2] Kroetz's avowed disinterest in the people is a long way from his publicly held positions from the early to mid-seventies. His 1976 contribution to the DKP convention in Bonn emphasizes his commitment to the suffering of the people:

> Aber eines war mir doch schon immer klar: Mich haben die Menschen interessiert, ihre Not, ihr Elend, ihre Demütigungen, und ich habe nie in den geistigen Exkrementen des bürgerlichen Formalismus gewühlt, und ich habe mich nie um den Beifall der großbürgerlichen Verleger und ihrer Kulis gekümmert.[3]

As indicated in the introductory section on realism in chapter one, Kroetz here restates the relationship between his chosen formal aesthetic means and his concern for the needs of the oppressed. The "mental excrement" to which he refers is abstract or absurdist aesthetic strategies, which he clearly associates with opportunism and capitalist exploitation. The fact that Kroetz's supposed rejection of the *Volk* corresponds to a redefinition on his part of both an appropriate aesthetic and a revised political vision is thus not surprising.

There are, however, indications that his expressed break with overtly political drama and with its audience is not as clean as it would seem. In fact it is my contention that these emphatic pronouncements are just a dramatic gesture. Both the prologue and scene five of *Bauern sterben* reveal a continued preoccupation with art's political or non-political character.[4]

Kroetz admits that his move away from politics and back to art stems both from confusion about and disappointment in the developments within the (West) German political landscape. In the television interview cited above, Gaus asks Kroetz whether or not he regrets his return to "radical" art,[5] i.e. his decision to give up on committed literature. Kroetz replies:

> es ist schon bedauerlich, weil ich mit meinen Entschuldigungen, warum ich Politik nicht mehr mache, auch eigentlich nicht weiterkomme. Ich habe es nicht verwunden, 1980, als ich mit der Politik aufgehört habe. Es tut mir weh, daß ich es nicht verwunden habe. Aber ich weiß nicht, wo ich hingehen sollte.[6]

Noteworthy in the passage is the tone of personal loss, emotional suffering and lack of direction. The personal crisis his departure from the DKP caused has a parallel in the renewed search for new means of aesthetic expression. This search, as well as his political and personal disillusionment, are foregrounded against the belief that the author has virtually no import, impact or status in (West) German society. The increasing pessimism apparent in Kroetz's work culminates in *Bauern sterben*. Its negative tenor reflects, among other things, the perceived absence of any potential for politically committed artists to attain the goals they set for themselves. Kroetz writes: "Dann könnt ich an der Wand hochgehen vor lauter Wut, daß der Künstler, der Dichter in dieser Bundesrepublik ein Scheißdreck ist und nichts zählt. . . . Hier in dieser Scheißrepublik haben wir Null-Stellenwert."[7]

Kroetz criticizes the media, among others, for ignoring the opinions of authors on contemporary issues in favor of technical experts from the field in question. These remarks are overtly political, at least in terms of art's political voice in contemporary West German society. Unfortunately, another possible reading of this statement is as an attempt to privilege artistic as opposed to general opinion. In other words, Kroetz seems to claim for himself and for other interested authors an expert status that has no readily apparent justification. In so doing, he relegates the general populace to a lower rung on the ladder of political intelligence. What this would mean is that, merely by virtue of his being an author, Kroetz sees himself better able to respond to political issues than the ordinary citizen. When it becomes clear that the media do not accept him as a political expert, he becomes disenchanted and indignant.

Of course, one can explain such a comment in yet another way. Authors/artists provide a special perspective on current issues that could be helpful within the arena of active politics. However, in the post-*Tendenzwende* republic[8] the authorial voice falls on deaf ears. We could, therefore, view Kroetz's vehement attack on the Federal Republic as the disappointment of an author committed to the political role of literature in a society increasingly resistant to such a concept. The SPD's reform politics of the seventies may have diffused more radical leftist critiques of German society, but the success of the CDU/CSU conservative government during the economic and ideologically "up-beat" eighties has effectively silenced the German left. Despite Kroetz's avowed turn from politics, though, *Bauern sterben* as a whole addresses directly and indirectly several contemporary political issues, as well as various questions of public participation in the political arena.

The Art of the Theater: The Prologue to *Bauern sterben*

Although the play has been criticized as being too cliché-ridden, a tired rehashing of a very old problem,[9] the prologue and scene five explicitly address the relationship of art to politics. The first of three monologues covers art as a purification of reality and as a thorn in the side of the apparent and hidden governors of contemporary society. The second expresses the alienation of the aesthetic realm from the world within which it exists and the desire to explode the walls surrounding and restraining artistic production. At the same time, it questions the honesty of this desire. The third culminates in a mockery of the theater as mere clownery.

Kroetz assigns the explication of the theater's traditional function to an old comedian, evoking with his age conservative visions of art and the theater as a palliative for reality. He explains to the audience how theater works. The theater in question here is both a theater and a mortuary, a rather crass metaphor to underscore the distance between art and life itself. The director of the mortuary is, however, an *Intendant*, a title most commonly used for the chief executive of cultural institutions. The director insists that his actors make the corpses, i.e. the characters they play, as life-like as possible: "Diese Leiche ist ihre [*sic*] bisher schönste, weil sie schaut so lebendig aus. So müssen alle Ihre Leichen ausschauen, sagte der Intendant, wenn Sie bei mir alt werden wollen" (IV,219). The beautification and vivification of the dead body as the object of theatrical art reinforces the idea that the theater has no connection to life. At the very most it is an artificial one, as the concept of the lifelike here is a fabrication.

The perspective of the old comedian differs slightly from that of the *Intendant*. He tells his public that the theater shows human beings not as they are, but rather as they would be. Lest art be accused of an actual falsehood, he quickly adds that the theater does not conceal anything, it merely distributes the truth differently than life itself does outside of the theater walls. The old comedian (re)presents the idea that the importance of art is its preservation of the utopian, or of life as it truly is beneath the coarse and deceptive surface of reality: "Unsere Kunst ist wichtig, denn wir geben dem Leben seine Wahrheit und Schönheit zurück" (IV,219). Whereas the theater director admits to producing only the illusion of reality, the old comedian equates the beauty of art with truth, relegating empirical reality to the status of inadequate representation. Life becomes real only through art.

Unfortunately, art's ability to smooth out the wrinkles of empirical reality is just what blurs its ties to the society with which we are most familiar, i.e. to the arena in which the powerful exploit and systematically destroy their social and financial inferiors. Art estranges reality to the point where the exploiters and the exploitees are no longer compelled to recognize themselves in the works before them: "Die Mächtigen beklatschen schenkelschlagend unsere Darstellung ihrer Opfer. . . . Nur wenige erkannten sich wieder, meist Hausfrauen, die sich mit allem identifizieren" (IV,220).[10] But the comedian continues:

> Da wechselte zuerst die Regierung, dann die Intendanz. Plötzlich hieß es, wir hätten über das Ziel hinausgeschossen. Unsere Kunst hätte die Zuschauer zusehends schockiert. Sie hätten ihre nächsten Angehörigen nicht mehr erkannt. Pfarrer, Ärzte und Staatsanwälte ließen sich mit der Vermutung vernehmen, unsere Leichen seien überhaupt nicht tot. (IV,220)

A change in the directorship brought about or was a consequence of both a political and an aesthetic shift in perspective. The inherently critical character of art *vis-à-vis* society surfaced to haunt its very benefactors.

As a virtual contradiction to the notion that art prettifies, thereby softening the harshness of life, this passage is difficult to untangle and to clarify within the monologue of the old comedian. An explanation of the discrepancy must point out that the monologue contains both references to historical developments in post-war drama, as well as a theoretical question as to the societal function of the aesthetic product.

In the fifties and sixties the West German theater developed from an attack on the society which seemed all too eager to welcome fascism to an attack on capitalism, particularly post-war Germany, and again particularly the Germany of the "economic miracle." The theater shed its role as the source of solace and comfort for the cultured bourgeoisie. It became, instead, an open attack on its own public. When the theater attempted to expose the oppressive structures of capitalist society the subtle, but potent censorship of capitalist market relations, both external and internal, came crashing down (at least according to the old comedian): "Unsere Verträge liefen aus und wurden stillschweigend nicht verlängert" (IV,220). The censorship of capitalist democracies is not explicit: disapproval voices itself in silence and the withholding of funds.

In turn, drama of the seventies, at least in Kroetz's view, turned back in on itself and gave in to pathetic self-absorption, debunking the radical politics it so fervently expressed a few years earlier as mere pretense. Kroetz writes in a journal entry published in *Furcht und Hoffnung der BRD*, "'Theater heute' und das heutige Theater sind derart entpolitisiert, daß es schon gar nicht mehr zu beschreiben ist: das Innerste von Innen aus dem Innern."[11] In essence, the theater has made censorship superfluous. To those who claimed that the insidiously covert censorship of capitalism absorbs and defuses the political power of art, Kroetz's young comedian answers scoffingly: "Da ist dein Publikum, und dort bist du. Die Rampe ist dazwischen, sonst nichts. Gar nichts. Schau hin, du alter Narr, ist was dazwischen? Eine Zensur, ein Staatsanwalt, ein 'halt so nicht!'" (IV,220)[12] Although the old comedian's suspicions of censorship may be exaggerated, the young comedian's response represents in a certain sense an acquiescence in or compliance with the more subtle forms of censorship in late capitalist democracies. Thus, the generational differences between the old and the young actor also illustrate the changing political attitudes of the young in a post-*Tendenzwende* Germany.

On the level of aesthetic theory, this passage further alludes to the double character of art. Does art function as a mere *Leckerbissen* for the social and economic elite or does it incite to riot? Are the corpses in the mortuary really dead or are they only pretending to be? There are various perspectives on how art actually functions in society. Does art truly maintain the privileges of the autonomy bourgeois society has granted it, tending to the appearances of a dead world? Does art in a sense use its autonomy to mock and critique the social world trapped in the constrictive net of exchange value?[13] Or does it completely deny its autonomous character, insisting on both its immanent implication in society and its contingent right actively to engage in society's struggles? None of these questions has a definitive answer. It is clear that art does have political ramifications and consequences. It is not clear how they are created and directed. This enhances substantially the sense that the monologue of the old comedian is self-contradictory. One could even conclude that it is less the monologue that is contradictory than art itself.

The young comedian also addresses the issue of art's function in society, albeit in a decidedly different fashion. He seems to reject any claims the theater might make to have an active role in societal change when he blurts out, "Theater ists und nur Theater!" (IV,220). The young and the restless, burning for action and social importance, struggle to escape the plastic world of the theater with its plastic rewards and exchange them for the exciting realm of real life: "Ich will hier raus! Ich will endlich einen echten Rausch und eine echte Fotze, und wenn ich sterben soll, dann von der Mafia Hand und nicht der Sehnsucht Palmenwedel. ... Ich will aufs Titelblatt und nicht ins Feuilleton" (IV,221). The superlative character of his language (e.g. "von der Mafia Hand sterben," "der Sehnsucht Palmenwedel") would, however, appear to betray a goal that has little to do with the desire to experience life directly, i.e. not through the mediation of the aesthetic. Indeed, as the young comedian continues his diatribe against the theater it becomes increasingly clear that this melodramatic speech is nothing more than self-stylization on the part of the actor – just more theater. The members of the audience can conclude from this that the theater's occasional claims to political commitment, even political relevance, i.e. a commitment to the world outside of art, are pitiable attempts at self-aggrandizement.

Is this a permanent component of the aesthetic product? If one shifts the perspective somewhat, the question becomes one of the degree to which ridicule and the ridiculous (whether directed inwardly or outwardly) are essential elements of an artwork. In his *Ästhetische Theorie* Adorno maintains that the most meaningful works of art contain a moment of clownery.[14] For Adorno, this element of the silly turns against the destructive rationality of empirical reality, and functions as only one of the weapons in art's critical arsenal. For Kroetz, this silliness has only negative consequences for the potential effect of, in this case, drama on its audiences. Kroetz once stated that the theater can never escape its propensity to render harmless and endearing what it places on its stage. In an essay for *konkret* Kroetz wrote, "Theater an sich hat eine verniedlichende Komponente, die sich zuerst einmal auf alles überträgt, was mit den Mitteln des Theaters dargestellt wird" (WA, 543f). Although one might question whether the trivializing potential of the theater work really affects all theatrical representation, there are many sections of *Bauern sterben* that highlight moments of artistic clownery or folly.

Nonetheless, whether "das Alberne"[15] in art functions critically as ridicule or acritically merely to lighten an evening's theater fare, one need not come to the conclusion that the whole of the theater can be reduced to foolish clowning around in a three-ring circus. Yet the prologue closes with the speech of a young comedienne that would seem to do just that. Reflecting on her options now that she has been fired by the company she says:

> Und wenn alle Stricke reißen, kann ich mich in einen Affen verwandeln, der 12 kleine Äffchen gebiert. Und das glaubwürdig vom ersten bis zum letzten Augenblick. Das ist vielleicht eindrucksvoller, als wenn irgendein Fritzchen durch den Don Carlos stolpert. Und Theater oder Zirkus, das ist mir wirklich scheißegal. (IV,223)

Through its mockery of both the traditional theater of Schiller's *Don Carlos* and its reduction to a circus side-show, the theater contemporary to the young comedienne, this passage underscores the author's ambivalence toward the institution for which he writes. The plaintive quality of her speech indicates that Kroetz is himself still reluctant for this to be the final word on the theater's social function.

Kroetz's prologue presents the audience with three differing positions on the character and function of the theater. The old comedian offers us the view of art as ideally untouched by the realities external to it. The young comedian then seemingly laments this isolation and pleads for the opportunity to escape the prison of autonomy. However, his clownish delivery and affectation unmask these pleas as self-congratulatory and vain rhetoric. Finally, the young woman's desperate search for work points out the lengths to which the theater will go to insure its continued existence. In so far as the prologue subjects each of the three positions to ridicule, it is clear that none of them is adequate. The prologue does not offer a fourth option and the main portion of the work continues to poke holes in the polished veneer of the art world's self-complacency.

In scene five, a scene Kroetz did not include in his own stage production of the piece for the Münchner Kammerspiele, a poet futilely attempts to capture the attention of the play's two main characters as they make a fevered attempt to reach the land of their dreams: the big city. The poet, referred to as "Der Eilige," considers himself vital to the city, to mankind. Bestowing him with the title of "the hurried one," the text indicates that the artist rushes about, never staying in one place (aesthetic harbor?) for very long, and further implying perhaps that he does not waste much time on self-reflection. It takes a great deal of effort not to interpret this segment as a bit of self-irony on the part of the dramatist. In such a case, the artist's frenetic character would point to Kroetz's own career-long experiments to locate both a style with which he feels he can accomplish his aesthetic goals, as well as a social class within which he can pursue and achieve his broader political project.

The poet's oration on the necessity for art to engage in class struggle, actively to take the part of the working class, illustrates this point quite well: "Was nützt die Kunst, wenn sie nicht den Interessen der arbeitenden Menschen dient. Deshalb schreibe ich vom Menschen für den Menschen. Von einem gesicherten Klassenstandpunkt aus" (IV,234). But how does this commitment voice itself in the first few lines of a poem he tries to read to the brother and sister? It voices itself in a pretentious and contrived language that cannot serve to open a dialogue with the uncomprehending silence of the siblings. Despite the fact that they really have no interest in him or his work, the poet harangues them with his creative efforts:

Über Puri
der heiligen
geht die Sonne
zum Meer.

Wie ein
Votivbild
schau, sagt A.
(IV,234)

The poet pauses to reflect on what his poetry is for him. He asks why God, who is disappointed in his muse, commits suicide. Then he continues his reading:

Warte schau die Uhr.
Naziland ich komm.
Wieder ist die Aktentasche
voll mit Literatur.
Schreiben, schreiben.
Warum?
Die hier können nicht lesen.
Denen hab ich
nichts zu sagen.
Was ich
in den letzten drei Jahren
daheim publiziert hab
wäre es nicht genug

gewesen die Republik
zu sprengen zu zerreißen
zu rühren bloß?

(IV,236)

Evoking a theme prominent in post-war German literature, namely the Nazi past and art's relationship thereto, the poet wonders at the ineffectuality of political aesthetics. The poet's questioning is, however, less an intellectual pursuit of art's failure to have the impact he wishes it did than an existential desperation: he is hurt. When he stops once again to ponder his existence "Warum treffe ich nie ein Herz mit einem Wort. Ich bin verzweifelt" (IV,237), the two on the tractor respond by hurriedly leaving the self-absorbed poet behind in the dust.

The confrontation in this scene depicts a total breakdown in communication, or, rather, the complete failure to establish dialogue. Not only is the poet not telling our brother-and-sister team anything they want to hear, he is also telling it to them in a language to which they have no access. He elicits no response from them other than their unrelenting silence. "Schweigen – die Antwort für einen deutschen Dichterl Schweigen aus Deutschland?" (IV,236). The hasty poet does not understand why his words do not reach them and they simply do not understand him. The artist, in his desperation, throws a hand grenade after them. He turns against those for whom he had thought himself in battle.

Kroetz, too, turns against his long-targeted public, berating it with his rejection. In his public pronouncements, such as those made in the Gaus interview, he does not, however, indicate those areas in his own production that could be hampering effective communication between his work and his audience as he does in the case of the hurried poet. And it would be useless conjecture to insist that Kroetz is indeed implicating himself in the ineffectuality of political art. The analogy of Kroetz to "der Eilige" serves merely to point out that his public comments on art at the time this work first appeared underscore similar sentiments as to the ability of art to fulfill any political mission.

More importantly, *Bauern sterben* mocks the politically committed artist, criticizing his (or her) failure to reflect on both the nature of the audience as well as the extent to which the author is actually committed to that audience. Although Kroetz begins around 1980 to publish the idea that he has never really done anything other than write about his own life, it is not until *Furcht und Hoffnung der BRD* that he has a character accuse a politically committed author of fraud. Although the accusation comes from an editor, who is himself the subject of a biting critique, it is, nonetheless, worthy of consideration in this instance. The

editor says to the author, who is trying to have the former publish an
article he has written on a demonstration against the AGFA plant:

> Sie! – der so stolz ist, daß er ein Gewerkschaftsbuch haben darf, der sich
> mitten drin fühlt in den Kolleginnen und Kollegen – der den Zug der Zeit
> im Kreuz spürt – den Wind (*lächelt, nickt*) wenn die andern frösteln im
> praktisch leeren, nullgradigen, nächtlichen Fußballstadion. (*Kleine Pause.*)
> Sie haben nicht von der Wirklichkeit, sondern von Ihrer Sehnsucht
> geschrieben nach – Solidarität (*freundlich*) nach Mut und Kampf und Kraft
> und Streik und Betriebsbesetzung! – Ich glaub, Sie sind ein kleiner
> "Wahrheitsunterdrücker" – denn die, denen man es immer vorwirft, sie
> würden nur von sich schreiben, die geben es wenigstens zu, aber Sie –
> Sie – Sie jubeln sich in etwas hinein, was Sie erträumen, Sie benutzen die
> Arbeiterschaft für Ihre Träume, für die Abreagierung Ihrer Ängste, Ihrer
> Frustrationen, Ihrer Komplexe – Sie benutzen die Arbeiterschaft für sich!
> (IV,144f)

The editor's words echo the sentiments of Peter Schneider's student
movement activist in *Lenz*. The title character, disillusioned with the
political rhetoric and the asceticism of the student leaders, explores the
hypocrisy of students who seek and then exploit a relationship with the
working class in order to alleviate their own existential boredom and
liberal guilt. Lenz eventually strives to combine political activism and
a more sensuous existence in the mountains of Italy. What is so striking
about the comparison is that Schneider wrote his book in 1972, ten years
before *Bauern sterben*.[16] Kroetz attributes his intellectual and aesthetic
isolation to his persistent pursuit of a Marxist political agenda, and this
isolation finds expression in both the hasty poet's desperate attack on his
listeners and the editor's accusations against the author quoted above.

These statements, however, do not as yet take full account of how
Kroetz belittles his own (West) German audiences in the interview from
the Hamburg program. The disparaging remarks about the *Volk* are only
one side of a double-edged sword, and his bitterness toward the German
public occasionally gives way to less emotional assessments of the
audience. In an interview with *Die Welt* Kroetz acknowledges the
distance of the theater from the lives of most individuals:

> Ich stelle fest, daß 80–85 Prozent der Menschen Kunst überhaupt nicht als
> eine Form der Auseinandersetzung mit dem Dasein sehen. Sie sind einfach
> ungeübt darin, und deswegen bin ich auch resigniert. Ich kann nicht mehr
> für diese 85 Prozent schreiben. Wenn ich das täte, müßte ich mich als Autor
> für die 'Schwarzwaldklinik' verdingen.[17]

The inability of the aesthetic realm to transcend its own boundaries and
to extend its influence into a broader public leaves the individual artist

to grapple with the passivity of the public, which is at least partially the result of art's relatively insulated position within social reality. Although artists have occasionally tried to tear down the walls of the institution, they have never been more than marginally and/or fleetingly successful. Attempts to reintegrate art and aesthetic practice into everyday living have run afoul of a long-standing insistence on art's autonomy. The passage above expresses directly the quandary a politically committed artist will inevitably face, and the one that Kroetz began to acknowledge at the end of the seventies.

The reviews of *Bauern sterben* are interesting for many reasons, but for now their titles will only lead into the end of this introduction. Elisabeth Fischer entitles her review "Kroetz stellt seine Wunden aus,"[18] Benjamin Henrichs calls his review "Kroetz voll Blut und Wunden,"[19] and Peter von Becker, writing for *Theater heute*, calls his "Die Stadt, das Land und der Tod. Kroetz und Achternbusch inszenieren Kroetz und Achternbusch in München."[20] It is obvious in these and other reviews that this work was received in the media as Kroetz's personal statement about his career in the theater, about his battles with the institution, which have, if we are to believe the critics, left him scarred and bleeding.

It would, nonetheless, be incorrect to reduce this piece completely to a public display of this dramatist's emotional wounds. Another, perhaps dialectical, way of approaching this play is to see it as the expression of the alienated political author faced with the implacable lethargy of the current public, as a political analysis of this venerable institution in its present state. So, has Kroetz surrendered in his struggle to write politically committed drama or has he simply altered his tactics once again? What an analysis of *Bauern sterben* yields depends on how one prefers to answer these questions.

Bauern sterben: Structure

The prologue and scene five aptly demonstrate Kroetz's thoughts *vis-à-vis* committed literature and his perception of his own work since the early eighties. The play's own thematization of the theater's socio-political role would suggest that it forms a central focus for *Bauern sterben*. Nonetheless, both the author and the work put up certain resistances to a political reading. Therefore, my analysis of this work approaches it as an example of not only political drama, but also the dilemma of political theater in the mid-eighties.

Bauern sterben is a compilation of loosely related scenes. The author in fact characterizes it as a "dramatisches Fragment" (IV,215). As it appeared in the program to the Munich production, the text consists of the prologue and fourteen individual scenes. After the prologue, the piece opens to a seemingly typical Kroetzian kitchen: father, mother, grandmother, son and daughter are gathered together around the family stove. Although elements of Kroetz's earlier works continue to reappear throughout the course of the production, their function does not seem to go beyond merely a teasingly macabre reference to the author's previous thematic and stylistic emphases.

Despite its apparently fragmentary character, there are well-defined sections of the play. The first is, of course, the prologue, which has been the central focus of this chapter up to this point. The second is the world of the characters' rural *Heimat*, and the third is the impersonal, overwhelming metropolis. In the second section, Kroetz establishes the framework for the developments to come.

Bauern sterben constructs its *dramatis personae*, i.e. their (stage) identities, through the comparison of particular forms of production, through language and through references to past, which include religion and ancestry. Each one of these aspects reinforces and intersects with the others. The following discussion, therefore, will often not progress in a clearly linear fashion, proceeding from one issue to another, but will instead view the scenes in question from various perspectives, in order to create a more accurate picture of this second section as a whole.

The Rural Idyll?

The play centers first on the conflicts within a family of four: father, mother, son and daughter.[21] When the curtain opens on the family gathering, the audience is confronted with the son chanting a hypnotic litany of modernization. He insists that the family farm will go under if his father does not switch from dairy to beef cattle, if they do not install electricity, put on a new roof, put in a telephone and buy a car. In the very first sentences of this play two virtually opposite modes of production clash in the conflict of the father and the son over the issue of modernization.

> Sohn: (*verzweifelt*) Mia brachan a   Wassaleiding, ohne a
> Wassaleiding gäds nirgands mea. A Wassaleiding hoda jeda.
> Mia brachan a neichs Doch, ohne a neichs Doch gäds
> nirgands mea. A neichs Doch hoda jeda. Mia brachan an
> richtign Schdrom fia richtige Maschina. Ohne richtige
> Mashina gäds nirgands mea. (*sehr laut*) Mia brachan a
> Heizing, mia brachan an Delefon und a Auddo brachma aa.
> Und umschdein miaßma von da Milli afd Buinmast, afd
> Buinmast. (IV,225)

The world of modern technology shimmers in this character's eyes, promising the good life, complete with leisure time and sex:

Sohn: Und a Wei kriagt i nachat aa, wenn umschdeid werat und modernisiad, weis gern kamat des Wei, a jäde, wenns sigd: im Schdoi hoda umschdeid, ois is dodal modernisiad! . . . Koa Schdoiarbad dengdsese und gfreitse. (IV,225)

The father is not merely resistant to the idea of modernization. He is adamant in his refusal to do so; he even expresses his intent legally to prohibit his heirs from switching to beef cattle from dairy cattle:

Vater: Und wenne amoi iwagib, 'nachad machmas nodarisch daß die Millikia bleim, daß bleim wia as Milligeid und wia meine Hosn aa. Daß ois ois aso bleibd wias etzan is. (IV,226)

The father, however, as the representative of the traditional small landowner, is essentially visibly bleeding to death. A mysterious medical condition causes him to bleed from vesicles on the skin, and his blood has seeped into everthing around him: into his clothing; into his house; and, above all, into the very milk they sell. He no longer has the strength to resist the forces of progress, nor does the author seem to suggest that such resistance would necessarily be a good thing.

Kroetz portrays the father as enmeshed in the spirit of capitalism, if not in its profitability. He views everything and everyone in his household as his personal property. In response to his son's threat to abandon him, he replies:

Vater: Du gäsd ned, du gäsd nia, weie di ned laß. Du gheasd aa mei, wia meine Kia und da Fernsäa aa.
Sohn: (brüllt) I ghea mia.
Vater: Mei ghärsd, ois is no mei, du und da Fernsäa aa. (IV,226)

He can conceive of interpersonal relationships only in terms of commodities. The grandmother, his last tie to his past, has passed away without anyone having taken notice. Her body, their heritage, is riddled with worms, and the stench of decay pervades the family's common space. The father reacts to his mother's death by securing for himself the remote control for the television, which she has gripped fiercely in her hand. Although the others urge him to let her keep it, he insists on his right of ownership:

Vater: Awa da Fernsää ghead mei. I nimm de Fernbedienung mid
ins Baradies. (*reißt sie ihr weg*) Mia hodses gem. I hobs. I
hobs! Etz ghead ois wida mei. Ois. De hobe iwalebd. Jung
und oid, groß und kloa, ois mei. Bluad und Milli, Viech und
Mensch, ois mei. (*Er schaltet genußvoll den Fernseher aus.*)
(IV,228)

Although rigor mortis has set in, the father still manages to break his
mother's hold. Reasserting his ownership of all that he surveys, he
revels in his imagined sovereignty. By literally breaking the bones of his
dead mother, the father severs the ties binding his generation to the past
and exposes those ties as reified, as unable to provide the present with
an emotionally sustaining base.

Indeed, both the past and the future of this socio-economic class is
dead or dying. While the daughter and the mother clean and prepare the
grandmother's corpse for burial, the daughter has a miscarriage. She
puts the aborted fetus into the stomach of the corpse, which worms had
already eaten through. The daughter explains to her unborn child that it
will spare itself the pain of life by going straight from non-being to
death:

Tochter: Gäsd do eine, do is warm und guad. Werstas schon seng.
Von oam Bauch in andan. Des is sche. Werstas seng,
wosida sog. Brachst gorned afd Weld, bleibta daschbart da
Umweg, und du versamst nix. (IV,229)

She reduces the whole of life to an unnecessary and unpleasant detour.
A comparison of this miscarriage with the numerous attempts at self-
performed abortions in Kroetz's early works reveals not only a
continued focus of the author on the child, particularly the unborn child.
It also contrasts to the unborn child as the locus of hope for a better
future. In *Oberösterreich*, Anni successfully wards off an attempt
against the life of her unborn child and swears that its life will be better
than theirs has been. In *Bauern sterben*, the hope engendered by a
pregnancy is very literally stillborn.

When the family gathers again at the grandmother's graveside in
scene three, the sense of disconnection and the permeation of
commodity relations broadens to a realm, conventionally viewed as the
source of emotional solace, of one's identity within the universe: The
father extends the boundaries of his property to include Christ. He says,
"Ois is no mei, und du schdehst aa uaf meim Grund und Bodn, des
muaßta oiwei vor Aung hoitn!" (IV,230). Just as he has brutalized his

family, he cuts the ties to his soul by tearing the figure of Christ from his cross. He has destroyed all that has functioned historically in the formation of the individual's identity: the family, a sense of personal chronology and man's connection to the world as a whole. This situation becomes truly intolerable for the children, and they take off on the family tractor, carrying with them the body of Christ, which their father had ripped from his cross. They leave behind their parents, who turn to skeletons even as the tractor is still in sight.

Although the dramatist strips the quality of the idyll from the countryside, he nevertheless endows it with a mystical quality.[22] This he does largely through language. As it constitutes the first locus of confrontation between the work itself and its audience, language is perhaps the most striking feature of *Bauern sterben*. The question of dialect use arose already in the discussion of *Oberösterreich*. In that context dialect functioned as a descriptive tool and as an attempt at authenticity, as well as an indication of constraint and limitation. It was a constitutive element, but it was not an essential element. In his earlier works, Kroetz generally directed the actors to model their speech on Bavarian dialect. If they did not possess the technical ability to do so, he suggested that they drop the dialect and speak in a manner natural for them.

In *Bauern sterben* Kroetz has expanded the structural role of a highly stylized dialectal form considerably.[23] The language of the pre-technology peasantry acts as a distinct barrier between the world of the characters' rural *Heimat* and the world of instrumental rationality as embodied in the austere world of the city. In the first scene, in which the brother recites his ritualized litany, the language spoken on the stage comes to resemble the anachronistic use of Latin in the catholic mass. In a sense, it enshrouds the scene before the audience, evoking an aura of primacy, that is to say, of a primal relationship between the peasant and the land.[24] Every time the characters in *Bauern sterben* consciously imitate the mode of communication operative in the city, they abandon dialect and assume standardized usage.

Not surprisingly, this most often occurs when they imitate the language of the media. In scene eight, the siblings play a game in which they try to guess the product from the slogan:

Tochter:	Eigentlich sehe ich ganz gut aus – nur diese fettige, unreine?
Sohn:	Clerasil –
Tochter:	Und nach dem Schulabschluß, Verlobung –
Sohn:	Volksbanken und Raiffeisenkassen – wir bieten mehr als Geld und Zinsen – (IV,241)

The culture industry structures the individual both physically and emotionally, offering both a "clear complexion" and a stable financial future. Furthermore, the transformation to which they are subjected in the city voices itself in an entirely different language than the logic of the country. It is a language foreign to the siblings. The use of dialect is necessary to underscore the barriers between these two worlds: barriers that will soon prove to be insurmountable.

Urban Blight

In the first three scenes of the play, the dramatist constructs a poisonous rural Eden. Yet, it is only the remnant of a paradise lost to those who live in it. The road out, however, leads to an urban nightmare. It is littered with the victims of the rational logic of technological progress. In the third section of the play, Kroetz raises such issues as the actual benefits of technological progress, the effects of instrumental rationality on the members of society, the individual's growing sense of isolation and, again, the increasing sense of a loss of self.

On their way to the city, brother and sister pass by a farmer trying to defend his forests from appropriation by the utilities commission. He is desperate and has resorted to his shotgun to salvage his land, to preserve his family's history:

> *Bauer*: (*tobsüchtig mit einem Gewehr herumfuchtelnd*) Wos vadeidigds an eß? Vadeidigds eß mi oda as Elegdrizidädswerg? Vadeidigds eß mein Woid oda vadeidigds eß de Iwalandmastn? I sogs eich: wea oan vo meine Baam oriad, den schiaße nieda. Wenn oana sei Modorsog owirft, nachat schdirbda. Fia mi gibds koa Enteignung. I bin i. Und mei Sach isas meinige. Und des seit 16 Genaraziona. Wea vun eich Hodalumbn hodn 16 Genaraziona, de woa nochweisn ko? Eß wißds ned amoi wea eicha Vattan is, aso werddes sei bei eich hoamadlose Hunt. . . . (*sieht die Geschwister auf dem Traktor kommen*) Nachbar, kimmsd grod zua rechtn Zeid! Sigstas wia ses mid mia dreim. Heit i moing du. Huifma! . . . Heifma zum, gega de ausda Schdod. De ausda Schdod han insa Untagang. De Schdod und as Land han Feinde! (IV,232)

The path to progress, or to increasing levels of consumption, has led to the destruction of any inanimate or reluctant animate objects. For sixteen generations, this man's family has tended the land. The farmer rightly questions whether the electricity company is willing to do the same. Yet neither the farmer's desperation nor his shotgun will ever have an appropriate target to attack. One cannot halt progress with a shotgun.

Just as starry-eyed with the much-touted benefits of technology to man as the engineers and architects of such projects, the siblings see this farmer as an obstacle to the good life. The daughter shouts down the angry farmer with the promises of the nuclear power industry: "Midm Schdrom kimmts Atom, midm Schdrom kimmts Atom, midm Schdrom kimmts Atom. Wenns Atom kimmt, bracht koana mea arbadn!" (IV,232f). The sister picks up her brother's litany from the opening of the text, reciting here the utopian promises of nuclear power. The rhetoric of technological progress reveals itself to be just that: rhetoric. Instead of the good life, human beings are faced with possible extinction.

They then pass a woman who has just lost her job. She describes for them the work she did for twelve years in the lighting division of AEG. The task she completed at least 128 times a day has been rendered obsolete and unprofitable: "Der Fortfall meiner Arbeit war eine Rationalisierungsmaßnahme zugunsten der Ertragslage des Gesamtkonzerns" (IV,238). The language the woman uses could have come straight from the company's annual report. She cannot explain their decision to lay her off with her own idiom, because the logic of capitalist rationalization does not correspond to her individual reality. After listening to the useless consolations offered by the politicians and the management of AEG, she decides her only option is to set herself on fire in protest against the way capitalism rationalizes human beings into non-existence.

In response, the daughter accuses the woman of indolence. Many of Kroetz's characters in the past leveled this same accusation against the unemployed until they found themselves in a similar situation. Brother and sister are as yet untouched by the rationality of production. They still harbor hope for the future and ignore the warnings of the human waste products they encounter.

The end of their journey is an unfinished, unfurnished apartment in an impersonal apartment complex. Apartment complexes themselves are the epitome of a highly rationalized, compartmentalized society. Living space is standardized and allows for very little individualized deviation from the norm. Kroetz has even pushed this structural symbol to the extreme in that the walls have not been plastered, there is no furniture and no carpeting – nothing to add warmth. There is running water – which so amazes the siblings, that they consider themselves to have found paradise. Running water and electricity in abundance:

Technology delivers the physical essentials for life to the finger-tips, but it is incapable of filling the emotional needs of human beings.

The siblings have been in the city only a short time, when the cries of cows in the cattle yards awaken in them nostalgia for the home they left behind them:

> *Sohn*: Schdui! Schdui soids sei – (*Er schnauft, horcht ange-strengt.*) Heasd du des? Heasd nix? Des hans, de han do! Heasdas ned? (*aufgeregt*) Des hans, des hans! (*macht leise und zart einen Kälberschrei nach*)
>
> *Tochter*: (*schaut ihn an, horcht, nickt*)
>
> *Sohn*: (*äußerst erregt, macht sehr lange, sehr leise Kälber-schreie nach, sehr zart*) (IV,244)

It is ironic that the siblings interpret the frightened calls of animals about to be slaughtered as a greeting. They strain to hear the cries, and attempt to return the greeting. Their as yet unfettered optimism blocks out the context of the cattle's call, a context that would allow them to hear the implicit warning.

In a concerted attempt to respond to their new surroundings, the siblings plunge into consumerism, memorizing ad slogans and littering the apartment with piles of canned goods. As mentioned above, they mimic the language of marketing. In a sense, it is their attempt to sell themselves, to make themselves viable commodities. The initially mesmerizing, mysterious character of the city, however, soon reveals its dark side: unemployment, isolation, exploitation.

In scene nine the daughter tells a story that resembles a fable. The story is of the camel, a proud animal. Indispensable for prosperity in the desert, he was both a beast of burden and a status symbol. The camel even allowed his master to beat him, secure in the knowledge that it was irreplaceable:

> *Tochter*: Freile is a gschlong worn. Awa es war notwendi, es war sehr notwendi, ma hods ghaut und gschundn, aba ma hods bracht. Es hodse dengt: hau nua zu, du haust ma grod recht, solangst me haust, brachst me, und hod glocht. Das Wüstenschiff! Des war sei Glick, es war unersetzlich, und obwois vui hod arbadn miaßn, war es wer, es war wer, wei mas bracht hod. A Ewigkeit long. Es hod wos glernt, es hod wos kenna, es hod an hohen Preis ghobt, man hats deswengpflegn miaßn. (IV,245)

The march of technological progress caught the camel off guard. Once the automobile and the truck were invented, he was no longer needed. Cut off from other camels, kept prisoner in a concrete stall with glaring neon lights, the camel now waits unsuspectingly until the moment the butcher is ready for him. His death is not a dignified one, and if it in any way makes the butcher's task more difficult, the camel's corpse is beaten and kicked:

Tochter: Da Schußabbarat schiaßt nei ins Kamei und na schdeds und schiadeid se und foid hi afn Bedon, und wenn so bläd foid, daß ses wos bricht, nachat haut da Metzga noch drauf aufs dode Kamei weila mehra Fieslarbad hod. Manche san gscheid und schwitzn, de schderm scho im Gang an da Aufregung, de machen am meisten Arbad, da muaß extra da Gabelstapfla kumma unds hoin. (IV,246)

The daughter's tale is, of course, similar to the plight of the siblings, even if they are not as yet aware of these similarities. The story of the camel, however, also parallels to a striking degree the history of the traditional working class. The proletariat was beaten, but it was needed. On this basis the workers' movement was able to secure some benefits from management. With the advent of robotics and the ever-increasing automization of production, the worker becomes less and less necessary. Isolated from other workers in the concrete compartments assigned to them by society, the individual worker waits, perhaps unsuspectingly, for the death of his or her class.

As he began to do in *Nicht Fisch nicht Fleisch*, Kroetz delves here even further into the changing character of the economy. The brother cannot find work because the jobs open are for engineers, chemists, computer technicians: not for ex-farmers or uneducated, unskilled factory workers. He reads from the want ads:

BMW sucht Entwicklungsingenieure. Fragen Sie Personalabteilung PM-10. Wir haben der Zukunft ein Ziel gesetzt. Compur, ein Unternehmen der Bayer AG. sucht Chemieingenieur. Steinstraße 15. MAN: CAD-Layouter, Dipl. Ing. Fachrichtung Werkstoff für Planung. (IV,246)

The work he learned to do, and the work that has shaped his identity, is no longer in demand.

Desperate for income, the brother begins to sell his blood for plasma. Even such extreme measures prove inadequate and he sees himself forced to draw his sister into his efforts. Although originally he had essentially kept his sister a prisoner in the apartment to avoid her exploitation, he eventually forces her into prostitution. She is ravaged physically for 20 marks while her brother is literally and figuratively bleeding to death. Gradually, but systematically, the city takes from the siblings the remnants of their former identities. It takes their blood, their dignity and their physical well-being.

Despite the hardships they face and the arbitrary character of success in capitalism, their innocent faith in Christ as the giver of life and the source of comfort remains strong. It has not, however, remained unchanged. Their religious roots have withered and they respond by attempting to resuscitate the body of Christ, by attempting to force the second coming of the messiah. Even as he lies in bed connected to a society that demands his blood in return for a minimum existence, the brother offers his own blood to Christ. The sister, in fact, tries to force-feed him:

> *Tochter*: (*nimmt Blut zum Opfern*) Dua niz vaschiddn, es is as Bluad vom Bruadan, es isas deirigste wosma no hom, du bisd koid und dirr, gei, du bliatst nimma! Sunsd kannst epps beisteian zim Lem. . . . Awa du saufsd as bloß, sogsd niz und gibsd nix! (*lauter*) Des muaß an End hom! (*leiser*) Es is da scho vagunnd, awa a es Heagodl muaß fia sei Lem sorgn und ned bloß saufa, wos erm andane hischdein!
>
> *Sohn*: Laß mein Heagod schde, es is mei Bluad und i gibs erm gern, wea gern gibd dea kriagd doppeid zruck. Wenna wieda a Grafd hod na gibda. (IV,252)

In their eagerness to revive a flagging source of spiritual comfort, they reinstitute the blood sacrifice of earlier historic periods. Nonetheless, even such a sacrificial gesture receives no response from the broken and battered Christ figure. The presence of Christ in the play is pervasive, but it does little more than remind the audience of unfulfilled promises.

In the face of a growing sense of isolation and loss, the siblings turn to other sources for emotional sustenance. For instance, they try to recreate within the concrete walls of their apartment the nurturing aspects of their life in the country. The brother hauls mounds of dirt home, buys rabbits and goats, and orders his sister to grow their own food. He even hangs a giant poster of a waterfall on a wall, but as his sister explains to him, "Af meine Händ is koa Seng mea–" (IV,258). At every level, the individual and the societal, there is no life. There is only stagnation and death.

Broken, the two attempt to return home with what little they have left: themselves and their god. Home, however, is now only the plot in which their parents lie. They come back to face the death of their past, their present and their future. As their last declaration of their own identity, they die: "Wie zum Schlafen legt sich der Sohn auf den niederen Grabhügel, die Tochter nagelt den Christus an ein Kreuz, dann setzt sie sich nieder, zieht ihre nassen Sachen aus, friert und läßt sich einschneien – alle sind heimgekehrt" (IV,262). Their quest to find paradise by means of technology and progress has ended in self-destruction. Theirs is a resolute and quiet suicide. After Edgar of *Nicht Fisch nicht Fleisch* strips himself naked and tries to swim himself clean, he returns to the warmth of the home. Although obviously not a source of ecstasy, Helga's kitchen does provide nourishment and warmth. The sister in *Bauern sterben* strips off her wet clothes, but only in order to embrace death. Her home is the frozen earth of her parents' grave.

This rendition of what happens in this play would give the impression that *Bauern sterben* offers its audience a coherent, cohesive narrative. In fact, the piece contains many elements of the fantastic and of heavily, sometimes glaringly blatant, symbolism: plasma donations, society as literally sucking the life blood from the siblings; prostitution as the metaphorical emotional violation of the sister; a wooden figure of Christ, broken off at the knees, dragged down from the cross and into the profane realm of man; and freezing death. It cites implicitly the world of the fairy tale, but fails to deliver the promised happy ending. It evokes the mystery plays of the Middle Ages, but offers no redemption. Moray McGowan sees in *Bauern sterben* the pattern of the expressionist *Stationendrama*.[25] Yet another critic describes the play as follows, "Bruchstücke spielen sich zu Welttheater auf."[26] In other words, the play's various elements create a cosmic scope, but it is a cosmos that does not cohere. With this play and *Der Nusser* (premiered in 1986[27]) Kroetz has radically departed from his erstwhile kitchen realism and has entered the realm of the surreal.

The Politics of *Bauern sterben*

The discussion in earlier chapters repeatedly brought up the restrictions that Kroetz's realist techniques had placed on his work. It is clear in *Bauern sterben* that he is trying to expand the boundaries of his previous pieces, in a sense subsuming the small nuclear family into the symbolic family of "man." He has dissolved the bonds he once constructed between his work and reality as he perceived it. In the program to his own production of the piece he writes: "Das Stück spielt irgendwo zwischen Landshut und Kalkutta." Instead of locating the story in a specific city such as Lienz, or Munich, or even a specific region such as Oberösterreich, Kroetz identifies the location of *Bauern sterben* as somewhere on earth. The geographical vagueness essentially raises a claim to universality – somewhere between Landshut and Calcutta could be anywhere.

However, it also brings up questions about his intended audience and about the general validity of the symbols he employs. The basic conflict presented here is indeed broad enough to accommodate its application to several different and distinct concrete situations, each, in turn, giving rise to varying interpretations. However, in brief it is the clash of the rural and the urban, of sensuous religiosity in the simple, backward world of *Heimat* and the instrumentalization of reason by the domineering, all-consuming demon: the city.

Problems arise, though, when one attempts to apply this metaphorical juxtaposition to a select reality. Can the play really fulfill its grandiose claim that it could take place anywhere from Bavaria to India? The answer to this is a definite no. Wolfgang Hammer makes a suggestion that might help the audience deal with Kroetz's dichotomized world:

> Er will ja nicht das Bauernsterben in Bayern darstellen (das hätte auch wenig Bedeutung, da die Entwicklung in der Bundesrepublik weitgehend abgeschlossen ist und die wenigen Bauern zu Agrarunternehmern geworden sind, die für den Markt produzieren). Kroetz will den globalen Zusammenhang herstellen, will zeigen, was den Menschen zwischen Mexiko-Stadt, Lagos, Ankara, Calcutta durch die Landnahme und -flucht, durch die Auslöschung traditioneller Lebensweisen angetan wird.[28]

Hammer specifically calls attention to Kroetz's global intentions and implies that the dramatist was on some kind of pedagogical mission to show (the question is whom) what capitalism's effect on rural culture has been. Although Hammer's explanation of Kroetz's intent provides an interesting point of departure for an analysis of the play, it does not really answer any questions about its self-posited location in the cosmos. Hammer himself realizes this, quickly bringing up the difficulties involved in symbols which are abstract enough to contain the universe, but also potentially so abstract that they lose any relationship to physical reality, remaining as it were on a metaphysical plane. Should any sense of a coherent universe still linger in the minds of the viewers, the chaotic artistic veil of *Bauern sterben* easily clouds the image.

The multiple interpretive possibilities here all raise other questions. For instance, if what Kroetz is truly trying to do is to show the Mexicans, Indians, Turks, etc. the correlations between their development and what has long since happened in Germany, a German audience would seem somehow inappropriate. If what he wanted to do is show the Germans what is happening in Mexico, India, Africa, why does he germanicize to this extent? What is the substance of the comparison?

Does Kroetz's *Bauern sterben* exceed the interpretive capabilities of a theater audience? Or does the piece abdicate its guiding role in its own reception, in the sense that it simply offers a range of symbols, applying only a minimum of conscious structuration? On a more general level, must politically intentioned literature and drama be more explicit and, in a sense, more dictatorial than this piece is? Why are these questions important?

The danger of Kroetz's "irgendwo zwischen Landshut und Kalkutta" is that it runs the risk of being caught between nowhere and Grimm's world of fairy tales. Hammer maintains that Kroetz tried to get around this "drohende blasse 'Irgendwo'" by resorting to a magical realism, a mythologization of reality designed to mediate between the general and the specific. I believe that this mediation fails or is altogether absent, and that one of the consequences of Kroetz's globalization of oppression is political vagueness. Equating Calucutta with Landshut blurs their very different economic and political structures and slurs over the exploitive relationship of the West to the Third World. This equation would not have been possible for the communist Kroetz.

The political multivalence of *Bauern sterben* again brings to mind Adorno's critique of committed art and, in particular, of Brecht in his essay "Zur Kritik des Engagements." Adorno maintains that the illustration of fundamental structural characteristics of capitalism on the stage requires a level of abstraction that reduces the analysis at best to self-understood truths, and at worst to inaccuracy and misinformation. This is indeed the most formidable hurdle political art must face: it must strike a balance between the blatant and the overly abstract.

The Parable: Part I

As a tool for the aesthetic abstraction of a particular subject matter, it might be useful here to take a brief look at Brecht's employment of parables to portray contemporary society. Brecht felt that contemporary events did not belong on the stage in their immediate form, because the audience is always too close to such issues, this closeness preventing it from recognizing the "general" behind the "specific."[29] By removing the fable from the here and now, Brecht hoped to denaturalize the structures beneath certain societal transactions, allowing the members of the theater public to recognize that such transactions are not ordained by God, but rather alterable, subject to human planning and manipulation. In Brecht's *Der Messingkauf* the philosopher explains that the task of the theater is not just to present reality, it must also reveal reality, dissect it in a sense: "Daß die Realität auf dem Theater wiedererkannt wird, ist nur eine der Aufgaben des echten Realismus. Sie muß aber noch durchschaut werden. Es müssen die Gesetze sichtbar werden, welche den Ablauf der Prozesse des Lebens beherrschen" (GW16, 520). The famous Brechtian *Verfremdungs-Effekt* was burdened with this tremendous responsibility, and it is in this context that Brecht attributed such efficiency to the parable.[30] However, Brecht's understanding of this form was such that the parable must always and continuously construct itself in relationship to the "non-aesthetic" realm, i.e. reality. Klaus-Detlef Müller describes this relationship as follows: "Die Parabel ist Vermittlung der unmittelbar erlebten zur gedeuteten und verstandenen Wirklichkeit, ein ästhetisches Medium in einem in seiner Ganzheit außerästhetischen Vorgang."[31] The parable is not structured merely to effect a recognition of reality, rather it is intended as a provocation to change the circumstances portrayed. It is designed to assist the public in its efforts to master its own situation. In other words, it is intrinsically bound to social practice. What results when the parable is divorced from this practice is an empty abstraction.[32]

Müller claims that post-Brechtian authors have done just this: they have broken up the indivisible duo of theory and practice because of their scepticism about drama's ability to change anything, let alone social practice: "Unter dieser Prämisse wird die Aufklärung um ihre praktische Dimension verkürzt . . . Skepsis und Resignation sind im Appell immer schon mitenthalten."[33] It is possible to interpret this scepticism and resignation in terms of socio-political changes, but that would not necessarily invalidate the critique, it would only serve as an explanation.

Kroetz's relationship to Brechtian aesthetic theory has been highly ambivalent. Early in his career, Kroetz claimed not to have been familiar with Brechtian aesthetics, but a growing dissatisfaction with his work up until *Oberösterreich*, and Brecht's reputation as a communist, led him to look in Brecht's work for answers to his aesthetic dilemma.[34] He writes in a notation to *Münchner Kindl*:

> Der Radikal-Realismus ist nicht in der Lage den 2. Schritt zu tun. Zum zweiten Schritt eignen sich am besten die Mittel Brechts, daß die Darsteller, losgelöst aus ihrem soziologischen Hintergrund, frei sind und Informationen, Appelle, Zusammenfassungen und geschichtliche Zusammenhänge direkt an das Publikum weitergeben können.[35]

Nonetheless, his first published attempt to interpret Brecht was riddled with misunderstanding and revealed an overly simplistic understanding of the principles behind the Brechtian *Lehrstück*, not to mention Brecht's understanding of the political subject.[36] Although he makes a few awkward attempts to apply what he considers to be Brechtian aesthetic techniques in both *Dolomitenstadt Lienz* and *Sterntaler*, he obviously does not feel comfortable doing so. By 1977 and the writing of *Der stramme Max*, Kroetz had already abandoned his interest in a replication of Brechtian aesthetics, defending instead his own preferred limited realism. In an interview with Richard Blevins Kroetz states:

Von dem [großen Parabel] bin ich also längst weggegangen. Ich habe mich eben hier wieder zu meiner Form entschlossen, wobei ich der Meinung bin, daß es eine reaktionäre Position ist, diesen Stücken die Größe sozusagen abzusprechen, und sie nur als kleine, individuelle Dramen gelten zu lassen. Diese Stücke sind sehr wohl, im wahrsten Sinn des Wortes, große, die Gesellschaft betrachtende Stücke, und es ist ganz und gar nicht notwendig, daß der Unternehmer auftritt, der die Figur (den Max) in diese Dinge bringt.[37]

Driven onto the defensive by an increasing and almost pervasive rejection of his realism, Kroetz seeks to justify his refocusing on his more established aesthetic form, discrediting objections to his aesthetic paradigm that he had previously accepted as valid. One could argue, in fact, that Kroetz's earlier attempt to write a parable-like work, namely *Agnes Bernauer*, failed because he could not overcome his still largely realist aesthetic.[38] Rolf-Peter Carl argues that *Agnes Bernauer* lacks the distance from empirical reality it would need to exhibit to qualify as a parable.

These renewed efforts to legitimize the realist aesthetic and rather limited focus of his most successful works mark an increasing insecurity about his own work that was brewing, but did not come out completely until 1980. When Ursula Reinhold reinterviewed Kroetz then, he was attempting to realign his aesthetic strategy with the historical *Volksstück* of a playwright like Nestroy, going back beyond both Horváth and Fleißer, his stated aesthetic models at the onset of his career:

Als Methode ... interessiert mich heute Brecht nicht mehr. Dieser letzte Satz impliziert, als Methode habe er mich schon einmal interessiert. Meine Einschränkung: In meinen Aufsätzen sicher, im realen Schreiben wenig. (Denn auch dort, wo ich zum Beispiel Songs verwende, hab ich immer mehr an Nestroy als an Brecht gedacht.)[39]

This last citation represents yet another of Kroetz's strategic theoretical discrepancies, and it would not be wise to attribute too much significance to it as an accurate rendition of the aesthetic intentions behind *Sterntaler* or *Dolomitenstadt Lienz*. However, they are helpful as guides to an interpretation of *Bauern sterben*, insofar as it demonstrates his continued search for an adequate aesthetic form, a search that led him to the parable-like form of this work from 1985. An essay by Martin Walser from 1962 suggests that the parable constitutes an aesthetic response to the inadequacies of more traditional aesthetic modes (such as realism): "Die freischwebende Fabel, dieser absurde Vogel, ist entstanden aus der Einsicht in die Unbrauchbarkeit überlieferter Abbildungsverhältnisse."[40] In other words, Kroetz apparently began in the eighties to approach the position of the anti-realists in the realism debate of the late sixties and early seventies.

Without implying that Kroetz's *Bauern sterben* must be viewed as a parable in the *Brechtian* sense, we are clearly faced with a highly abstract, symbolically laden work. Walter Hinck's definition of the parable differs slightly from that of Müller. He writes:

> Sie erspart der sozialen Dramatik den Zwang zur naturalistischen Form. Indem sie aus der Realität nur ihre Strukturen, nicht ihr Außen übernimmt, genauer: indem sie eine bestimmte gesellschaftliche Wirklichkeit nicht in sklavischer Bestandsaufnahme abschildert, sondern an einem Gleichnisfall demonstriert, ermöglicht sie die poetische Umschreibung.[41]

Absent from Hinck's description is the assertion that the parable is a "provocation to change the circumstances portrayed," which allows one to label a work a parable without attaching to it the moment of activism. This, however, does not obviate the question of whether Kroetz's parable inherently calls for social change. Does it instead only contain the author's scepticism and resignation when confronted with the loss of the rural tradition as an area in which human beings at one time formed and located their historical and social identity? The answer to such a question and to whether *Bauern sterben* is or is not a parable in a Brechtian sense, in a non-Brechtian sense or at all, must wait until the analysis of the piece has come a little further.

Obviously the play does not present either the city or the rural *Heimat* of these characters as a place where they can find themselves, so to speak. They cannot, therefore, function as positive models. Then how do these two polar opposites play themselves out and how are they described in this piece? As we have seen, the brother finds out, while desperately seeking work, that the city not only has no work, but also no place for him in its heart. He tells the sorry tale of looking for employment and of how his identity is taken from him systematically as the city buys and sells its labor force:

Sohn:	Mi hoaßns bei de Arbadslosn in da Großmarkdhalle an Bauan, und wenns amoi a bor Schdund an Arbad gibd, nachat sogi dem Iagavorsteha i hoaß Baua.
Tochter:	Hoaßd ned.
Sohn:	Reithmaringer moga ned schreim, des is erm zlong. . . . De Schdod mog mein Noma ned, de radiad erm aus. De Schdod nimmt oam s Gsicht. Zerscht an Nam, na de Schbroch, nachat as Gsicht, do bleibt nix, da Kopf werd zaquetscht. (IV,247)

Kroetz reenacts the experience of many immigrants to the United States, whose names were changed arbitrarily by immigration officials, who had neither the patience nor the interest in understanding their actual names. Here the search for work reduces the individual to a generic quantity: farmer (*Bauer*); any distinguishing characteristics are irrelevant to the city. The impersonal city literally squeezes the individual into a recognizable object. The brother speaks only of the psychological impact life in the city has had on him. In what seems to be a last-minute realization of why the calves were calling to them, the sister draws attention to the physical impact urban isolation has had on them. She reduces the characterization of the city as an evil entity to one sentence, "Die Stadt is der Metzger" (IV,251). The equation of city and butcher is unnecessarily reductive. What is at stake here is not an adequately differentiated portrait of the modern city, but rather its wholesale condemnation.

Kroetz is not necessarily, as some critics have implied, creating in contrast a rural idyll.[42] Life in the country hardly receives a more favorable treatment than does life in the city. Once brother and sister realize that there is no place for them in the land of their dreams, the brother packs his belongings, namely his sister and his god, on his back and sets out for home. It is eminently clear that this return will not end in happiness. Put simply and succinctly, the *Heimat* of *Bauern sterben* is death. It is in fact Christ alone who can actually return home, although in order to do so he must be nailed to his cross one more time. There are only two options presented here: death in the city and death in the country.

It is, I believe, safe to assume that neither alternative will strike an audience as desirable. If, just for the sake of argument, one decides to view this work as a provocation to change certain societal structures, what could be changed and how could one effect such a change? Does this piece demonstrate what happens to human beings when they allow their bond to nature (*Heimat*) and their commitment to an ever-rejuvenating mythology (Christ) to wither and die? In other words, have human beings obliterated the ties to those areas in which they have traditionally shaped their identity? Must humans freeze to death in the chilly wasteland of technology? If this is indeed what the play describes, then it shall surely have found sympathizers within any one of the many new social movements in West Germany during the first half of the last decade.

New Social Movements: The Dispersion of the Political

In the mid- to late seventies there arose, as was touched upon briefly in the preceding chapter, a number of issue-oriented political initiatives that sought to affect political practice and public policy on a very circumscribed level. There were, for instance, citizens' initiatives to stop the building of additional runways at the Frankfurt airport and a plethora of neighborhood initiatives for urban improvements – parks, community centers, etc. There were also groups whose focus was larger: the ecology movement (later institutionalized in the Green Party), the anti-nuclear power movement, and the peace movement – to name just a few. After the virtual dissolution of the extra-parliamentary movement in 1969, many of the students and participants became disillusioned with globalizing theories of revolution and dogmatic and/ or authoritarian political praxis. The early seventies are often described as a period in which these tired students turned away from politics and into themselves. Just as clear, however, is the fact that the seeds for localized political action had been around since at least the beginnings of the peace movement in the fifties. New venues for political activism came about with the increasing presence of these smaller initiatives. Within these new social movements various political constituencies – from the academic to the non-academic, and from the left to the right – found that they could work together toward a goal without submitting entirely to an all-encompassing political philosophy.

Direct comparisons to Kroetz's political and aesthetic experimentation may be impossible. Whether he intentionally incorporates concerns from, for instance, the ecology movement is questionable, particularly since Kroetz's artistic identity crisis seems to stem in the main from his perception of drama's political ineffectuality and from the public's apparent apathy. Furthermore, there is always the danger that such a direct comparison may reduce the multiplicity of voices, strategies and foci of such a wide variety of social groupings.

Nonetheless, there are thematic and argumentative similarities between Kroetz's work and certain factions within the broad range of new social movements that merit examination.

One area of similarity touches on the question of individual and social identity. In fact, Joachim Raschke locates the sociological origins of the new social movements in a profound identity crisis resulting from a change in values, growing prosperity and the concomitant increase in disastrous ecological and social consequences.[43] Elim Papadakis goes as far as to say that at least within the ecological movement "the greatest psychological burden of its supporters is the fear of isolation and loss of personal and collective identity."[44] The "progress at all costs" mentality of contemporary society was credited with the destruction of the basic means for the reproduction of human life. In this context, the search for an alternative ideological community, within which one could both escape from and confront society's self-destruction, would seem to represent the attempt to reestablish the identity in crisis mentioned earlier.

Since at least 1980 Kroetz too has been toying with the notion of identity, psychological, social and political – in general and in specific, i.e. his own. How is it formed and what is its current status? Is our conceptualization of our own identity intact or in crisis? In *Nicht Fisch nicht Fleisch* one of the main characters undergoes a very painful self-examination, the immediate culmination of which leads him to seek desperately his primal roots, to find *the* man, not a man in the completely rationalized technological world of the twentieth century. He seeks, in other words, to relocate himself as a human being, since he has lost his sense of who we are. The siblings of *Bauern sterben* also futilely try to create for themselves an identity apart from and yet part of both their conservative heritage and the thoroughly rationalized world of high-tech society.

This floundering sense of self has arisen against the backdrop of profound structural changes in human society. The omnipresent bureaucracy of contemporary society has developed into a political system, whose input structure is largely closed off to potential societal conflicts and new interest constellations. In fact, it seems to function quasi-autonomously. Institutional pathways for the individual to influence and/or to articulate political protest are severely restricted. This has at least contributed to the exodus of political protest from the traditional political arena. The reaction of the extra-parliamentary opposition of the seventies (later partially institutionalized in the Green Party) to the problems with which they saw themselves and society confronted was quite ambivalent.

In some quarters, a new catastrophism supplanted the revolutionary optimism of the student movement. And such pessimism pervades Kroetz's *Bauern sterben*. At the latest from *Der stramme Max* to *Nicht Fisch nicht Fleisch* and from *Nicht Fisch nicht Fleisch* to *Bauern sterben* we see the development of an increasingly overwhelming resignation *vis-à-vis* political activism. As Kroetz's characters develop intellectually, their options for resistance, for improving their own personal and, to an extent, society's lot become ever fewer. The only real option presented in *Nicht Fisch nicht Fleisch* was a return to the center of the traditional nuclear family. In *Bauern sterben* suicide is the characters' answer to or protest against the societal structures that have destroyed their past and ensured that they do not find a space for themselves in the technology-driven world of the city. Whereas many of the new social movements sought answers to this political impasse in localized and focused activities, Kroetz's parabolic vision ends in death.

Again, it would be indefensible to make dogmatic generalizations about such highly divergent social formations, but certain argumentative strategies within new social movements do take recourse to an individualistic emotional appeal, invoking the individual's psychological needs and fears. Raschke describes these strategies in the following way, "Argumentiert wird unter Bezugnahme auf Lebensformen, Werte, kulturelle Praktiken, Gefühle (z.B. Angst), Bedürfnisse, Identitätsansprüche, also lebensweltliche Argumentationen."[45] In other words, the systemic Marxist critique of capitalism gives way to a more focused critique of structures in contemporary society that stand between individuals and that illusive sense of self-fulfillment. A good example of this is the following passage from an early version of the Green Party's program:

> Ein völliger Umbruch unseres kurzfristig orientierten wirtschaftlichen Zweckdenkens ist notwendig. Wir halten es für einen Irrtum, daß die jetzige Verschwendungswirtschaft noch das Glück und die Lebenserfüllung fördere; im Gegenteil, die Menschen werden immer gehetzter und unfreier. Erst in dem Maße, wie wir uns von der Überschätzung des materiellen Lebensstandards freimachen, wie wir wieder die Selbstverwirklichung ermöglichen und uns wieder auf die Grenzen unserer Natur besinnen, werden auch die schöpferischen Kräfte frei werden für die Neugestaltung eines Lebens auf ökologischer Basis.[46]

Implicit to the critique of economically driven politics is a critique of capitalist economies in general, but the emphasis quickly shifts to the idea that our current socio-political philosophy and practice do not lend themselves to the self-realization of the individual. The given structures hamper rather than further the individual's creative potential and thwart efforts to envision and implement a less hostile relationship to our environment. It is less a structural critique of an exploitive capitalist system than a specific attack on particular phenomena seen to have been born of this society.

Kroetz's critical work has followed a similar path. The surety of *Das Nest* gradually weakened in the plays that followed. *Nicht Fisch nicht Fleisch* still offered a rigorous critique of capitalism, but it already brought out the limits of such a critique by depicting the concerns of individuals that did not fit into a highly structured analysis. *Bauern sterben* takes this even further in its portrayal of the emotional damage generated by the excessive processes of rationalization and technological progress. A comparison of the strategy in *Bauern sterben* with that found within new social movements would reveal in both the call for an alternative to the dichotomized choice between the pre-technological world of "the country" and the dangerous and unreflective world of incessant technological progress. Both also continue to seek other answers for society's problems than what Marxism has to offer.

Kroetz and Marxism

Although Kroetz's position in the mid-eighties bears striking similarities to the highly personalized and eclectic political strategies gathered within the various new social movements of the late seventies and early eighties, it would be misleading to conclude that he has rejected Marxist philosophy completely, simply because his plays no longer propagate Marxist solutions to contemporary societal problems. *Bauern sterben* does, after all, contain a typical Kroetzian critique of the problem of unemployment in capitalist societies. It remains, however, on a fairly abstract plane, as his main concern here is with personal identity and, in that context, with what he still perceives as labor's immanent role in the formation of that identity. Kroetz himself has played down the political character of the play's focus. When asked why he felt – as author – that the piece was too unpolitical he responded: "Es hat keinen konkreten Status. Die Stadt als anonymer Täter zum Beispiel: Das kann man schon ein bißchen genauer sagen, wer Flüchtlingselend und Arbeitslosigkeit erzeugt, was da los ist usw."[47] His own criticism of the work demonstrates how fundamental certain Marxist tenets are in his analytical thinking. He cannot comfortably brand the city as criminal without offering a characterization of what constitutes its criminality. His previous works at least made reference to those whom Kroetz saw as the engineers of socio-economic injustice, but *Bauern sterben* no longer seems able to specify the structural sources or the power brokers that have led to such vast physical and emotional destruction.

Indeed, the lack of an explicit political stance, or at least an explicitly Marxist stance, in this piece is a consequence of more than just aesthetic imprecision. There is yet another political dimension to *Bauern sterben* which has not been the central focus of this analysis, but which deserves at least a brief examination. The discussion up to this point has treated this play as an expression of post-materialist values and also as a post-Marxian work in the author's own development. However, another aspect of this work underscores both the degree to which Kroetz's political thinking was shaped by the orthodox Marxism of the DKP and the extent of his disillusionment with this constrictive doctrine. That aspect is the opposition of agriculture and industry.

The confrontation of the largely agricultural countryside with the proletarian dominance in the large cities was an item of contention already for Marx himself. Marx, Engels and Lenin all believed that the proletariat would lead the revolution and also communist society after the means of production had been wrested from the hands of the bourgeoisie. They further believed that the agricultural wage laborer and the small landowner would be driven out of economic existence with the advance of large-scale farming, which itself, as a correlation to industrial production, seemed the logical progression in agricultural production. According to Lenin, once dispossessed and on the verge of extinction, these factions of the peasantry would join the urban proletariat in their struggle to overcome the strictures of capitalist class society. The younger Kroetz seemed to share or at least accept this vision of the future. In the 1977 interview with Richard Blevins Kroetz paints a rather optimistic picture of the effects an industrialization of agriculture would have:

> Erst wenn die Industrialisierung der Landwirtschaft wirklich durchgeführt ist, dann wird eben dieses Stadt-Land-Gefälle angleichbar sein. Gerechtigkeit und Gleichheit wird dadurch durchsetzbar sein: das ist die Hypothese, die ich für richtig finde. Das war hochinteressant, anhand der DDR Landwirtschaftsentwicklung diese Industrialisierung zu studieren – wobei die Projektionen für die Zukunft, teilweise, interessanter waren als die Teilergebnisse der Gegenwart.[48]

Indeed, the positive projections Kroetz mentioned never overcame whatever partial results were attained in Marxist-oriented economies. The Marxist-Leninist promise of social unity among the exploited classes during and after the glorious revolution never materialized. Kroetz does portray the tradition of the small landholder as bleeding dry-faced with the wide-scale purchase of land by corporate agricultural enterprises, but the peasant in *Bauern sterben* seeks solace and support in the city in vain.

The Marxist hope for a proletarian revolution has been subverted from many angles, and Kroetz addresses some of these in *Bauern sterben*. The growing emphasis on non-materialist values in the new social movements conflicts with the realization of materialist goals in orthodox Marxist political strategies. They were assaulted from another side through the integrative powers of the capitalist economy, which provided the working class with an ideological home within the larger community. As discussed above, the actual character and composition of the traditional working class has changed so radically in this century as to call into question its very existence. In fact, the traditional proletariat is rapidly dwindling in number as industrial production gives way to a post-industrial, service-oriented economy. The vision of a classless communist society that informed Kroetz's dramatic production since the early seventies has gradually fragmented, in a sense, into the still relatively well-delineated collage of the various citizens' initiatives and issue-oriented social movements.

The argumentative strategy in *Bauern sterben* relies heavily on its creation of the mythic cosmic subject who is empty enough for Kroetz to pour into him[49] all of the fears and problems of the modern individual. This modern man must, it appears, die if he cannot successfully mediate between tradition and progress, between the past, the present and the future. The play provides no such mediation and the audience watches as the world in which the cosmic individual lives gradually freezes over.

The Parable: Part II

The analysis of this play has now come far enough to address again the question of whether *Bauern sterben* is a parable, and, as such, a radical departure from his previous aesthetic models. The abstract character of the play's plot, the relatively generic nature of the brother and sister figures, and the absence of any really meaningful historical references all combine to legitimize the label parable for *Bauern sterben*. I would argue, however, that the pervasive resignation of the work and its overwhelming negativity preclude reading it as an experiment in Brechtian aesthetics. C.D. Innes offers what could be an apt description of *Bauern sterben* as parable: "The negative parable is so forceful that, instead of leading to the rejection of specific social evils, the impression is of cruelty as a universal, unchangeable human condition."[50] The problem with the description is that Innes was not writing about Kroetz, but rather Heiner Müller, an (East) German playwright, whose importance for the German stage began in the seventies and continued to increase throughout the eighties.

With works such as *Der Lohndrücker* (1956) and *Der Bau* (1963/64), Heiner Müller established a reputation as a political dramatist. As his work developed, Müller, like Kroetz, began to experiment formally, although unlike Kroetz he never returned to the formally realist aesthetic that characterizes *Der Lohndrücker*. Instead he pursued an increasingly abstract and non-representative aesthetic, whose often hermetic character makes any easy interpretation impossible. In the late seventies Müller articulated a definition of a political aesthetic that strains the confines of the word "political." He says to Bernard Umbrecht, "ich glaube schon, so bescheiden das klingt, die politische Hauptfunktion von Kunst ist jetzt, Phantasie zu mobilisieren." Borrowing a phrase from the philosopher Wolfgang Heise, he further describes the theater as a laboratory of social fantasy.[51]

Ten years later Kroetz offers *Die Welt* a new definition of his aesthetic project that seizes on essentially the same terminology as Müller: "Heute möchte ich gerne mit dem, was ich tue, Phantasiebomben legen."[52] In a very broad sense the furtherance of social fantasy could be construed as a political project, but it in no way resembles a structural critique of society, such as was Kroetz's goal in the pieces from *Oberösterreich* and *Das Nest* to *Der stramme Max*. The fact that both Müller and Kroetz come to this conclusion about the possibility for political aesthetics is odd. Even more peculiar is that they are only two in a long list of once committed authors who reach this point.

Peter Handke, who acted as something of an aesthetic nemesis for Kroetz in the seventies, noted in 1968 that the theater could not function as the locus for the contestation of political programs. Theater, he argues, is *Spiel*, it formalizes, i.e. aestheticizes everything. Handke writes:

> Wozu es taugen könnte (wozu es bisher auch getaugt hat): als Spielraum zur Schaffung bisher unentdeckter innerer Spielräume des Zuschauers, als ein Mittel durch das das Bewußtsein des einzelnen nicht *weiter*, aber *genauer* wird, als ein Mittel zum Empfindlichmachen: zum Reizbarmachen: zum Reagieren: als ein Mittel, auf die Welt zu kommen.[53]

Theater as a means to explore undiscovered inner territories, to expand consciousness, to make the individual more sensitive differs only slightly from Müller's fantasy laboratory and Kroetz's fantasy bombs. (They are all, furthermore, tantalizingly close to Adorno's idea that art's function is to hold open a space for a humanity undamaged by the instrumentalization of reason and the culture industry.) And yet, Handke's position was an extremely unpopular one in 1968, and one that Kroetz emphatically rejected as elitist. How can one account for this shift in position?

Some of the historical developments that have accompanied Kroetz's career have already been the focus of at least a cursory examination, developments that could explain in part Kroetz's new definition of his aesthetic project, but his search for a political aesthetic has also repeatedly trained his attention on the nature of the political subject. Perhaps a summary of how his views on the subject have changed will explain how Kroetz could come to embrace a concept of the theater he so decidedly turned away from almost twenty years earlier.

Kroetz and the Political Subject

In fact, in a discussion of political aesthetics it would be irresponsible, perhaps even impossible, to exclude a thematization of the political itself, or, in this case, of the political subject.[54] The possibility for political action depends on an agent. Without that agent the concept of politics becomes a conglomeration of letters void of any significance. I would argue that both changes to an aesthetic program and changing views of the political subject are inseparable in a description of Kroetz's development.

In 1971 Kroetz wrote the following about the political nature of the theater: "Theater soll politisch sein, es muß es sein, denn es spielt vor Volk und es zeigt Volk und das ist ein Vorgang, der permanent politisch ist" (WA, 521). Such a conception of the necessarily political character of the theater may not inform his very earliest works. However, by the time Kroetz wrote *Oberösterreich* he was adamant in his assertion that art served an important political function and that to deny this or to attempt to circumvent it was tantamount to support for the oppressive structures he saw prevalent in contemporary society. *Oberösterreich*, and, *de facto*, the first one-act plays constitute an attempt on Kroetz's part to portray the structural violence endemic to capitalist society. Various aspects of these pieces, however, thwarted the author's intentions.

One major limitation of these works is their lack of a clear perspective. This absence is a result of both structural elements and factors related to the content of the plays. Kroetz's realist techniques impose on the audience a particular interpretation of reality that closes itself off to contradiction: what you see is what you get. The characters the dramatist portrays are, however, virtually incapable of resistance.

Hardly more than the puppets of an exploitive capitalist consciousness industry, they cannot act as agents of politically conscious behavior. *Oberösterreich*'s realist style leaves little room for alternative readings of empirical reality and it leaves the audience without a viable political subject.

Das Nest takes up the problem of the political subject, attempting to locate the source of political consciousness. In a personal confrontation with the destructive logic of capitalist production, the major protagonist recognizes that prevailing societal structures have, in a sense, blinded him to the exploitive and dangerous aspects of a production-at-all-costs mentality. He chooses to take a stand against his employer. He consciously decides to act in a political manner, but he opts to do so in a very specific context: that of the labor union.

With the citation of union activism, Kroetz places *Das Nest* solidly within the framework of the class-based theory of social structure in orthodox Marxism. This view of identity formation as embedded in the economic stratification of society offers the individual a framework for political action. It also provides the individual with a battery of interpretive tools necessary for the development of a strategy of resistance. Chapter two discussed at length the adequacy of an orthodox Marxist analysis of contemporary society. Kroetz himself seems to have recognized that persuasive arguments hold Marxism to be an anachronistic and exclusionary (in the sense of disallowing competing explanations) theory of social organization. *Nicht Fisch nicht Fleisch* offers evidence of the author's uneasiness with a rigid application of Marxist social theories and with traditional labor politics. Thus, as Kroetz creates a more viable political subject in his dramatic world, the once clearly defined boundaries of that world begin to dissolve.

In *Nicht Fisch nicht Fleisch*, post-materialist values and conflicts confront Marxism with the limits of its own explanatory powers. Among the inadequacies the play calls to the fore is the inability of a collectivist, comprehensive social theory to address effectively the needs of individuals in a post-industrial world. *Nicht Fisch nicht Fleisch* uncovers the structural limits placed on potential political action with the increasingly anonymous administration of social being. The work portrays futile attempts at resistance, but the status quo prevails. Although the characters in the play are reasoning, intellectually competent human beings, they simply cannot combat the pervasiveness and efficiency of oppressive structures. Moray McGowan phrases this development as follows, "he now shows that the step out of object existence lays bare the painful conflicts between individual and social existence, conflicts which the progress from object to subject may intensify rather than resolve."[55] As Kroetz's political subject grows into what resembles Kantian *Mündigkeit*, its options for self-expression (for publicity) dwindle. It is in this work that the concept of an autonomous, effective political subject itself enters a crisis stage.

The individual in *Bauern sterben*, recently dislodged from center stage in the cosmos, sets off to locate and/or relocate a certain or sure identity. In the evil metropolis Kroetz's characters confront in its absence a materialist, proletarian utopia. The promised urban Eden proves to be an anachronistic, exclusionary and inadequate fiction. Capitalism continues to ban those who do not fit into one of the roles predetermined to ensure its continuing success.

On the other hand, the piece also rejects a naturalist, spiritualist tradition (*Heimatliebe* and occidental Christianity). The bonds to the land and to God have become brittle and threaten to, or, as in most cases, have already snapped. Just as reified as human experience in Kroetz's urban nightmare, the image of the idyllic peasant home has frozen over into an icy grave. The past, the present and the future all fall silent as the roar of technological progress overpowers any sounds of dissent.

What conclusions about the status of the political subject can one draw from the development it has undergone up to this point in Kroetz's work? The progress of society toward the safeguarding of human life has done irreparable harm to the emotional being of the individual. The demands of an all-pervasive bureaucracy and the logic of capitalist production and distribution have, in effect, forced a virtual mutation of the species. The structural limits placed on behavior resistant to the will of administration have successfully channelled such behavior away from effective political opposition. Whereas Kroetz once sought to portray the viable political agent, he now registers its absence. It is perhaps not the total absence of a viable subject, but the absence of viable venues for political and personal expression. But is this melancholic rejection of autonomous political action necessarily a rejection of the political or of political agency altogether?

It might appear that Kroetz has revised his views on the integrity of the political subject completely, bringing him much closer to Adorno, who has repeatedly emphasized the virtual absence of any human autonomy. This is, however, not quite the case. Kroetz is instead attempting to redefine the process of subject-formation by making use of societal configurations that do not coincide entirely with a Marxist social analysis. The characters in *Bauern sterben* may not be able to effect the changes in lifestyle they seek, but they are far from being unsuspecting pawns in the game to determine who controls the means of production. Their suicide is both an act of despair and an act of defiance. One might question the desirability of their decision, but one cannot deny that it is an absolute refusal to participate any further in their own exploitation. It is unlikely that Kroetz will eventually reject Marxism entirely as an interpretive tool, but it is clear that he is searching for new perspectives on the issue of identity and subject in a post-materialist context.

There are hints, in fact, that Kroetz is simply retooling his particular vision of the political landscape. Once he abandoned his attempts to fit the world into a Marxist analysis, his work began to open up space for social forces that had not received attention before.[56] Theoretical rigidity has given way to political eclecticism. In the program to *Bauern sterben* Kroetz states:

> Ich unterstütze nun immer, wo es eben geht, die Grünen oder die Friedensbewegung. . . . Nach meiner eigenen politischen Überzeugung hätte ich ohne weiteres im Saarland Oskar Lafontaine unterstützen können. Genauso habe ich hier in München, eine 'Bürgerinitiative Künstlerliste' unterschrieben und zur Wahl der DKP aufgerufen. . . . Und genauso hatte ich bei den Bundestagswahlen die Grünen unterstützt.[57]

This political patchwork quilt corresponds to the reduction of the political in his aesthetic project mentioned above. Although he has not turned completely from an emphasis on the political commitment of the author, he has reshaped that commitment considerably. In a 1986 interview with *konkret* Kroetz states: "Ich habe mich damit abgefunden, daß Literatur nicht eingreifen kann. Wenn überhaupt, dann nur über das radikale Ich des Autors. . . . Nur das Bekenntnis des Autors zu sich selbst wird noch Spuren von Wirkung bei den Menschen hinterlassen."[58] This foregrounding of the artist's self constitutes an extreme personalization of the political. Political conflict as mediated through the ego of the author finds its way into the artwork as the expression of personal alienation and isolation.

Bauern sterben demonstrates that Kroetz has definitely lost his faith in the traditional political subject as it developed in liberal theory. Or rather, he has lost faith in that facet of the liberal individual that made possible autonomous, self-determined political action. Nonetheless, it would be a mistake to assume from this that Kroetz agrees with post-structuralism's gleeful observation of "man's" death. McGowan is correct to emphasize the still immense distance between Kroetz's views of the subject and those of a contemporary like Botho Strauß.[59] In fact, Kroetz's thoughts on the subject are much more empirically bound than the more conceptual, i.e. abstract, construction of the subject in post-modern philosophy, for instance in the work of Michel Foucault. It is, therefore, not surprising that Kroetz's efforts to zoom in on the "radical" authorial self remain focused on behavioral problems rather than on the construction of subjectivity itself. The concluding chapter will continue to explore the questions of political subjectivity and aesthetic strategy, using the three plays *Zeitweh*, *Der Dichter als Schwein* and *Bauerntheater* as referents to look back and forward to Kroetz's dramatic career.

Notes

1. "Franz Xaver Kroetz im Gespräch mit Günter Gaus," Broadcast of the Westdeutscher Rundfunk. 14 Dec. 1986.
2. Zadek, *Franz Xaver Kroetz. Bauern sterben*, pp. 156f.
3. Franz Xaver Kroetz, "Zur Diskussion: Beiträge vom Bonner Parteitag der DKP," *kürbiskern*, no. 3 (1976): p. 164.
4. An analysis of these two sections will follow at a later point in the discussion of this work. (See pp.163–172)
5. "Radikalität" is the term Kroetz uses to describe the way in which art must be produced. In this case, however, it is not politically radical, but rather radically unpolitical, or radically self-absorbed.
6. See also his remarks: "ich kann die Bewegung des westdeutschen Volkes nicht nachvollziehen"; and: "Es ist in den 20 Jahren, in denen ich da bin, politisch nicht vorwärts gegangen. Es ist rückwarts gegangen. Das schafft mir auch den Ekel. Ekel vor Politik und eben auch Ekel vor Leuten, die dafür sorgen – es sind auch Wähler –, daß es zurückgeht. Ich find' mich heute weniger zurecht als vor 20 Jahren."
7. Zadek, p. 160.
8. In chapter one this term applied to a significant refocusing of aesthetic experimentation. Here it refers to the political shift from the social-liberal coalition to the Christian Democratic-liberal coalition that began with Kohl's appointment as chancellor in 1982.
9. See e.g. Renate Schostack, "Landshut am Ganges," *Frankfurter Allgemeine Zeitung*, 12 June 1985.
10. The ridicule of housewives in this passage as individuals unable to control their emotions or maintain an integral sense of self reflects what I would argue is a pervasive misogyny in Kroetz's work throughout his career.
11. Franz Xaver Kroetz, *Furcht und Hoffnung der BRD* (Frankfurt/M.: Suhrkamp Verlag, 1984), p. 228.

12. Although this young comedian would deny the presence of censorship in today's society, the developments related to a play by Kroetz's contemporary, Herbert Achternbusch, which was running concurrently with *Bauern sterben*, would seem to indicate otherwise. At the time these plays were running, the West German government invited two South African dignitaries to visit the Federal Republic. The government did so despite the recent arrest of a West German minister in South Africa, whose only crime was burying two black Christians. To protest against the West German government's implicit sanction of South African politics through its invitation of the two South African diplomats, Sepp Bierbichler, the actor playing the lead role in *Gust*, interrupted his performance to read a statement against apartheid and to distance himself and the theater group from the politics of his government. The reaction of the Bavarian government was to forbid any such political actions in the theater and to threaten the director of the theater with dismissal. See e.g.: *Der Spiegel*, no. 52, 23 Dec. 1985, pp. 153f; *Die Süddeutsche Zeitung*, 9 Dec. 1985; and Joachim Kaiser, "Müssen Künstler vor der 'Kunst' kuschen?" *Die Süddeutsche Zeitung*, 13 Jan. 1986.

Even *Bauern sterben* met with calls for its removal from the season's bill. CSU politicians publicly asked the director of the Münchner Kammerspiele to discontinue the performances of the play. Using logic similar to that employed by Jewish citizens who objected to Fassbinder's *Der Müll, die Stadt und der Tod*, these individuals asserted: "Als Bürger und Christen sind wir . . . zu der Auffassung gelangt, daß hier die Wahl der 'dramatischen Mittel' weit über das Maß hinausgeht." The *Frankfurter Rundschau* quotes the CSU general secretary: "Handelte es sich in dem Frankfurter Stück um die Verletzung der Gefühle unserer jüdischen Mitbürger, einer religiösen Minderheit in der Bundesrepublik Deutschland, so handelt es sich hier beim Kroetz-Stück um die Verletzung der Gefühle von Christen, der religiösen Mehrheit in der Bundesrepublik Deutschland, die sich lediglich nicht so lautstark artikuliert wie die jüdische Minderheit in Frankfurt." He further argued that it was simply not permissible that a theater supported by tax monies should treat its constituency in such a manner. Obviously, censorship, or at least attempted censorship, is indeed still a threat to artistic production. In: *Frankfurter Rundschau*, 23 Dec. 1985.

13. See numerous passages in Adorno, *Ästhetische Theorie*.

14. Ibid., pp. 180f.

15. Ibid.

16. Peter Schneider, *Lenz* (Berlin: Rotbuch Verlag, 1973).

17. *Die Welt*, 5 Oct. 87.

18. *Süddeutsche Zeitung*, 11 June 1985.

19. *Die Zeit*, 14 June 1985.

20. *Theater heute*, no. 7 (1985): p. 22.

21. The family also includes a grandmother, but she is already dead by the time the curtain opens.

22. This is both a reference to his earlier works such as *Das Nest*, as well as a renunciation thereof. Hajo Kurzenberger writes of Kroetz's work up until 1978: "Durchgehender Zug freilich bleibt Kroetzens Sehnsucht nach Positivem: sein Harmoniebedürfnis, sein Verlangen nach Geborgenheit, seine Neigung zur Idylle sprechen aus allen Stücken und ihren Personen, die solches Verlangen teilen." *text + kritik*, no. 57 (Jan. 1978): p. 12. Clearly this search for a protected space has not been successful.

23. Kroetz did eventually write a standardized German version of the work, which is included in volume four of the collected plays.

24. The evocation is, of course, dysfunctional as the relationship between the peasant and the land has already begun to crumble.

25. McGowan, "Botho Strauß and Franz Xaver Kroetz," p. 72.

26. Fischer, "Kroetz stellt seine Wunden aus."

27. First published in: Rudolf Rach (ed.), *Theater* (Frankfurt/M.: Suhrkamp Verlag, 1986), pp. 385–435. Although this piece does not represent a decided retreat from expressly political drama, as one might have expected, the political issues in *Der Nusser* are not constitutive elements. This may stem more from the fact that the play is based on another work, Ernst Toller's "Der deutsche Hinkemann," than from any authorial intent. What it might indicate, therefore, in terms of Kroetz's further development is unclear. Given Kroetz's limited success with the Hebbel adaptations *Maria Magdalena* and *Agnes Bernauer*, I suspect *Der Nusser* will remain an isolated episode in Kroetz's experimental pattern.

28. Wolfgang Hammer, "Verkleinert und verzuckert," *Frankfurter Rundschau*, 2 Dec. 1986.

29. In a discussion with Ernst Schumacher Brecht presented the following argument: "Wenn man das falsche Bewußtsein zerschmettern und das richtige formen will, dann muß man die Menschen vor sich selbst . . . zu sich selbst bringen. Das kann man nicht, indem man ihnen ihresgleichen vorsetzt. Josef kennt Josef so gut, daß ihm alle Josefe schnuppe sind." Ernst Schumacher, *Brecht. Theater und Gesellschaft im 20. Jahrhundert* (Berlin: Henschel Verlag, 1975), p. 16.

30. "Die Parabel ist um vieles schlauer als alle anderen Formen. Lenin hat die Parabel doch nicht als Idealist, sondern als Materialist

gebraucht. Die Parabel gestattete ihm, das Komplizierte zu entwirren. Sie stellt für den Dramatiker das Ei des Kolumbus dar, weil sie in der Abstraktion konkret ist, indem sie das Wesentliche augenfällig macht." Schuhmacher, p. 17.

31. Klaus-Detlef Müller, "Das Ei des Kolumbus? Parabel und Modell als Dramen-Formen bei Brecht, Dürrenmatt, Frisch, Walser," in *Zu Bertolt Brecht: Parabel und Episches Theater*, ed. Theo Buck (Berlin: Henschel Verlag, 1976), pp. 203f.
32. See also ibid., p. 215.
33. Ibid., p. 214.
34. Ursula Schregel describes Kroetz's turn to Brecht as follows: "he associates with Brecht above all the fact 'that he was a Communist.' But Kroetz turns to Brecht the 'fable-maker,' although Kroetz's reduced dramaturgy at first appears to have scarcely anything in common with Brecht's great historical themes. He arrives at Brecht via the common background of a materialist view of life. When Kroetz turned away from the catastrophic events in his plays, he took his first step towards the Brechtian perception of fable." Schregel, p. 475.
35. Rpt. in Riewoldt, *Franz Xaver Kroetz*, p. 103.
36. See "Über DIE MAßNAHME von Bertolt Brecht," WA, 570–582.
37. Rpt. in Richard Wayne Blevins, *Franz Xaver Kroetz: The Emergence of a Political Playwright* (New York, Berne, Frankfurt/M.: Peter Lang, 1983), pp. 275f.
38. Carl, *Franz Xaver Kroetz*, p. 121.
39. Reinhold, pp. 376f.
40. Martin Walser, "Vom Theater, das ich erwarte. Was nötig ist: Nicht die elfenbeinerne sondern die aktive Fabel," in Helmut Kreuzer, *Deutsche Dramaturgie der Sechziger Jahre* (Tübingen: Niemeyer Verlag), p. 21.
41. Walter Hinck, "Von der Parabel zum Straßentheater. Notizen zum Drama der Gegenwart," in Arnold, *Positionen des Dramas: Analysen und Theorien zur deutschen Gegenwartsliteratur,* ed. Heinz Lundwig Arnold (Munich: C.H. Beck, 1977), p. 29.
42. See Fischer, "Kroetz stellt seine Wunden aus."
43. Raschke, pp. 414, 420.
44. Papadakis, p. 25.
45. Raschke, p. 421.
46. *Die Grünen: Das Bundesprogramm* (Bonn: Die Grünen, 1984), p. 4.
47. Zadek, p. 165.
48. Blevins, p. 461. Kroetz recounted his experiences with GDR agricultural policy in a report entitled "Sozialismus auf dem Dorf"

(WA, 427–515). His publisher, the Suhrkamp Verlag of Frankfurt, refused to publish the work because they considered it distorted and amateurish. As a result, Kroetz temporarily severed his relationship with Suhrkamp and published the report in the volume *Weitere Aussichten*. Kroetz himself later criticized the piece as propagandistic.

49. I have intentionally identified the gender of this subject as male. Whether this is a conscious or subconscious decision on the part of the dramatist is of little importance, but it is virtually always a male character who acts as the fulcrum of societal conflict and development in Kroetz's work.

50. Innes, p. 157.

51. Heiner Müller, *Rotwelsch* (Berlin: Merve Verlag, 1982), p. 111.

52. *Die Welt*, 10 Oct. 1987.

53. Peter Handke, "Straßentheater und Theatertheater," in Kreuzer, pp. 126f.

54. I use this term with full knowledge of its problematic character. The concept of the subject and/or individual will be the object of focus at a later point in this chapter.

55. McGowan, "Subject, Politics, Theater," p. 87.

56. The women's movement and its effects on society is one notable example of this.

57. Zadek, pp. 158f.

58. *konkret*, March 86, p. 71.

59. McGowan, "Botho Strauß and Franz Xaver Kroetz," pp. 64 and 73.

—5—

Conclusion: *Zeitweh, Der Dichter als Schwein* and *Bauerntheater*

To what kind of a political subject does Kroetz direct his attention after *Bauern sterben*? Clearly the concept of the political in Kroetz is on the retreat. Just how far it will draw back is impossible to predict. Furthermore, what Franz Xaver Kroetz as an individual does eventually decide also borders on the irrelevant. His decision is relevant only in terms of the political subject his artistic production manifests. That is to say, the way he perceives the status of the political subject is important only within the broader context of a theory of political aesthetics.

Kroetz's work since *Nicht Fisch nicht Fleisch* definitely makes him a participant in the endeavor to redefine the (political) subject. *Bauern sterben* manages finally to rescue the subject from the constraints society places on it, but does so only by killing it off. It seems, however, that a politically committed aesthetic product must engage the individual in a productive manner, it must address him or her in a way that leaves room for more than one response. The following discussion of *Zeitweh* (1986), *Der Dichter als Schwein* (1987) and *Bauerntheater* (1989–1991) considers what has become of *Bauern sterben*'s radical questioning of the individual subject's viability in today's world and whether Kroetz's own project of mediating the political through the artist's radical self actually does what it sets out to do.

The Self and the Subject

Zeitweh was the author's first attempt to realize or concretize his newly discovered interest in the person of the artist, but this development left many of its own traces in the works that preceded it. The previous chapters have already stumbled over a few: the "poor poet" from *Furcht und Hoffnung der BRD*, the "hasty poet" and the comedic trio from *Bauern sterben*, and the various references from interviews in the late eighties. The ancestors of *Dichter Kroetz*, the sole character in *Zeitweh*, all bear autobiographical references, but generally do not go beyond that.

Zeitweh, however, explicitly names "Kroetz"[1] as its main focus. The author's *self-presentation* occurs through an extended monologue, which takes place completely in the playwright's kitchen. Obviously, a direct equation of the character and the person would be problematic, but Kroetz definitely tempts his audience/readers to do just that. The combination of a literal self-reference and the setting of the kitchen, the site of so many Kroetz works, make this piece into another episode in his long-pursued and very problematic practice of self-referentiality.

Whereas works such as *Das Nest*, *Mensch Meier* and *Der stramme Max* all presumed the audience possessed a certain level of familiarity with their predecessors, *Zeitweh* goes one step further by expecting the audience members to be familiar not only with the author's oeuvre, but also with the author himself, and to be able to employ that knowledge in their interpretation of the scene before them. The character *Kroetz* refers to his earlier work as "die kleinen feinen stories, die überschaubaren, die wo, der Onkel Brecht sagt bipifax Schulfunk-stories, genau, DER GUTE MENSCH VON PASING" (IV,357), an obvious allusion to the first one-act plays that centered on small two-to-three person families and that cemented Kroetz's theatrical fame. Describing himself, *Kroetz* uses some of the most frequent epitaphs critics have attached to Kroetz's name: "Ich glaube kaum, daß heute noch jemand bezweifeln würde, daß Sie zu den führenden deutschen – der derzeit bedeutendste deutsche Dramatiker sind – jaja – (*große Pause*)" (IV,367). Kroetz even allows *Kroetz* to refer back to a much-repeated comment he made about the relationship of the artist to politics in 1973. At that time Kroetz said: "Entweder man hat Charakter, dann setzt man sein Talent für die Unterdrückten ein, oder man hat keinen Charakter, dann ist man das, was ich einen Musenficker nenne" (WA,591). Torturing himself about personal responsibility, the *Kroetz* of *Zeitweh* murmers: "Naja, man muß da dann auch wieder durch, es gibt Zustände, in denen man eigentlich – wenn man Charakter hätte, jetzt ist es vorbei das wars" (IV,376). *Kroetz*, unlike Kroetz in the early seventies, can no longer even finish such a sentence: The time for such assured pronouncements has passed. In fact, one wonders whether the structural self-references of these three plays do not come under Kroetz's own category of "Insider-Scherz" (WA,543) for the intellectual elite, an impotent moment of self-derision.

The self-referential passages that fill the pages of all three plays are often interspersed with distancing mechanisms, such as "jaja," "naja," long pauses and various dashes. Such mechanisms force the reader familiar with the playwright's career to read them as self-questioning, if not self-criticism. They form a running intra-textual commentary on the artist's aesthetic project from the early seventies until the late eighties. The Kroetz the audience sees on the stage is the one who claimed in 1986 to have written himself out. No longer interested in or capable of focusing on questions of labor – unemployment, exploitation, alienation – the playwright sits in his kitchen anguishing over his inability to come up with one good sentence. Running back and forth between his dictaphone, the telephone, a pot of spinach on the stove and the kitchen sink, Kroetz creates a theatrical frenzy centered on the solitary figure of the playwright.

Kroetz reincarnates this solitary and frenzied figure in his two following works, *Der Dichter als Schwein* and *Bauerntheater*. In a pattern typifying his entire aesthetic production, he recycles various elements from *Zeitweh* into these two later works, creating a trilogy about "the artist." Kroetz prefaced *Zeitweh* with the following claim: "das ist nicht nur ein Stück über MICH – nein, nein, das ist schon auch ein Stück über EUCH," a comment directed to fellow theater people (IV,355). At the very least, he believed that *Zeitweh* pertained to the artistic community more generally.

On the other hand, he clearly perceives the danger the kind of portrait he is creating presents. *Kroetz* pointedly asks a question that addresses exactly the potential pitfalls of Kroetz's focus on the playwright: "Man müßte immer immer [*sic*] wissen wie weit die private Einlassung gehen darf wie weit sie drin sein darf – (*sieht das Diktafon, schaltet es an*) – wie weit man sich in sich hinein einlassen darf, ohne daß es kindisch wird" (IV,359). Kroetz's above-mentioned fascination with the author's self followed on the suicide of the political subject in *Bauern sterben*. The probing of the artist as subject was to yield a radicalization of experience to open up room for social fantasy. The exaggerated concentration on what one could call the concrete self of the artist can lead, however, to what then appears to be only childish self-absorption. The problematic distinction becomes that between *one's* self and *the* self, between *an* individual and *the* individual. Kroetz attempts in these three works to strike a balance between the private and the abstract, and it appears that his critical audiences believed he failed. Several passages reveal the sources of their displeasure.

The dramatist's introduction to *Zeitweh* prefigures the interpretive stumbling blocks he sets up for a reading of *Kroetz* as a representative, i.e. more abstract dramatic character. Kroetz writes of *Kroetz*: "Man merkt, daß er während der ganzen Szene keinen Standpunkt hat außer dem durchzukommen," and "Man muß sehen, wie er merkt, daß alles Schrott ist, was er heute sagt" (IV,354). *Kroetz* is there, in other words, to babble. He will not offer answers to social problems, but rather prove his own inanity. Do such comments constitute a biting critique of the artist as social being, or are they just a clever form of self-apology?

Kroetz rebukes his self for not being the *stuff* of literature, "der Ich gerinnt nicht mehr zur Literatur der Schlaffi –" (*sic*, IV,361). Attributing this apparently to laziness, rather than any inherent inability, the playwright cannot find in his "I" a markable substance. One could certainly argue along with Foucault that the individual subject does not hold definition, rather a stream of masks point to momentary configurations of the self, all of which give way in time to new externalizations of reconfigurations.[2] Nonetheless, Kroetz's preoccupation with the artist's self does not seem to approach the philosophical abstraction of Foucault's masquerade. Instead he gets bogged down very literally in *his* self. The plethora of autobiographical references tie *Kroetz* far too closely to Kroetz himself, forcing a personalization of self that impedes its own generalization. When *Kroetz* states: "Ich habe Angst, daß der Schreibprozeß, der mein Lebensprozeß geworden ist, austrocknet, und ich meinen Tod bei lebendigem Leibe erlebe und überlebe" (IV,369), the emphasis falls far too heavily on Kroetz's own fears of having outlived his fame, of watching his own literary demise rather than the life process of the radical self he so fervently evoked at the end of the eighties.

Although this may sound rather harsh, Kroetz himself seems aware of the ambiguity he has invested in his author-characters. Lorenz, a colleague of *Kroetz*'s reincarnation as "der Dichter" in *Der Dichter als Schwein*, articulates the dilemma quite precisely: "Das Problem is doch: Ein Schriftsteller schreibt immer über sich. Man steht in einem manischen Zusammenhang mit sich selber. Thats the problem!" (IV,456). Furthermore, Kroetz subjects this manic self-examination to repeated ridicule. The *Dichter*'s rather rustic neighbor exposes Lorenz as both overinvested and affective:

> *Lorenz*: An mich glaub ich überhaupt nimmer. Ich glaub, ich bin mein größter Irrtum.
> *Rosl*: Des is awa etza "fölleton," was du schmazt, oder? (IV,464)

Rosl's response to Lorenz evokes the self-centered affectation of the young comedian in *Bauern sterben* as well as Kroetz's own manifold and often overly dramatic contributions to the cultural pages of multiple journals. Beyond that, the term "feuilleton/fölleton," which has almost become synonymous with socio-cultural irrelevance, represents another jab at the solipsistic figure of the artist. In other words, Rosl says not only that Lorenz takes himself too seriously, but also that he does so despite his social inconsequentiality.

The three works Kroetz has written around the artist's self become grotesque comic self-dissections rather than an exploration of the creative process. A passage from *Der Dichter als Schwein* underscores aptly why this holds true. While Max, a companion of the playwright, describes a meeting they had with the director of a theater, he also comments on the playwright's relationship to his most prominent dramatic ancestor: "Das macht Brecht zum meistgespielten Dramatiker, daß er auf den Scheiß-Biographismus verzichtet. ICH BIN NICHT BRECHT, sagen wir" (IV,470). Kroetz's views on Brecht's work and the changes those views undergo in the course of the seventies and eighties was the subject of extensive discussion in the previous chapter. Here the desperation that comes out in the sentence "ICH BIN NICHT BRECHT" draws out both the playwright's apparent frustration with the ceaseless comparisons of his own work to Brecht's as well as his own admission that he has failed to go beyond himself: Brecht can make do without "Scheiß-Biographismus", the *Dichter* cannot.

Kroetz expressly criticizes playwrights who dwell too long on personal pain. Of Thomas Bernhard he says:

> mein Gott das interessiert doch kein Schwein, das ist doch DICHTERGEWICHSE, das is es (*leise*) – neinnein, die sind eben näher dran, das is die die haben was voraus, während du dir – ja sag es doch – während du dir für die Gewerkschaften und die Poli – die Politik den Arsch aufgerissen hast. (IV,358)

On the one hand, *Kroetz* acknowledges that an all too intense represent-ation of the personal does not lend itself well to drama. On the other hand he cannot distinguish between the personal or the subjective and the biographical. Although Thomas Bernhard's work often repeated itself, it never attached itself clearly to the dramatist's person. *Kroetz* blames the time he spent as a political activist for a distance from himself that blocks him from effectively representing his self in a work of art. One could, however, also easily suggest that the playwright's inability to generalize the (artistic) subject beyond his own personal boundaries hampers his thematization of the subject.

Art, Politics and Society

Even where the plays explicitly try, for instance, to talk more generally about the relationship of art and society, of art and politics, Kroetz's own turbulent career path shadows the text too closely. The three playwrights are all torn between pursuing a political aesthetic course in their work and acknowledging that such a pursuit is futile. Two passages from *Bauerntheater* illustrate the conundrum.

Dichter: Genau. (*kleine Pause.*) Man muß es sich einfach ganz
bewußt machen und eiskalt sagen (*Gurgelnde Laute*): der
Verlust von ein bißl Poesie zugunsten einer total
revolutionären Aussage (*laut, fast hysterisch*): ja, der kann
doch hingenommen werden, fruzefix [*sic*].[3]

Although unable in fact to say anything in the decisive fashion he hopes
to affect ("eiskalt sagen"), indeed almost choking on his statement, he
still clings to the hope that one can mediate between the aesthetic and
the political. Somewhat further in the text this hysterically frantic plea
turns over into a flight from the political because it seems so terribly
futile:

Dichter: Aber wenn es nicht einmal den Protest eines Protestes
gibt, weil der revolutionäre Blutrausch in der Kunst
höchstens Ostereier produziert, dann, ja Himmel noch
einmal, dann laß ich doch die Finger davon: Dann bleib
ich beim Bauerntheater, und wenn es micht umbringt.
(*Schnappt nach Luft.*) (14)

Through the conjunction *weil*, the *Dichter* here attributes the absence of
public interest in politics or political protest to art's inability to produce
more than decorative prettiness ("Ostereier"). Despite the playwrights'
apparent obsession with art's relationship to the political, their ability to
shape politics into the (more abstract) political is limited to
telegrammatic citation. *Kroetz* plows through the newspapers looking
for material, but he only manages to string the items together. A short
excerpt of his three-page reading follows: "anführungszeichen. schon
dreizehntausendneunhundertfünfundsiebzig. der ford taunus hats. kurz
gemeldet punkt. uganda hat einskommafünf millionen waisen punkt.
südafrika ruft bahnpersonal zurück punkt. politische häftlinge im
hungerstreik punkt. kämpfe in mosambique punkt" (IV,363). Differing
from the aesthetic possibilities of montage, in which political
commentary could be both an aesthetic element unto itself as well as a
commentary on the other elements of the collage, the political here
simply punctuates the personal, making its way into the artist's
consciousness and into the work of art only as fragment. Desperate as
Kroetz's dramatists often seem to be to establish a connection between
the fragments, they never manage to do so.

Kroetz also juxtaposes many of the serious comments on art with
remarks on some totally mundane subject, reaffirming what seems to be
the texts' main insight into the relationship of art and politics, i.e. that

none obtains. *Kroetz*'s obsession with the spinach cooking on the stove is a good example from *Zeitweh*, but such moments become even more frequent in *Der Dichter als Schwein* and *Bauerntheater*. While the *Dichter* of *Bauerntheater* muses over his own work and whether he has fulfilled his responsibilities to society, his mother fixates on household appliances:

> Dichter: – Ist meine Todesangst nur Vorwand, um mich aus der sozialen Verantwortung der Wirklichkeit wegzuschleichen, oder –
> Mutter: (*zufrieden*): Der Toaster ist das einzige auf das Verlaß ist. Der ist uralt aber er funktioniert. (*Beißt genußvoll.*) (18)

His puzzling about the "revolutionäres Gewicht" (9) of his work evokes from his mother only the response: "Ob die Eier fertig sind?" The playwright's self-absorbed contemplations on the nature of aesthetics and its relationship to the political are almost always succeeded by remarks that illustrate the gulf between aesthetic theory and everyday experience. The mother's reference to eggs has a double thrust in this context: eggs are both food as well as a derogatory colloquialism for incompetent or overly esoteric intellectuals. Kroetz has her go even further with the following interchange:

> Dichter: (*laut*) Kunst will bewegen, ich will etwas vorwärts treibn –
> Mutter: In mir rumort es, da ist ein Furz, der will heraus! (10)

Her response reduces the playwright's confession of his political aesthetic aspirations to so much hot, smelly air.

At times such juxtapositions mark occasions when the characters are simply not talking to each other. At other times the responses comment directly on the theoretical or philosophical speculations of the various artists. One instance from *Der Dichter als Schwein* finds Lorenz attempting to create of *the simple life* a quasi-metaphysical moment:

> Lorenz: Einfach Kartoffeln schälen und die tiefe Befriedigung spüren. Innerlich. Tun. Gut tun. Herrlich.
> Rosl: Depp. (IV,472)

Kroetz thus subjects to ridicule (*Depp*) not only the playwrights' theoretical speculations, but also their attempts to aestheticize everyday reality. At every turn the three plays reveal the aesthetic (and political) sensitivity of the artist as pathetic childishness. In one of the rare moments of *Der Dichter als Schwein* where the reader has some sense that the dialogue is not simply ironic or satirical, Lorenz and the *Dichter* talk about their careers and the way they view them from their current positions:

> *Lorenz*: Wir können doch, heute nacht, wenn es sein muß, zusammen ein Stück schreibn, so von Arbeiter und Streik und Arbeitsplatzvernichtung und Partei – wie in der guten alten Zeit. Des können mir doch sofort.
> *Dichter*: (*nickt*.)
> *Lorenz*: Aber wir TUN es nicht. Weil es unsern gewachsenen Ansprüchen, der Ehrlichkeit, dem Selbst, dem Seins-Lebensgefühl – weil wir nicht lügen wollen. Ich schreib doch heut nicht schlechter wie vor 20 Jahr, des wär ja –
> *Dichter*: (*angeekelt*): widernatürlich.
> *Lorenz*: (*nickt*.)
> *Dichter*: Ich find, es passiert mir nix mehr Wesentliches, nix mehr, was ein ANLASS wär zum – Schreibn – (IV,524)

Not only have the twenty elapsed years changed their views on the appropriateness of their earlier material, Lorenz explicitly states emotional maturity as the reason for this new assessment. They seem to believe that only childish naiveté could explain why they wrote what they once did. Fixated, however, on the notion that the stuff of literature comes from the artist's personal biography, they no longer find anything to aestheticize. As mentioned above, this notion of art as biographically driven is highly problematic. In Kroetz's particular case, it becomes an even more limiting factor through its coupling with what is still largely a realist aesthetic.

Realism and the Grotesque

Even though *Zeitweh*, *Der Dichter als Schwein* and *Bauerntheater* all often appear too preposterous to merit the adjective realist, Kroetz nonetheless indicates many times that he still considers his work in this fashion. In the stage directions at the beginning of *Bauerntheater* Kroetz notes on the way the actors should deliver their text: "Hier fällt jeder jedem inbrünstig ins Stich-Wort. Es gibt einiges an Unverständlichem, wie im Leben auch" (7), and "Die Figuren fühlen keine unmittelbare Verantwortung für das, was sie sagen, wie im Leben auch" (8). In a similar vein, *Der Dichter als Schwein* contains a scene in the third act in which four different conversations take place simultaneously (IV,462–472). The author's introduction to the first act of *Bauerntheater* indicates that the audience will understand only about one-third of the spoken text (9). Although it is not included in these last two passages, one can almost hear a Kroetzean caveat here: "wie im Leben auch."

One could legitimately argue that "true to life" and "realism" are not necessarily synonymous, but Kroetz explicitly refers to the realism of even these works. He writes in the opening of *Bauerntheater* about casting the various roles: "Da kleine Kinder in diesem Stück eine große Rolle spielen, kann man es kaum aufführen. Sonst müßte man die Kinder mit Erwachsenen besetzen und das würde den Realismus antinaturalistisch machen" (8). Both Kroetz and his more benevolent critics took pains in the early seventies to distinguish his work from naturalism. Here he not only adopts the label realism, but also conflates it with naturalism. The result is a certain amount of aesthetic confusion, and the fact that Kroetz uses the term realism still does not force us to accept his assessment at face value. Nonetheless, Kroetz goes to great lengths in all three works to create a stage picture that resembles a more mundanely conceived notion of reality.

In addition to the above-listed examples, Kroetz breaks down the characters' speech into spoken fragments, rather than producing the illusion that human beings talk in complete and eloquent sentences. He has also added stage-props familiar to us from earlier works, such as the kitchen stove, some food items like spinach and catfood in *Zeitweh* or canned sausages in *Der Dichter als Schwein*, which link the characters on stage to what one might call a "supermarket reality." Extensive dialogues about false teeth, problems with incontinence (*Der Dichter als Schwein* and *Bauerntheater*), repeated interruptions of dialogue or monologues by telephone calls enhance the temptation to read these plays as at least quasi-realist works. However, as with every other aspect of these plays, a moment of self-reflective irony pushes one to question just how fair the realist label is.

Essentially, the answer depends on how willing a reader or audience is to take seriously the distance between the *Kroetz/Dichter*-characters and Kroetz himself. An intriguing telephone conversation in *Zeitweh* illustrates the dilemma a reader familiar with Kroetz's previous work faces here. Having been asked several times to write a play about the nuclear power plant accident in Chernobyl in 1986, the playwright vents his frustration with such a topic and states why he thinks it is essentially an adramatic event:

> ja es ruft dauernd ein Arschloch an und fragt, ob ich ihm nicht das Stück Nach Tschernobyl schreiben will, und ich sag, das SIEHT MAN DOCH NICHT –

die Strahlung sieht man doch nicht, das ist doch ganz ungeeignet für das Theater . . . ich weiß nicht, was übrig bleiben wird, Tschernobyl oder die private Katastrophe. . . (IV,374)

The fact that one could not *see* the radiation emitted from the nuclear power plant made it, in *Kroetz*'s eyes, an unacceptable topic for the theater. The only aspect he can imagine recovering for the stage is the private catastrophe, biographical moments.

The discussion of *Das Nest* in chapter two indicated that the topic of toxic industrial waste was so complex as to render reductionist its thematic exploration in a realist work. *Kroetz* here seems to have realized this when he acknowledges that he cannot adequately portray Chernobyl dramatically. On the other hand, he insists here that he cannot do so because he cannot see it, i.e. he cannot mimic something aesthetically that is so abstract, so inconcrete. That there exist aesthetic means to thematize or to approach such a topic never occurs to him.

Interestingly enough, *Das Totenfloß*, a play by Harald Mueller[4] that is a grotesque exploration of society in a world already contaminated by nuclear accidents, premiered shortly after the Chernobyl accident.[5] *Theater heute*, (West) Germany's most influential theater journal, hailed the work as the play of the year. Mueller's use of non-realist aesthetic representation in *Totenfloß* allowed him to examine through his mutant characters not only the possible ramifications of a world poisoned by nuclear toxins, but also less historically specific social conflicts such as discrimination, exploitation and exclusion. The point here is simply that one obviously need not be able to see something in order to stage it, if one does so within an aesthetic construct that does not pretend to be roughly equal to empirical reality.

The question remains, however, whether *Kroetz*'s frustration with Chernobyl as a dramatic issue is also Kroetz's frustration. The question requires an answer because only so can one make visible any distance between the two figures, and only such a distance would allow us to assume that Kroetz has managed to move beyond his earlier understanding of realism. Furthermore, only the assumption that none of these three plays are realist works moves them out of the realm of "Kraftkitsch," as Gerhard Preußen described *Bauerntheater*, and into the realm of a highly stylized grotesque parody of the artistic self.

All three plays do contain manifold moments of what someone might call the grotesque. In *Zeitweh Kroetz* repeatedly urinates in the kitchen sink, always also explicitly drawing attention to the fact that he is doing so. In *Der Dichter als Schwein* the third act takes place in the *Dichter*'s neighbors' farmhouse, in which the family dog has left numerous piles of feces that the various characters then track through the house. One of the characters, naked from the waist down, lies on the living-room couch face down while farting in the air. The final scene in *Bauerntheater* has the *Dichter* set his typewriter on or next to his son's dead body while he frantically tries to capture the illusive one good sentence. I could cite numerous other examples as well.

Kroetz has also explicitly expressed his fascination with the grotesque. During his interview with *Die Welt* Kroetz describes his current perception of reality as follows: "Ich führe heute eine andere Existenz, und sie möchte ich gerne satirisch, ja grotesk darstellen. Die Groteske ist das, woran ich wieder glaube."[6] He has insisted that directors have missed or overlooked the radical substance of his work:

> Es ist nicht meine Schuld, wenn Regisseure nicht sehen, wo die Stücke böse werden, ins Absurde überschlagen, und sie nicht mit der ganzen Radikalität der Substanz arbeiten, die in den Stücken enthalten ist, sondern liebenswürdige Studioaufführungen im Genre des Fernsehrealismus machen.[7]

Kroetz here implies that his plays have always been more absurdist and grotesque than they have seemed. In fact, he goes so far as to say that the many directors who have staged his work are largely responsible for his reputation as a realist author. Another 1987 interview with the playwright gives Kroetz the opportunity to pinpoint the grotesque as the substance of real human existence and that the theater is dependent on this grotesqueness: "Das Theater geht nur dann nicht unter, wenn es unsere Defekte ausbeutet; rücksichtslos ist: Fette, Wasserköpfige, Krüppel und Huren müssen zeigen, was sie haben . . . Raus aus der Ästhetik, rein ins volle Menschenleben."[8] Wolfgang Schneider even attributes Kroetz's long-running success to the fascination of generally bourgeois theater audiences with the sordid, the absurd and the grotesque. He writes: "die Reizwörter 'Ohnmacht', 'Trivialität' und 'Blut' verweisen nachdrücklich auf jenes Gefühlsgemisch aus Selbstzufriedenheit, voyeuristischer Lust und Ekel, das die Kroetz-Stücke beim zumeist gutbürgerlichen Publikum hervorzurufen in der Lage waren und das bis heute ihren Erfolg garantiert."[9] The power of voyeuristic temptation is well known, and Schneider's commentary on Kroetz's theater career has a certain validity, but the playwright's statement about the position of the grotesque in human life draws a rather curious circle back to the question of Kroetz's realism-concept. The representation of what he sees as the grotesque constitutes for him a departure from aesthetic configuration: "Raus aus der Ästhetik, rein ins volle Menschenleben."

Human existence may or may not be inherently grotesque. However, Kroetz's apparent understanding of human life as grotesque would mean that the grotesque moments in these three plays do not necessarily mark a departure from the dramatist's otherwise largely realist aesthetic. Furthermore, although Kroetz mentions cripples, hydrocephalics and whores in conjunction with the grotesque, the examples listed from the plays themselves point more in the direction of the scatological than the grotesque. The use of scatological elements may have always been a popular tool with satirists, but it is still different from the monstrous and/or magical terror of a grotesque distortion and deformity of human or animal form. Bernard McElroy notes in *Fiction of the Modern Grotesque* that the grotesque "combines the fearsome with the ludicrous," but always "contains some awareness of the monstrous."[10] The *Dichter* of *Bauerntheater* argues at one point that the incredible and the ludicrous are almost indistinguishable: "Das Unglaubliche und das Lächerliche sind immer so nah beieinander, das ist es, was mich lähmt" (28). One cannot, however, equate the incredible with the fearsome and Kroetz's fascination with bodily functions never rises above the unpleasant. The various incarnations of the playwright also cannot possibly come under the category of the monstrous. Precisely the distance from the grotesque, in its more traditional definition, makes possible an evaluation of *Zeitweh*, *Der Dichter als Schwein* and *Bauerntheater* as pathetic, if not ridiculous self-display, which in turn prompted Gerhard Preußen's sarcastic "Ecce homo Kroetz."

To use yet another formulation for why these works found such a cool reception in the theater world: Kroetz's focus on the artistic or creative self gets enmired in the mundane. Nowhere do these pieces display an assurance of their relevance beyond Kroetz's own personal experience. This assessment should not, however, suggest that such relevance is not there at all, but rather that *Zeitweh*, *Der Dichter als Schwein* and *Bauerntheater* become much smaller works than they would otherwise have to be. If, as I implied earlier, Kroetz's reintroduction of the scatological does not represent a substantial aesthetic shift in the author's work, but rather merely a reevaluation of what constitutes a realist depiction of a particular aspect of reality, then one of the factors limiting these three plays is Kroetz's continued reliance on a primarily realist aesthetic.

This examination of Kroetz's work has repeatedly returned to the question of realism as an aesthetic paradigm. The playwright's conversion to Marxism in 1972 and his subsequent attempts to refocus his dramatic lens from his variedly disabled (therefore probably more aptly labeled grotesque) characters in his earliest staged one-act plays ran afoul not only of his somewhat anachronistic understanding of contemporary West German society, but also of the limitations his realist aesthetic imposed on the breadth or generalizability of his theater works. Both *Nicht Fisch nicht Fleisch* and *Bauern sterben* (along with *Furcht und Hoffnung der BRD*, to a certain extent, and *Der Nusser*) represented various attempts to get beyond those constraints. *Bauern sterben* is in fact Kroetz's first thoroughly non-realist work, but the examination of this play highlighted the risks involved in its generally parabolic form. If Kroetz's realist works could not attain the social scope he hoped for, *Bauern sterben* became too abstract, losing sight in the process of its relationship to the political praxis that still informed it.

Thus it does not seem surprising that Kroetz returned in *Zeitweh* and the two plays that followed to another variant of the extended realism of *Nicht Fisch nicht Fleisch*. In these three plays, however, both the author's apparent inability to conceptualize the subject beyond a particular individual and his realist strategy that so eloquently evokes memories of his earlier realist plays combine to reduce what he conceived of as a radical and grand questioning of the artistic self to a rather pitiful and painful exhibition of Kroetz's theatrical frustration.

Although the analysis of this playwright's work has underscored the limitations his own aesthetic strategies have placed on his political-aesthetic project, nowhere does it condone a wholesale rejection of realism as either an outdated or an aesthetically inferior representational strategy. Instead the intent of each reading has been to localize what in the plays discussed here pushed the dramatist to revise his strategy as he sought to create an effective political aesthetic. As such my attempt has been to generate a functional examination of each work and not a valuative judgment. In other words, it is of little interest to me whether some critics call *Oberösterreich*, *Das Nest* or any of Kroetz's other plays "good" or "bad" according to what must ultimately remain rather nebulous criteria.

In order to illustrate the approach this examination of Kroetz's work has taken, let me highlight a few points from Peter Bürger's *Theorie der Avantgarde*. Of prime interest for this study has been his treatment of aesthetic means – *Kunstmittel*. Bürger claims that the project of the historical avant-garde made possible a recognition of aesthetic means as such. Once the avant-garde began to employ a variety of techniques, conscious of them as *Kunstmittel* and not as bound to particular aesthetic practices and programs, artists were freed to choose from a tremendous array of means and techniques. Bürger writes: "Erst die Avantgarde . . . macht die Kunstmittel in ihrer Allgemeinheit erkennbar, weil sie die Kunstmittel nicht mehr nach einem Stilprinzip auswählt, sondern über sie *als Kunstmittel* verfügt."[11]

The ramifications of the avant-garde's decoupling of *Kunstmittel* from particular styles are numerous. Especially important here is the fact that any discussion of the current state or level of aesthetic means has become irrelevant. The multitude of styles and techniques available to an artist is so great as to render any boundaries to style invalid. In direct opposition to Adorno's insistence on non-representational art as the only acceptable aesthetic form, Bürger argues that no one artistic movement or aesthetic strategy can claim a greater degree of historical legitimacy or accuracy. As an example of this, Bürger asserts that today one cannot argue against the application of realist techniques simply on the grounds that they do not represent the most progressive aesthetic form.[12]

On the basis of his study Bürger ultimately comes to promote the aesthetic strategy of montage, given that in such a construction each element can function both separately from the others and together through them. However, he underscores the impossibility of claiming an historical prerogative for any one aesthetic strategy. In closing, Bürger suggests that an analysis of function replace a normative study of art. A functional analysis would take as its object the social impact or influence (*Wirkung*) of a work as the confrontation of the various elements in a particular artwork with a particular audience:

> An die Stelle der normativen Betrachtung tritt die Funktionsanalyse, die die gesellschaftliche Wirkung (Funktion) eines Werks aus dem Zusammentreffen von im Werk angelegten Stimuli mit einem soziologisch bestimmbaren Publikum innerhalb eines vorgegebenen institutionellen Rahmens (Institution Kunst) zum Gegenstand der Untersuchung machen würde.[13]

Rather, therefore, than attempt to judge the aesthetic merit of Kroetz's work, my analysis sought to demonstrate how the various aesthetic strategies Kroetz employed intervened in what he considered to be his political-aesthetic project. On this point, however, Bürger also issues a warning about any mistaken notion that analytical surety can ever be complete. The following passage served as a guide for my own study of Kroetz's efforts to create a functional political aesthetic:

> Die Bestimmung dessen, was gesellschaftlich relevant ist, hängt mit dem politischen Standort des Interpreten zusammen. Das bedeutet: die Frage, ob ein Gegenstand relevant ist oder nicht, kann in einer antagonistischen Gesellschaft nicht durch Diskussion *entschieden*, wohl aber kann sie *diskutiert* werden.[14]

One could add here that the determination of what is socially and aesthetically relevant or appropriate can never reach a final conclusion. This is particularly true for an analysis of a contemporary author such as Kroetz. In fact, a recently staged work, *Der Drang*, while pursuing elements familiar from all of the various permutations his plays have revealed over the last twenty years, moves in a new direction completely, namely toward satirical sexual comedy. Despite its still biting critique, this would actually position *Der Drang* closer to the less critical, more entertaining *Volksstück*-tradition, of which Brecht wrote so disparagingly: "Da gibt es derbe Späße, gemischt mit Rührseligkeiten, da ist hanebüchene Moral und billige Sexualität" (GW 17,1162). In lieu, therefore, of a conclusion, the following review offers preliminary answers to questions raised about the possibilities for and of a political aesthetic that the theater has in the work of this very prolific and influential playwright.

Conclusion

The development of Kroetz's dramatic efforts represents a search for an effective expression of political reality. The search forced him to experiment. Kroetz sought a subject capable of political action and an aesthetic strategy that could address the needs of that subject adequately. Over the years he has modified his conceptualization of the political subject and refashioned his aesthetic strategy to address the changing character of that subject. He adjusted the ultrarealism of the earliest one-act plays somewhat in both *Oberösterreich* and *Das Nest* in order to create a more generally "valid" portrait of contemporary German society. *Nicht Fisch nicht Fleisch* departs from a strictly realist aesthetic opening up more room for an exploration of human existence in the late twentieth century, still using but already seriously questioning the analytical validity of the political philosophy informing the plays from 1972 to 1980, namely Marxism. From *Oberösterreich* to *Nicht Fisch nicht Fleisch* the political subject gradually becomes more and more competent, but the social context, in which this individual acts and interacts, slowly begins to crumble. In this process the elements of a political agent about to coalesce scatter. A secure or fixed sense of individual identity disintegrates in *Bauern sterben*, while at the same time opening new venues for aesthetic expression. Nonetheless, a viable subject for political praxis is once again absent.

That is to say, a subject is absent in terms of a traditional political strategy. Kroetz has responded to the demise of the autonomous agent with a retooling of his political project that entails both a new political eclecticism and a reduction of the political itself. The trilogy of *Zeitweh*, *Der Dichter als Schwein* and *Bauerntheater* focused in again on the subject, but this time via the artist's self. Kroetz hoped in these works to generate through their examination of the artist as radical subject new spaces for creative expression – for himself and theater audiences, but both the still largely realist aesthetic and Kroetz's chronic practice of self-citation cause these latest works to transgress the line between the aesthetic abstraction of the creative subject and the banality of autobiographical introspection.

Where his latest works will lead him is unclear. *Der Drang* revolves around sexual tensions that are familiar from his earliest works, but that he has recontextualized outside of his once rigidly Marxist interpretation of social reality. When this study reached an end, Kroetz had also just come out with a new work for the theater entitled *Ich bin das Volk*, a collection of scenes from contemporary German society that revolve around issues of racism and xenophobia and the violent confrontations that sprang up in the early nineties.[15] The two plays differ from each other substantially. Structurally *Der Drang* resembles the earliest one-act plays, while *Ich bin das Volk* recreates the scenic collage of a work like *Furcht und Hoffnung der BRD*.

The montage construction of *Ich bin das Volk* allows the playwright to generate a more comprehensive, broad-scale social landscape than the highly focused social Petri dishes of plays like *Heimarbeit* and *Wildwechsel*. In contrast, however, to *Furcht und Hoffnung*, any sure-footed, dogmatic political judgement of the figures that people these brief scenes – from skinheads, to supreme court justices, to German tourists, to teachers and pupils and even to the first German army recruits for service as United Nations peace keepers – is markedly absent. In fact, more often than disapproval the reader gets a sense of the author's sympathy for the limited perspectives of the individuals he portrays. In the interview that accompanies *Theater heute*'s publication of excerpts from *Ich bin das Volk* Kroetz states that he no longer has the moral certitude that would allow him to condemn a whole array of his fellow citizens, but rather that his interest lies in hinting at the sources of racism, xenophobia and hate, while bringing to light their pervasiveness.[16]

If anything in Kroetz's development as a dramatist has been representative of the general trends in post-sixties German theater it is this gradual waning of a determined and defined political program. He has tended to reach certain benchmarks on his path toward a politically undogmatic theater much later than his contemporaries like Botho Strauß, Peter Handke and to a certain extent the prominent East German playwright Heiner Müller, but his latest pronouncements also no longer reveal a clearly delineated political philosophy that would or even could find expression in a well-defined aesthetic program.[17] This state of productive disarray is symptomatic for German drama today. One could arguably trace this stylistic plethora back to the early seventies, when the new critical *Volksstück* first experienced a revival. Its renaissance in the late sixties/early seventies marked the end of the grand political narratives that characterized German documentary theater, and helped to usher in (however mutedly and unsuspectingly) a less globalizing, restrictive period of aesthetic experimentation.

Furthermore, aesthetic plurality is undoubtedly absolutely essential to express the ever-changing constellation of social practices and structures that constitute contemporary society. Although art cannot expect to *speak* to every individual that is part of its public, the artist must choose an aesthetic strategy that takes into account the various moments of the aesthetic process. This includes a reconceptualization of the political subject. A political aesthetic today must work with a concept not of an integral, autonomous political subject, the hallmark of enlightenment political philosophy, but rather with a concept of political agency, as a meeting point of many structures and discourses. A functional aesthetic would then be conceived of as plural and non-exclusionary. It would take into consideration the targeted and real audience, production constraints, and the socio-political backdrop of the artwork during production and reception. Finally, it would address the new forms of experience of a post-industrial age. The search for innovative combinations of already familiar aesthetic techniques and for new aesthetic techniques should not, however, ignore the institutional constraints placed on the efficacy of politically committed art. One cannot expect art to have a direct political effect. Kroetz's disappointment with the response he received to his work in the early to mid-eighties was to a large extent simply an over-assessment of the theater's sphere of influence.

In line with this, the study of politically engaged art should represent the attempt to analyze, as Peter Bürger suggests, the social functioning of the work of art, to measure the means against the ends and to contribute in an indirect fashion to an understanding of how certain techniques function in certain contexts. This spirit informed my examination of the developments in Kroetz's dramas from *Oberösterreich* to *Bauerntheater*. No matter what direction Kroetz follows in the future, the work he has already written for the theater offers a rich and unexhausted source for the exploration of the problematic and highly involved relationship between the aesthetic and the political.

Notes

1. Because of the possible confusion between the character and the dramatist himself, I will italicize all references to the character *Kroetz*, and leave the name in plain text with every mention of the actual person Kroetz.

2. Michel Foucault, "Nietzsche, Genealogy, History," rpt. in *The Foucault Reader*, ed. Paul Rabinow (New York: Pantheon Books, 1984), p. 94. The influence of such philosophy reverberates throughout the works of Kroetz's contemporaries. For instance, Heiner Müller's theater pieces from the late seventies and eighties, such as *Hamletmaschine* (1977) or *Verkommenes Ufer Medeamaterial Landschaft mit Argonauten* (1982) incorporate what one could almost call explicit references to Foucault's work. The moments in *Hamletmaschine* when the Hamlet-character literally tears up a photograph of the playwright loudly echoes Foucault's short, but very influential essay "What is an author?" in *The Foucault Reader*, pp. 101–120.

3. Franz Xaver Kroetz, *Bauerntheater* (Frankfurt/M.: Suhrkamp Verlag, 1991). All further citations of this work will be followed simply by the page number from this edition. Here p. 12.

4. Mueller, a playwright once associated with the new critical *Volksstück*, had essentially disappeared from the theater scene until this piece appeared.

5. The play is very reminiscent of Beckett's *Endgame*, but is less hermetic and claustrophobic than the Beckett work.

6. *Die Welt*, 7 Oct. 1987.

7. From an interview with Anke Roeder, "Der Luxus der vollkommenen Identität: Franz Xaver Kroetz als Autor, Schauspieler und Regisseur," *Forum Modernes Theater* 2, no. 1 (1987): p. 59.

8. Cited in Wolfgang Schneider, "Der Musenficker," *konkret*, no. 1 (1988): p. 48.

9. Ibid.

10. Bernard McElroy, *Fiction of the Modern Grotesque* (London: Macmillan, 1989), pp. 12, 14.

11. Peter Bürger, *Theorie der Avantgarde* (Frankfurt/M.: Suhrkamp Verlag, 1974), p. 25.

12. Ibid., p. 121.

13. Ibid., p. 122.

14. Ibid., p. 9.

15. As of May 1995 only a few segments from this work had appeared in print. See Franz Xaver Kroetz, "Ich bin das Volk," *Theater heute* (Oct. 1994): pp. 44–51.

16. Franz Xaver Kroetz, "Mit dem alltäglichen Faschismus selbstverständlich umgehen," *Theater heute* (Oct. 1994): pp. 4–8.

17. One might object here that Botho Strauß's work since the mid-eighties may in fact be returning gradually to a well-defined moral/political aesthetic, but I believe such a conclusion would still be premature.

Select Bibliography

Primary Texts

Kroetz, Franz Xaver. *Bauerntheater*. Frankfurt/M.: Suhrkamp Verlag 1991.

——, "Der Drang". *Theater heute* (July 1994), pp. 31–40.

——, *Furcht und Hoffnung der BRD*. Frankfurt/M.: Suhrkamp Verlag, 1984.

——, *Stücke*. Vols. I–IV. Frankfurt/M.: Suhrkamp Verlag, 1989.

——, *Weitere Aussichten . . . Neue Texte*. Berlin: Henschel Verlag, 1976.

Interviews and Essays

Kroetz, Franz Xaver. "Bin ich das einzige Schwein?" *Spiegel*, no. 22 (30 May 1994): pp. 199–202.

——, "Eigentlich bin ich ein christlicher Autor: Gespräch mit Franz Xaver Kroetz über sein Stück 'Bauern Sterben.'" *Süddeutsche Zeitung*, 23 Dec. 1985.

——, "Es ist phantastisch für 'Bild" zu schreiben: Interview mit Manfred Kriener." *taz*, 16 July 1989.

——, "Franz Xaver Kroetz Interview." *konkret* (March 1986): pp. 70–73.

——, "Franz X. Kroetz: Der liebe Gott ist noch viel rücksichtsloser. Interview mit Lothar Schmidt-Mühlisch and Horst Stein." *Die Welt*, 5 Oct. 1987.

——, "Franz X. Kroetz: Was sollte ich denn machen ohne Bayern? Interview mit Lothar Schmidt-Mühlisch und Horst Stein." *Die Welt*, 7 Oct. 1987.

——, "Ich schreibe nicht über Dinge, die ich verachte. Ich bin für mich sehr interessant." *Theater heute* (July 1980): pp. 18f.

——, "Interview mit Franz Xaver Kroetz." With Ursula Reinhold." *Weimarer Beiträge* 22, no. 5 (1976): pp. 46–59.

——, "Mit dem alltäglichen Faschismus selbstverständlich umgehen." *Theater heute* (October 1994): pp. 4–8.

——, "Zweitausend Lichtjahre von Gott entfernt. Franz Xaver Kroetz über die Kunst, das Kreuz und die Radikalität der Liebe. Publik-

Forum-Gespräch von Karl-Josef Kuschel." *Publik-Forum*, no. 20 (9 Oct. 1987): pp. 23–26.

Secondary Literature

Adorno, Theodor W. "Der Artist als Statthalter." In *Gesammelte Schriften*. Vol. XI. Frankfurt/M.: Suhrkamp Verlag, 1974, pp. 114–126.

——, *Ästhetische Theorie. Gesammelte Schriften*. Vol. VII. Frankfurt/ M.: Suhrkamp Verlag, 1970.

——, "Culture Industry Reconsidered." *New German Critique*, No. 6 (Fall 1975): pp. 12–19.

——, "Engagement." In *Gesammelte Schriften*. Vol. XI. Frankfurt/M.: Suhrkamp Verlag, 1974, pp. 409–430.

——, "Erpreßte Versöhnung." In *Gesammelte Schriften*. Vol. XI. Frankfurt/M.: Suhrkamp Verlag, 1974, pp. 251–280.

——, "Offener Brief an Rolf Hochhuth." In *Gesammelte Schriften*. Vol. XI. Frankfurt/M.: Suhrkamp Verlag, 1974, pp. 591–598.

——, "Standort des Erzählers im zeitgenössischen Roman." In *Gesammelte Schriften*. Vol. XI. Frankfurt/M.: Surhkamp Verlag, 1974, pp. 41–48.

Arac, Jonathon (ed.). *Postmodernism and Politics*. Minneapolis: University of Minnesota Press, 1986.

Arato, Andrew and Eike Gebhardt (ed). *The Essential Frankfurt School Reader*. New York: Urizen Books, 1978.

Arendt, Hannah *Walter Benjamin und Bertolt Brecht; Zwei Essays*. Munich: R. Piper, 1971.

Arnold, Heinz Ludwig (ed.). *Als Schriftsteller Leben*. Reinbeck bei Hamburg: Rowohlt Verlag, 1979.

——, *Franz Xaver Kroetz*. Munich: *text + kritik* (57), 1978.

Arnold, Heinz Ludwig and Theo Buck (ed.). *Positionen des Dramas: Analysen und Theorien zur deutschen Gegenwartsliteratur*. Munich: Beck, 1977.

Arnold, Heinz Ludwig and Volker Sinemus (ed.). *Literaturwissenschaft*. Vol. 1 of *Grundzüge der Literatur-und Sprachwissenschaft*. Munich: Deutscher Taschenbuchverlag, 1974.

Aronowitz, Stanley. *The Crisis in Historical Materialism*. New York: Praeger, 1981.

Aronson, Ronald. "Sartre and the Radical Intellectual's Role," *Science & Society* 39, no. 4 (Winter 1975/76): pp. 436–449.

Auffermann, Verena. "Bundesdeutsches Elend – Glanzlos und Grausam." *Theater heute* (August 1984): p. 47.

Aust, Hugo, Peter Haida and Jürgen Hein. *Volksstück. Vom Hanswurstspiel zum sozialen Drama der Gegenwart*. Munich: Beck, 1989.

Baumeister, Thomas and Jens Kulenkampff. "Geschichtsphilosophie und philosophische Ästhetik. Zu Adornos ästhetischer Theorie." *Neue Hefte für Philosophie*, no. 5 (1973): pp. 74–104.

Becker, Peter, von. "Die Stadt, das Land und der Tod. Kroetz und Achternbusch inszenieren Kroetz und Achternbusch in München: 'Bauern sterben' und 'Gust.'" *Theater heute* (July 1985): pp. 22–26.

——, "Zur Bonner Autorendramaturgie." *Theater heute* (May 1983): p. 22.

Benjamin, Walter. *Gesammelte Schriften*. Edited by Rolf Tiedemann and Herman Schweppenhauser. Frankfurt/M.: Suhrkamp Verlag, 1972–.

Berg, Jan, et al. *Einführung in die Dramenanalyse. Von Lessing bis Kroetz*. Kronberg/Ts.: Scriptor Verlag, 1976.

Berghahn, Klaus. "Auch eine Politologie des westdeutschen Gegenwartsdramas." *Basis*, no. 10 (1980): pp. 233–238.

Berman, Russell. "Adorno, Marxism and Art." *Telos* 34 (Winter 1977-1978): pp. 157–166.

——, *Modern Culture and Critical Theory*. Madison: University of Wisconsin Press, 1989.

Blevins, Richard Wayne. *Franz Xaver Kroetz: The Emergence of a Political Playwright*. New York: Peter Lang, 1983.

Boa, Elizabeth. "Kroetz's *Nicht Fisch nicht Fleisch*: A Good Red Herring?" *German Life and Letters* 38, no. 4 (1985): pp. 313–322.

Brand, Karl-Werner (ed.). *Neue soziale Bewegungen in Westeuropa und den USA. Ein internationaler Verleich*. Frankfurt/M.: Campus Verlag, 1985.

Brauneck, Manfred. *Literatur und Öffentlichkeit im ausgehenden 19. Jahrhundert*. Stuttgart: J.B. Metzlerscher Verlagsbuchhandlung, 1974.

Brecht, Bertolt. *Arbeitsjournal*. Edited by Werner Hecht. Frankfurt/M.: Suhrkamp Verlag, 1973.

——, *Gesammelte Werke*. Frankfurt/M.: Suhrkamp Verlag, 1967.

Brüggemann, H. *Literarische Technik und soziale Revolution. Versuche über das Verhältnis von Kunstproduktion, Marxismus und Literarischer Tradition in den theoretischen Schriften Bertolt Brechts*. Reinbek bei Hamburg: Rowohlt Verlag, 1973.

Bubner, Rüdiger. "Über einige Bedingungen gegenwärtiger Ästhetik." *Neue Hefte für Philosophie*, no. 5 (1973): pp. 38–73.

Buddecke, Wolfram and Helmut Fuhrmann. *Das deutschsprachige Drama seit 1945*. Munich: Winkler Verlag, 1981.

Bügner, Torsten. *Annäherungen an die Wirklichkeit. Gattung und Autoren des neuen Volksstücks*. New York: Peter Lang, 1986.

Bürger, Peter. *Theorie der Avantgarde*. Frankfurt/M.: Suhrkamp Verlag, 1974.

Bullivant, Keith. *Realism Today*. Leamington Spa: Berg, 1987.

Calandra, Denis. *New German Dramatists*. London and Basingstoke: Macmillan, 1983.

Carl, Rolf-Peter. *Franz Xaver Kroetz*. Munich: C.H. Beck, 1978.

———, "Franz Xaver Kroetz: 'Der stramme Max.'" *Literatur für Leser*, no. 1 (1981): pp. 53–55.

Certeau, Michel de. *The Practice of Everyday Life*. Translated by Steven F. Randall. Berkeley: University of California Press, 1984.

Claas, Herbert. *Die politische Ästhetik Bertolt Brechts vom Baal zum Caesar*. Frankfurt/M: Suhrkamp Verlag, 1977.

Clark, John. *The Modern Satiric Grotesque and Its Traditions*. Lexington: University of Kentucky Press, 1991.

Cocalis, Susan L. " 'Mitleid' and 'Engagement.' Compassion and/or Political Commitment in the Dramatic Works of Franz Xaver Kroetz." *Colloquia Germanica* 14, no. 3 (1981): pp. 203–219.

Cohen, Jean. *Class and Civil Society: The Limits of Marxian Critical Theory*. Amherst: University of Massachusetts Press, 1982.

Demetz, Peter. "Zur Definition des Realismus." *Literatur und Kritik* 16/17 (1967): pp. 333–345.

Drews, Jörg. "Wider einen neuen Realismus." *Merkur* 29(1) (1975): pp. 29–39.

Dubiel, Helmut. "Farewell to Critical Theory?" Translated by B. Gregg. *Praxis International* 3, no. 2 (July 1983): pp. 121–137.

Eagleton, Terry. *Criticism & Ideology*. London: Verso, 1975.

Eggers, Ulf Konrad. *Aspekte zeitgenössischer Realismustheorie*. Bonn: Bouvier, 1976.

Eichholz, Armin. "Butter, Blut, Boden und Beerdigung." *Die Welt*, 11 June 1985.

Enzensberger, Hans Magnus. "Die Bewußtseins-Industrie." In *Einzelheiten I*. Frankfurt/M.: Suhrkamp, 1962, pp. 7–17.

Ernst, Gustav. "Literatur und Leben. Zum (neueren) literarischen Realismus." *Wespennest*, no. 74 (1989): pp. 3–39.

Ettinger, Albert. "Franz Xaver Kroetz: *Mensch Meier*." In *Deutsche Gegenwartsdramatik*. Edited by Lothar Pikulik.Göttingen: Vandenhoeck & Ruprecht, 1987, pp. 99–140.

Fischer, Eva-Elisabeth. "Kroetz stellt seine Wunden aus. 'Bauern sterben' – Uraufführung an den Münchner Kammerspielen." *Süddeutsche Zeitung*, 11 June 1985.

Foster, Hal. *Recodings – Art, Spectacle, Cultural Politics*. Port Townsend, Washington: Bay Press, 1985.

Foucault, Michel. *Discipline and Punish*. Translated by Alan Sheridan. New York: Pantheon Books, 1975.

———, *The Foucault Reader*. Edited by Paul Rabinow. New York:

Pantheon Books, 1984.

——, *The Order of Things*. New York: Random House, 1970.

François, Jean-Claude. "Franz Xaver Kroetz et le neo-realisme theatral." *Allemagne d'aujourd'hui* 44 (1974): pp. 52–60.

Fraser, Nancy. "The French Derrideans: Politicizing Deconstruction or Deconstructing the Political?" *New German Critique* 33 (Fall 1984): pp. 127–154.

Fuchs, Hans Joachim. "Theater als Dienstleistung." *Universitas* 41, no. 6 (1986): pp. 621–630.

Fülberth, Georg. *KPD und DKP 1945–1990*. Heilbronn: Distel Verlag, 1990.

Gabel, Joseph. *False Consciousness*. Translated by Margaret A. Thompson and Kenneth A. Thompson. Oxford: Basil Blackwell, 1975.

Gorz, André. *Farewell to the Working Class: An Essay on Post-industrial Socialism*. Translated by Michael Sonenscher. London: Pluto Press, 1982.

Grohotolsky, Ernst. *Ästhetik der Negation – Tendenzen des deutschen Gegenwartsdramas: Versuch über die Aktualität der "Ästhetischen Theorie" Theodor W. Adornos*. Königstein/Ts.: Athenäum, Hain, Hanstein, 1984.

Habermas, Jürgen. *Legitimationsprobleme im Spätkapitalismus*. Frankfurt/M.: Suhrkamp Verlag, 1973.

——, *Die Neue Unübersichtlichkeit*. Frankfurt/M.: Suhrkamp Verlag, 1985.

——, *Strukturwandel der Öffentlichkeit*. Darmstadt and Neuwied: Hermann Luchterhand Verlag, 1962.

——, *Theorie des kommunikativen Handelns. Handlungsrationalität und gesellschaftliche Rationalisierung*. Vol. I. Frankfurt/M.: Suhrkamp, 1981.

Hammer, Wolfgang. "Verkleinert und verzuckert: 'Bauern Sterben' von Kroetz, jetzt am Schiller-Theater." *Frankfurter Rundschau*, 2 Dec. 1986.

Haslinger, Josef. "Der proletarische Selbst-Zerstörungsroman – Über den Wirklichkeitsverlust der neueren österreichischen Literatur." *Wespennest*, no. 76 (1989): pp. 55–59.

Haug, Wolfgang. *Bestimmte Negation*. Frankfurt/M.: Suhrkamp Verlag, 1973.

——, "Brecht oder Aitmatow? Positionen zur gesellschaftlichen Kompetenz/Inkompetenz von Literatur." In *Aktualisierung Brechts*. Edited by W.F. Haug, K. Pierwoß and K. Ruoff (*Argument-Sonderband*, 50), pp. 19–43. Berlin: Argument-Verlag, 1980.

Hermann, Siegfried. "Die Deutsche Kommunistische Partei." In

Parteienhandbuch: die Parteien der Bundesrepublik Deutschland 1945–1980. Edited by Richard Stöss, pp. 901–981. Opladen: Westdeutscher Verlag, 1983.

Hein, Jürgen, "Formen des Volkstheaters im 19. und 20. Jahrhundert." In *Handbuch des deutschen Dramas.* Edited by Walter Hinck. Düsseldorf: A. Bagel, 1980.

——, *Franz Xaver Kroetz: "Oberösterreich" – "Mensch Meier."* Frankfurt/M.: Diesterweg, 1986.

——, *Theater und Gesellschaft: Das Volksstück im 19. und 20. Jahrhundert.* (Literatur in der Gesellschaft 12). Düsseldorf: Bertelsmann, 1973.

Henrichs, Benjamin. "Bayerischer Kommunismus, nestwarm: Über Franz Xaver Kroetz." In *Beruf: Kritiker.* Munich: Carl Hanser Verlag, 1978.

Hensel, Georg. "Mythen, Moden, Privatsachen. Beobachtungen in der Spielzeit 1985/86." *Jahresring* (1986/87): pp. 269–278.

——, "Der Schlaf der Liebe gebiert Ungeheuer. Beobachtungen in der Spielzeit 1984/85." *Jahresring* (1985/86): pp. 254–265.

Hinck, Walter. "Deutsche Dramatik in der Bundesrepublik seit 1965." In *Deutsche Literatur in der Bundesrepublik seit 1965: Untersuchungen und Berichte.* Edited by Paul Michael Lützeler and Egon Schwarz, pp. 62–84. Königstein/Ts.: Athenäum, 1980.

Hoffmeister, Donna L. "'Ich kann nur schreiben, von dem, was ich sehe, nicht von dem, was ich sehen möchte.' An Interview with Franz Xaver Kroetz." *Modern Language Studies* 11, no. 1 (1980–1981): pp. 38–48.

——, *The Theater of Confinement. Language and Survival in the Milieu Plays of Marieluise Fleißer and Franz Xaver Kroetz.* Columbia, S. Carolina: Camden House, 1983.

——, "'Zamhaltn muß man dann.' Reassurance Displays in Franz Xaver Kroetz's *Oberösterreich.*" *German Quarterly* 54, no. 4 (1981): pp. 447–460.

Hohendahl, Peter Uwe. "Autonomy of Art: Looking Back at Adorno's *Ästhetische Theorie.*" *German Quarterly* 54, no. 2 (1981): pp.133–148.

Hohoff, Curt. "An der Sprachlosigkeit entlang. Das Theater des Franz Xaver Kroetz."
Merkur 30, no. 2 (1976): pp. 189–193.

Hollier, Dennis. "The Handbook of the Intellectual." *Raritan* (Fall 1981): pp. 73–88.

Hunter, G. Frederick. "Commitment and Autonomy in Art: Antinomies of Frankfurt Esthetic Theory." *Berkeley Journal of Sociology* 30 (1985): pp. 41–64.

Huyssen, Andreas. "Introduction to Adorno." *New German Critique* 6

(Fall 1975): pp. 3–11.

Innes, C.D. *Modern German Drama. A Study in Form.* Cambridge: Cambridge University Press, 1979.

Ismayr, Wolfgang. *Das politische Theater Westdeutschlands.* Meisenheim am Glan: Hain, 1977.

Jaeggi, Urs. *Literatur und Politik.* Frankfurt/M.: Suhrkamp Verlag, 1972.

Jay, Martin. *The Dialectical Imagination. A History of the Frankfurt School and the Institute of Social Research 1923–1950.* Boston: Little, Brown and Company, 1973.

Jones, Calvin. *Negation and Utopia. The German Volksstück from Raimund to Kroetz.* New York: Peter Lang, 1993.

Kässens, Wend and Michael Töteberg. "Fortschritt im Realismus? Zur Erneuerung des kritischen Volksstücks seit 1966." *Basis* 6 (1976): pp. 30–47.

———, "'Nest und Käfig' Zu der Trilogie von Franz Xaver Kroetz: 'Oberösterreich,' Das Nest' und 'Mensch Meier.'" *Spectaculum* 30 (1979): pp. 287–294.

Kafitz, Dieter. "Die Problematisierung des individualistischen Menschenbildes im deutschsprachigen Drama der Gegenwart (Franz Xaver Kroetz, Thomas Bernhard, Botho Strauß)." *Basis* 10 (1980): pp. 93–126.

Kiebuzinska, Christine Olga. "Revolutionaries in the Theater: Meyerhold, Brecht, and Witkiewicz." Diss., University of Maryland 1984.

Kluge, Gerhard (ed.). *Studien zur Dramatik in der BRD.* Amsterdam: Rodopi, 1983.

Knopf, Jan. "'Eingreifendes Denken' als Realdialektik." In *Aktualisierung Brechts.* Edited by W.F. Haug, K. Pierwoß and K. Ruoff (*Argument-Sonderband*, 50), pp. 57–74. Berlin: Argument–Verlag, 1980.

Koch, Hans, Klaus Jarmatz, Hermann Kähler, Werner Mittenzwei et al. (eds). *Zur Theorie des sozialistischen Realismus.* Berlin, GDR: Dietz Verlag, 1974.

Kohl, Stephan. *Realismus: Theorie und Geschichte.* Munich: Wilhelm Fink Verlag, 1977.

Kotze, Astrid von. "Monopolisierung von Sprache in *Mensch Meier* von Franz Xaver Kroetz." *Acta Germanica* 13 (1980): pp. 165–174.

Krauss, Henning. *Die Praxis der "litterature engagée" im Werk Jean-Paul Sartres 1938–1948.* Heidelberg: Carl Winter Universitätsverlag, 1970.

Kreuzer, Helmut (ed.). *Deutsche Dramaturgie der Sechziger Jahre.* Tübingen: Niemeyer Verlag, 1974.

Laclau, Ernesto and Chantal Mouffe. *Hegemony and Socialist Strategy. Towards a Radical Democratic Politics.* Translated by Winston Moore and Paul Caminack. London: Verso, 1985.

Laemmle, Peter (ed.). *Realismus – Welcher?* Munich: Edition *text + kritik*, 1976.

Lehnert, Detlef. *Sozialdemokratie zwischen Protestbewegung und Regierungspartei: 1848–1983.* Frankfurt/M.: Suhrkamp Verlag, 1983.

Link, Werner (ed.). *Schriftsteller und Politik in Deutschland.* Düsseldorf: Droste Verlag, 1979.

Lüdke, W. Martin. *Literatur und Studentenbewegung.* Opladen: Westdeutscher Verlag, 1977.

——, (ed.). *"Theorie der Avantgarde." Antworten auf Peter Bürgers Bestimmung von Kunst und bürgerlicher Gesellschaft.* Frankfurt/M.: Suhrkamp Verlag, 1976.

——, (ed.). *Nach dem Protest. Literatur im Umbruch.* Frankfurt/M.: Suhrkamp Verlag, 1979.

Ludwig, K.H. *Bertolt Brecht. Philosophische Grundlagen und Implikationen seiner Dramaturgie.* Bonn: Bouvier, 1975.

Lukács, Georg. *Essays on Realism.* Translated by David Fernbach. Cambridge, Massachusetts: MIT Press, 1980.

——, *Geschichte und Klassenbewußtsein.* Darmstadt and Neuwied: Hermann Luchterhand Verlag, 1968.

Marcuse, Herbert. *Eros and Civilization.* Boston: Beacon Press, 1955 and 1966.

——, *One Dimensional Man. Studies in the Ideology of Advanced Industrial Society.* Boston: Beacon Press, 1964.

McCarthy, Patrick, "Sartre, Nizan and the Dilemmas of Political Commitment." *Yale French Studies*, no. 68 (1985): pp. 191–206.

McElroy, Bernard. *Fiction of the Modern Grotesque.* Macmillan, 1989.

McGowan, Moray. "Botho Strauß and Franz Xaver Kroetz: Two Contemporary Views of the Subject." *Strathclyde Modern Language Studies*, no. 5 (1985): pp. 58–75.

——, "Das Objekt entdeckt seine Subjektivität: 'Innerlichkeit' in den neueren Kroetz-Stücken?" In *Subjektivtät – Innerlichkeit – Abkehr vom Politischen? Tendenzen der deutschsprachigen Literatur der 70er Jahre.* Edited by Keith Bullivant, Hans-Joachim Althof et al, pp. 263–276. Bonn: DAAD, Dokumentationen & Materialien, 1986.

——, "Subject, Politics, Theatre – Reflections on Franz Xaver Kroetz." In *A Radical Stage.* Edited by W.G. Sebald, pp. 77–92. Oxford: Berg, 1988.

Mennemeier, Franz Norbert. "Volkstheater gegen den Strich." In *Modernes deutsches Drama.* Munich: Wilhelm Fink Verlag, 1975.

Motekat, Helmut. "Das 'Neue Volksstück'." In *Das zeitgenössische deutsche Drama*. Stuttgart: Kohlhammer Verlag, 1977.

Müller, Gerd. *Das Volksstück von Raimund bis Kroetz*. Munich: Oldenbourg, 1979.

Nevin, Donald J. "Franz Xaver Kroetz: The Dialectical Development of a Dramatist." Diss., University of Minnesota 1980.

Ollman, Bertell. "Toward Class Consciousness Next Time: Marx and the Working Class." *Politics and Society* 3, no. 1 (1972): pp. 1–24.

Papadakis, Elim. *The Green Movement in West Germany*. London: Croom Helm, 1984.

Prendergast, Christopher. *The Order of Mimesis*. Cambridge: Cambridge University Press, 1986.

Preußen, Gerhard. "Portrait des Künstlers als Alte Sau." *Theater heute* (June 1991): p. 26.

Raschke, Joachim. *Soziale Bewegungen. Ein historisch-systematischer Grundriß*. Frankfurt/M./New York: Campus Verlag, 1985.

Reinhold, Ursula. *Tendenzen und Autoren: Zur Literatur der siebziger Jahre in der BRD*. Berlin: Dietz Verlag, 1982.

Riewoldt, Otto (ed.). *Franz Xaver Kroetz*. Frankfurt/M.: Suhrkamp Verlag, 1985.

——, "Franz Xaver Kroetz. Der lange Weg zum Volksstück." In *Studien zur Ästhetik des Gegenwartstheaters*. Edited by Christian Thomsen, pp. 268–291. Heidelberg: Carl Winter Universitätsverlag,1985.

——, *Von Zuckmayer bis Kroetz*. Berlin: Erich Schmidt, 1978.

Rischbieter, Henning. "Vom Druck auf den Durchschnitt und vom Drang, auszubrechen." *Theater heute* (July 1981): pp. 1–5.

——, "Vom Leid der Arbeitslosigkeit: Franz Xaver Kroetz' neues Stück 'Furcht und Hoffnung der BRD' in Bochum und Düsseldorf Uraufgeführt." *Theater heute* (March 1984): pp. 28–30.

Roberts, David. "Changing Directions. West and East German Literature in the 70s." *Meanjin* 42, no. 2 (1983): pp. 167–174.

Roeder, Anke. "Der Luxus der vollkommenen Identität: Franz Xaver Kroetz als Autor, Schauspieler und Regisseur." *Forum modernes Theater* 2, no. 1 (1987): pp. 55–62.

Rucht, Dieter. "Neue soziale Bewegungen – Anwälte oder Irrläufer des Projektes der Moderne?" *Frankfurter Hefte* 39, no. 11/12 extra (1984): pp. 144–149.

Rühle, Günther. *Anarchie in der Regie?* Frankfurt/M.: Suhrkamp Verlag, 1982.

——, "Die Schwierigkeit, Theater zu machen, und das Versagen der Kritik." *Universitas* 42, no. 3 (1987): pp. 275–280.

——, *Theater in unserer Zeit*. Frankfurt/M.: Suhrkamp Verlag, 1976.

Ruoff, Karen. "Das Denkbare und die Denkware. Zum eingreifenden Denken." In *Aktualisierung Brechts*. Edited by W.F. Haug, K. Pierwoß and K. Ruoff (*Argument-Sonderband*, 50), pp. 75–83. Berlin: Argument-Verlag, 1980.

Rupp, Hans Karl. *Politische Geschichte der Bundesrepublik Deutschland*. Stuttgart: Kohlhammer, 1978.

Ryan, Michael. *Politics and Culture: Working Hypotheses for a Post-revolutionary Society*. Baltimore: Johns Hopkins University Press, 1989.

Sartre, Jean-Paul. *Black Orpheus*. Translated by S.W. Allen. Paris: Présence Africaine, 1963.

——, *Politics and Literature*. Translated by J.A. Underwood and John Calder. London: Calder & Boyars, 1965.

——, *Sartre on Theater*. Translated by Frank Jellinek. New York: Pantheon Books, 1976.

——, *What is Literature?* Translated by Bernard Frechtman. New York: Philosophical Library, 1949.

Schaarschmidt, Peter. "Das moderne Volksstück. Sprache und Figuren." In *Theater und Gesellschaft*. Edited by Jürgen Hein, pp. 201–217. Düsseldorf: Bertelmann Universitätsverlag, 1973.

Schäfer, Max (ed.). *Die DKP: Gründung, Entwicklung, Bedeutung*. Frankfurt/M.: Verlag Marxistische Blätter, 1978.

Schmitt, Hans J. and Godehard Schramm (ed.). *Sozialistische Realismuskonzeptionen. Dokumentationen zum I. Allunionskongreß der Sowjetschriftsteller*. Frankfurt/M.: Suhrkamp Verlag, 1974.

Schneider, Wolfgang. "Der Musenficker." *konkret*, no. 1 (1988): pp. 46–50.

Schödel, Helmut. "Der fliegende Hinkemann: Franz Xaver Kroetz inszeniert ein Stück von Kroetz: 'Der Nusser,' frei nach Ernst Toller." *Die Zeit*, 21 Mar. 1986.

Schostack, Renate. "Landshut am Ganges. Franz Xaver Kroetz: 'Bauern sterben' – Uraufführung in den Münchner Kammerspielen." *Frankfurter Allgemeine Zeitung*, 12 June 1985.

Schregel, Ursula. *Neue deutsche Stücke im Spielplan am Beispiel von Franz Xaver Kroetz*. Berlin: Volker Spiess, 1980.

——, "The Theater of Franz Xaver Kroetz." *Modern Drama* 23, no. 4 Special Issue (1981): pp. 472–483.

Schwab, Lothar. "'Wildnis der Meere' Zum Genrewechsel in 'Nicht Fisch nicht Fleisch' von Franz Xaver Kroetz." In *Deutsches Drama der 80er Jahre*. Edited by Richard Weber, pp. 51–64. Frankfurt/M.: Suhrkamp Verlag, 1992.

Skasa, Michael. "Alltag im Kopfstand: Kroetz inszeniert Kroetz' 'Nicht Fisch nicht Fleisch.'" *Theater heute* (Dec. 1983): pp. 13f.

———, "Der stramme Max, zur Essener Uraufführung des neuen Kroetz-Stückes." *Theater heute* (July 1980): pp. 20f.

Steinweg, Reiner. *Das Lehrstück. Brechts Theorie einer politisch-ästhetischen Erziehung.* Stuttgart: Metzler, 1972.

Šubik, Christian. *Einverständnis, Verfremdung und Produktivität. Versuche über die Philosophie Bertolt Brechts.* Vienna: Verlag des Verbandes der Wissenschaftlichen Gesellschaften Österreichs, 1982.

Thiele, Dieter. *Bertolt Brecht. Selbstverständnis, Tui-Kritik und politische Ästhetik.* Frankfurt/M: Suhrkamp Verlag, 1981.

———, "Brecht als Tui oder der Autor als Produzent?" In *Brechts Tui-Kritik.* Edited by W.F. Haug (*Argument-Sonderband*, 11), pp. 213–233. Berlin: Argument-Verlag, 1976.

Thieringer, Thomas. "Moral in reinem Raum: Kroetz' 'Weihnachtstod', uraufgeführt im Werkraum." *Süddeutsche Zeitung*, 20–21 Dec. 1986.

Thorn, F. "Die passive Schöpfung, zur Rolle des Publikums im Theater." *Süddeutsche Zeitung*, 8 Aug. 1986.

Timm, Uwe and Gerd Fuchs. *Literatur und Wirklichkeit. (Kontext I).* Munich: Bertelsmann Verlag, 1976.

Töteberg, Michael. "Der Kleinbürger auf der Bühne. Die Entwicklung des Dramatikers Franz Xaver Kroetz und das realistische Volksstück." *Akzente* 23, no. 2 (1976): pp. 165–172.

Tomberg, Friedrich. *Politische Ästhetik.* Darmstadt and Neuwied: Hermann Luchterhand Verlag, 1973.

Träger, Claus. *Studien zur Realismustheorie und Methodologie der Literaturwissenschaft.* Leipzig: Reclam, 1972.

Usmiani, Renate. *The Theatre of Frustration. Super Realism in the Dramatic Work of F.X. Kroetz and Michael Tremblay.* New York: Garland Publishing, 1990.

Walser, Martin. *Erfahrungen und Leseerfahrungen.* Frankfurt/M.: Suhrkamp Verlag, 1964.

Walther, Ingeborg. *The Theater of Franz Xaver Kroetz.* New York: Peter Lang, 1990.

Wellershoff, Dieter. *Literatur und Lustprinzip.* Cologne: Kiepenheuer & Witsch, 1973.

———, *Literatur und Veränderung.* Cologne: Kiepenheuer & Witsch, 1969.

———, "Realistisch schreiben." *Literatur und Kritik*, no. 91 (1974): pp. 21–24.

Wellmer, Albrecht. "Truth, Semblance and Reconciliation: Adorno's Aesthetic Redemption of Modernity." *Telos*, 62 (Winter 1984/85): pp. 89–115.

Wendt, Ernst. *Wie es euch gefällt geht nicht mehr.* Munich: Carl Hanser

Verlag, 1985.

Witte, Bernd. "Krise und Kritik. Zur Zusammenarbeit Benjamins mit Brecht in den Jahren 1929–1933." In *Walter Benjamin – Zeitgenosse der Moderne.* Edited by P. Gebhardt (et al.), pp. 9–36. Kronberg/Ts.: Scriptor Verlag, 1976.

———, "Über die Notwendigkeit des Schreibens. Plädoyer für einen produktiven Umgang mit der Literatur." In *Literatur als Praxis?* Edited by Roul Hübner and Erhard Schütz, pp. 14–24. Opladen: Westdeutscher Verlag, 1976.

Wolin, Richard. "The De-aesthetization of Art: On Adorno's *Ästhetische Theorie.*" *Telos* 41 (Fall 1979): pp. 105–127.

Wright, Elizabeth. *Postmodern Brecht. A Re-Presentation.* London: Routledge, 1989.

Zehm, Günther. "Jean Paul Sartre und das politische Drama." *Theater heute*, Sonderheft (1965): pp. 91–95.

Index

Index

Index

90–3, 104, 123, 129, 136, 154, 164, 174–6, 196, 198, 200
Ohnsorg-Theater, 13
Osterunruhen, 49n7

parable, 47, 163–4, 166, 173, 196
paritätisches Mitbestimmungsrecht, 102
Parteilichkeit, 42–4
Piscator, Erwin, 11, 32
political subject, the, 68, 93, 175–9, 184, 186, 198, 200
post-industrialsm, 9, 105, 108–9, 173, 176, 200
post-materialism, 172, 176, 178
pregnancy, 2, 61, 70, 73, 74, 95n19, 134, 154
proletariat (see also working class), 26, 64, 66–7, 76, 88–9, 92, 104, 159, 172–3, 177

racism, 199
Radikalenerlaß, 102
Randgruppen (see marginal social groups)
realism, 16, 19–20, 24–5, 30–3, 36–41, 47, 69, 78, 80–2, 86–7, 91, 96n25, 97n27, 100, 127, 129, 132–3, 163–6, 175, 191–5, 197–9
realism debate, 16, 20, 26, 32–6, 39, 45, 166
Reise ins Glück, 3
religion, 152, 160

scatology, 195
Scheel, Walter, 102
Schneider, Peter, 150
Second World War, 103
self-referentiality, 75, 87, 185
Social Democratic Party, 16, 19, 38, 88, 101–3, 143
social-liberal coalition, 101
socialist realism, 30, 33, 41–5, 83, 90, 98n43, 132
Sozialistischer Deutscher Studentenbund (SDS), 19
SPD (see Social Democratic Party)
Sperr, Martin, 12–13, 16
Spiegel-Affair, 102
Stallerhof, 2, 43, 61–3
Sterntaler, 2, 81, 90, 165–6
Stramme Max, 3, 70, 88, 93, 123–4, 128, 135, 165, 170, 174, 185

Strauß, Botho, 8–11, 96n26, 125, 178, 199
student movement, 7, 10–12, 14–15, 18–19, 32, 36–7, 52n34, 64, 102, 117, 150
Studentenbewegung (see student movement)
subject, the political (see political subject, the)

Taschau, Hannelies, 20
Taylorism, 89
technology, 105–7, 115–16, 130, 156–9, 161, 168, 170, 177
Tendenzwende, 6, 9, 16, 141, 143, 145, 179n8
theater of the absurd, 6–7
Third Reich, 7, 12, 18
Timm, Uwe, 20, 34–9
Tiroler Elegien, 33
Toller, Ernst, 3
toxic waste, 87, 122–3, 193
Turini, Peter, 4
Typische, das, 42–4, 83

union, 85, 86, 88–9, 104–6, 108–10, 119, 122–4, 128–9, 150, 176
urban (see city)

Verfassungsfeinde, 102
Verfremdungseffekt, 164
Volksstück, 2, 11–16, 47, 63, 165, 198–9

Walser, Martin, 1, 19, 166
Weimar Republic, 12, 18
Weiss, Peter, 6–7, 18
Weitere Aussichten, 3, 63, 90
Wellershoff, Dieter, 32–3, 38–9
Werkkreis Literatur der Arbeitswelt, 19
Wiener Gruppe, 32
Wildwechsel, 2, 54n43, 61, 63, 75, 199
Wirtschaftswunder, 17, 144
Wolf, Friedrich, 45
women, 111, 121, 130–1, 133–4, 136
women's movement, 112, 134, 136
working class (see also prolaetariat), 28, 46, 69, 88, 90, 100, 102, 104, 110, 148, 150, 159, 173

xenophobia, 199

Zeitweh, 4, 179, 184–6, 190–3, 195–6, 198
Zuckmayer, Carl, 6